Creating the Dropout

An Institutional and Social History of School Failure

Sherman Dorn

 PRAEGER

Westport, Connecticut
London

Library of Congress Cataloging-in-Publication Data

Dorn, Sherman.
 Creating the dropout : an institutional and social history of
school failure / Sherman Dorn.
  p.   cm.
 Includes bibliographical references and index.
 ISBN 0–275–95175–8 (alk. paper)
 1. High school dropouts—United States. 2. Education, Secondary—
Social aspects—United States. I. Title.
LC146.6.D67   1996
373.12'913'0973—dc20   95–45414

British Library Cataloguing in Publication Data is available.

Library of Congress Catalog Card Number: 95–45414
ISBN: 0–275–95175–8

First published in 1996

Praeger Publishers, 88 Post Road West, Westport, CT 06881
An imprint of Greenwood Publishing Group, Inc.

Printed in the United States of America

The paper used in this book complies with the
Permanent Paper Standard issued by the National
Information Standards Organization (Z39.48–1984).

10 9 8 7 6 5 4 3 2

Contents

Tables

Acknowledgments

This research project began several years ago when Michael Katz asked me when the word "dropout" came into common use. As co-convener of a faculty and graduate student seminar on work and welfare at the University of Pennsylvania, he also invited anthropologist Linda Burton to give a talk that suggested, to me, the links between age norms and social institutions. He prodded me to think clearly about the social construction of dropping out, and his advice and encouragement have been invaluable.

Many others have been helpful, in a variety of ways: Maya Amis, David Angus, Harry Bernhard, Nancy Bernhard, Ruth Bernhard, Dain Borges, Evelyn Brooks Higgenbotham, Amy Cohen, Steve Conn, Alfred Dorn, Jeanne Dorn, Murray Dorn, Rhea Dorn, Jack Dougherty, Richard Dunn, Susan Garfinkel, Tim Hasci, Alison Isenberg, debra kimmelman, Walter Licht, Bob Margo, John Noakes, Sam Preston, Jim Raths, Donna Rilling, Liam Riordan, Beth Rose, Marc Stein, and Marian Winship. The University of Pennsylvania and Andrew J. Mellon Foundation supported my work in 1991–92, and Doug Fuchs and Lynn Fuchs have provided a congenial home for me the last several years at Peabody College of Vanderbilt University. Bill Reese and anonymous reviewers for the *History of Education Quarterly* helped me refine my ideas about age-consciousness and the rhetoric of dropping out. Bob Engs and Michelle Fine, in particular, provided valuable criticism and encouragement early, and David Labaree did so at the very end of this process. Helen Oakes and Helen Faust shared with me their recollections of Philadelphia school history from the 1960s; those conversations helped shape my understanding of civic dynamics and the local definitions of dropping out.

I also owe thanks to many people who support researchers. The reference and interlibrary loan librarians at the University of Pennsylvania and Vanderbilt University give aid and comfort every day to students and faculty, without nearly enough recognition. Alan Divack at the Ford Foundation Archives and David Ment at Columbia University Teachers College's Special Collections facilitated my research in New York, as did Brenda Galloway-Wright and George Brightbill at Temple University's Urban Archives in Philadelphia. The Ford Foundation and the Urban Archives have graciously permitted me to use their materials here. The staff at the Atlanta Public Schools Archives, the Georgia State Department of Archives and History, and the Philadelphia School District pedagogical library were patient and forbearing with my requests and research needs. The Inter-University Consortium for Political and Social Research distributes the U. S. Census Public Use Microdata Samples and other data sets available to researchers worldwide, making secondary analysis like the one I present in Chapter 1 possible.

Elizabeth Margareta Griffith has been enthusiastic and wonderfully patient with my work, even as it interfered with her own writing. Kathryn Dorn and Vincent Griffith were not around when I began this research, but they have complicated the final work and enriched my life. I dedicate this book to them and their peers; may our expectations for them be marvelously irrelevant.

Introduction

One of the six goals of official education policy in the United States is to achieve a 90 percent graduation rate by the year 2000. Overlook for the moment the arbitrary threshold of 90 percent and the question of what a high school graduation rate might be. Politicians created the America 2000 education policy, and grandiose statements from them are not unusual. Think instead of why the second goal (90 percent graduation), as opposed to several dozen others one could mention, is one of the six highest priorities of official federal policy. At a summit of the nation's governors and the president in 1989, the *zeitgeist* or collective political instincts (depending on your interpretation) suggested that high schools should graduate the vast majority of students. The 90 percent graduation goal represents, at the very least, the importance we attach to high school completion (U. S. Department of Education 1991).

At least two ironies accompany this policy goal of 90 percent graduation. One is that the overwhelming majority of students already receive some sort of diploma. This should not obscure the existence of population groups whose members are much less likely to graduate than the general population. (In addition, there are questions about whether current statistics reflect the success of high schools or the growth in alternative diploma programs.) However, the policy target is for improvement in the general population, not reducing inequality in who receives diplomas. The graduation target is thus a marginal improvement over current conditions.

The second irony is that the goal of nearly universal graduation directly conflicts with other priorities in education reform over the past fifteen years. High among the views of many education critics in the recent past has been the belief that schools need to raise standards, set specific requirements for graduating from high school, and ensure that a diploma is a valuable credential. The only way for a diploma to have some comparative value, though, is to contrast those with diplomas to those without diplomas. The problem with this set of goals is that raising standards by definition means making it more difficult to earn a diploma (Hamilton 1987; McDill, Natriello, and Pallas 1987).

The policy focus on graduation is an oddity, therefore. Emphasized as a goal even though it would not improve much on official statistics, and in conflict with other goals of educational reform, the policy of 90 percent graduation from high school seems out of place in the list of national goals. Again, the question at the moment is not why we value graduation at all but why it is one of the highest priorities of stated federal policy. Imagine, for a moment, that instead of 90 percent graduation the second goal was "schools shall encourage every adolescent to become involved in local politics," and one can see that the question is of alternative priorities. America 2000 seemingly values a high school diploma more than (among the alternatives) education for participative democracy. Former President Bush, the nation's governors, and other policymakers and politicians chose high graduation above many other goals. The six national goals in America 2000 are sweeping generalizations, but they say something about how politicians (for themselves and for the public) see the role of schools. And, in that, the goal of high graduation is an enigma.

One can understand the graduation goal better if one looks at it as a statement of expectations for adolescents rather than educational policy. The target of 90 percent graduation depends on assumptions of what people earning diplomas can do for a society and states explicitly how many should graduate from high school. To some extent, beliefs about the salutary effects of education are deep-rooted in the United States. New England Puritans created education regulations in the seventeenth century based on their expectation that education would improve the morality of their society. Since the early nineteenth century, educators have fretted about the future of truants, and some have called for universal secondary education since the Progressive Era at the turn of the twentieth century. But the expectation of widespread high school graduation is relatively recent. Even those who concerned themselves at the turn of this century with "elimination from school" or "early school leavers" thought that leaving school in adolescence was a tragic but common event. Only in the last fifty years has high school graduation become the norm, in any sense of the word, in the United States. Only since World War II has a majority of teenagers graduated from high school or a diploma become required for most jobs.

Concurrent with the new expectation of high school graduation came the dominance of one word to describe those without diplomas: dropout. Dropping out became the rhetorical complement of high school graduation in the early 1960s. It is now the touchstone for many of the doubts we have about adolescents. As much as this society lauds graduation, it fears dropping out. Sometimes the fear begins in empathy or compassion for the dropout, sometimes in apprehension of what the dropout may become as an adult. Education is the ticket to a successful life, as folk wisdom puts it. Conversely, dropping out is not only ominous for the individual but dangerous for the society. As Lucius Cervantes, a sociologist at St. Louis University, colorfully claimed, "It is from this hard core of dropouts that a high proportion of the gangsters, hoodlums, drug addicted, government-dependent-prone, irresponsible and illegitimate parents of tomorrow will be predictably recruited" (Cervantes 1965: 197).

Educators and social critics have created, rather than discovered, the dropout problem. Many of the problems of dropouts are real, but the public debate over dropping out since the early 1960s has been fundamentally irrational in the way in which concerns over a "dropout problem" gelled. First, the dropout problem appeared despite improvements in the proportion of the population graduating from high school. Second, policies supposedly responding to the dropout problem were too small and isolated to have much influence on larger demographic trends. Third, the dominant construction of the dropout problem omitted issues (such as racial disparities in education) that would have been sensible components of any analysis of school attrition. The appearance of the dropout problem makes sense best as a reflection of the growing expectation of high school graduation. It also reflects the dilemmas of the high school as a mass institution. High schools became extremely successful in attracting adolescents. Their very success, however, created expectations at mid-century that led to criticism of the fact that they did not keep everyone until graduation.

Dropping out as a definition of a social problem, a reflection of expectations, and the target of social policies is the subject of this book. It begins with a brief summary of graduation experiences since 1940 and the changing role of high schools. The core of this book covers the early 1960s, when the phrase "dropout" emerged to become the dominant term describing those who leave school before receiving a diploma. The stereotype of high school dropouts that coalesced in the 1960s said much about how educators and social critics saw juvenile delinquency, labor markets, and gender roles. What schools did in response reflected their imperviousness to reform. The civil rights movement, and reactions to it, shaped what was said or not said about race and dropping out; and much about dropouts was not said. Dropouts continue to be spoken of as a social problem, and the language of dropping out reflects a deep ambiguity about the purposes of schools and the inability of schools both to socialize everyone and to act as meritocratic judges of ability and worth.

A brief word, first, of what I have omitted from this book. This does not include any oral history of dropouts, though exploring the historical conditions inside schools leading to dropping out would be a valuable project. I have focused instead on this society's expectations of high school graduation and the resulting policies. This book also does not discuss the educational disparities between whites and Hispanics or Native Americans, though they were as evident as the inequities documented here for African Americans. Finally, the events in Atlanta, Philadelphia, and New York are discussed primarily in the context of the narrow question of dropping out rather than the rich history of urban politics in each city. I understand that these omissions may disappoint some readers. I trust that the story I tell of educational expectations compensates for its limits.

SOCIAL PROBLEMS AND AGE NORMS

I see concerns over school dropouts as forming the social definition of a problem. The fundamental argument of this book is fairly simple: We have chosen the wrong way of looking at dropouts. Instead of seeing different educational outcomes as evidence of remaining inequities in schooling, we have focused instead on the social costs of dropping out, typically imagined as dependency, criminality, and lower economic productivity. Through this language, the social construction of dropping out has given high schools the burden of ameliorating poverty and preventing social chaos. As a higher proportion of teenagers attended secondary schools, this new mission for high schools and the expectation of high school graduation perhaps seemed natural. It was, however, an historical artifact that one can time by the rise of the dropout problem. Demography is important in shaping our views of social problems, but it is not restrictive. Several ways existed to shape the growing expectation of high school graduation, and we did not *have* to choose concerns about dependency as the primary metaphor for dropouts.

Others have examined dropping out as a social construction (Papagiannis, Bickel, and Fuller 1983), but the key is in its historical origins. Concern over dropouts, defined as a problem in itself, did not blossom until the 1960s. Most discussion of school attrition was subsumed under other issues (such as vocationalism) before then. An indication of this is the language used by writers. Generally, those before the 1960s used different (and interchangeable) terms: elimination from school or school leaving. The word "dropout" did not become the dominant label until the 1960s. That change in language reflects a real change in expectations and in the role of high schools. The central issue for me is why dropping out became a crisis issue in the 1960s. Was the concern a rational response to changing economic circumstances, as the Project on School Dropouts Director Daniel Schreiber would have said? Substantial evidence suggests that the construction of dropping out in the 1960s was far from an objective discovery of a new problem. Instead, one must see the dropout problem as a social construction.

The main problem with the dominant social construction of dropping out is the assumption that it is the burden of schools to socialize adolescents and prevent delinquency and dependency. There is nothing wrong with socialization being a part of schools' purposes. However, it is ahistorical to believe that high schools are the appropriate place to prevent social chaos. After all, attendance and high school graduation have increased or at least remained very high for teenagers while homicide rates have risen over the past several decades. While national rates of school attendance may mask some severe problems in cities, it is certainly true that more sixteen- and seventeen-year-olds in what are euphemistically called inner cities attend school than was the case with teenagers in cities 100 or even fifty years ago. Yet we (quite reasonably) conclude that teenagers are more likely to be violent with tragic results now than in the past.

We have become accustomed to thinking of high schools as the great socializers of adolescence. That, however, is a historical artifact. Even when James Bryant Conant was writing about high schools in the late 1950s, his assertion (Conant 1959: 7) that "the public high school is expected to provide education for *all* the youth living in a town, city, or district" (his emphasis) was a recent development. It did not even match demographics entirely (for a sizable minority of students, then as now, did not come close to graduating). We have assigned high schools this responsibility because, over the first half of the twentieth century, teenagers slowly withdrew from the labor market and instead attended school. What is surprising is that the high school became the dominant institution for adolescents who were not working. In the nineteenth century, relatively few attended high schools, and a variety of institutions claimed that they could prevent juvenile delinquency. None were nearly as successful as high schools, because no others had the draw of a valuable credential. Yet high schools' success in dominating other institutions of adolescence led to the expectation of high school graduation and, thus, the criticism that high schools were insufficiently socializing adolescents.

What is wrong is the assumption that some institution has to reform the poor. That is a common presumption as institutions have taken over the care of those outside the labor market. High schools are a special type of warehousing institution because they are attached to age-related expectations, or age norms. We use high schools as part of our justification for why certain people are not working and are dependent. Teenagers are in school, supposedly to prepare for jobs and adult life. Older people are retiring, supposedly to enjoy later years in life. The assumed functions of high schools ease our minds about dependency and appeal to us with the notion that these institutions will take care of dependency, prevent delinquency and urban chaos, and so forth. The truth of the matter is that twelve or more years of schooling is itself a rationalized form of dependency in our society, and schooling cannot solve the real problems poor people face, including violence.

This perspective on social problems relies in part on work by sociologists about how problems become recognized, visible, and urgent. As Stephen Hilgartner and Charles Bosk (1988: 57) explain, competition for attention shapes our views of problems:

[T]here is a huge "population" of potential problems—putative situations and conditions that could be conceived of as problems. This population, however, is highly stratified. An extremely small fraction grows into social problems with "celebrity" status, the dominant topics of political and social discourse. A somewhat larger number develop into lesser social problems; small communities of professionals, activists, and interest groups work to keep these problems alive on the margins of public debate. The vast majority of these putative conditions remain outside or on the extreme edge of public consciousness.

Hilgartner and Bosk argue that different social constructions of problems (both different problems and different views of a similar issue) compete for attention in various public arenas. Thus, the range of visible social concerns depends not only on concrete conditions but on the environment of public arenas, their capacity to carry debates about social issues, and the process of intellectual competition. This perspective suggests that the appearance of dropping out as a problem represents success in the public competition over concerns. The 1960s dropout problem is an example of a "lesser" social problem, where a small group of people actively publicized their views of the issue. Over the long term, the stereotype of dropping out from the 1960s has come to dominate this society's perspectives on high school graduation. It reflected some contemporary concerns, like juvenile delinquency and the consequences of workplace automation, while largely avoiding other issues commonly discussed at the time, such as civil rights and the Cold War.

The social construction of dropping out becomes more understandable when one sees it as an age-related historical development. To summarize the argument briefly, the creation of the dropout problem reflected the limits of age-specific institutions. Over the first half of the twentieth century, high schools became the dominant institution of teenagers—or, as it has become known, adolescence. As teenagers were less able to find work, and because secondary education had value in adult labor markets, adolescents increasingly attended high school. Educators willingly took on a new mission for high school to socialize entire generations of adolescents. The very success of high schools in attracting attendance, however, created growing expectations of attendance and graduation. The students leaving school without diplomas became a problem despite the fact that they represented a shrinking proportion of successive birth cohorts. The description of the newly discovered problem focused on the impending criminality and dependency of dropouts. High schools' success led critics to expect more and charge it with failure in the very mission (absorbing adolescents) that it had so successfully undertaken.

This understanding of the dropout problem rests on the work of historians who have traced the growth of American age-specific institutions (Chudacoff 1989; Graebner 1980; Haber 1983; Kett 1977). The evolution of age norms has often been concurrent with changing roles of American social institutions and the economy. For example, the first widespread medical literature on geriatric conditions originated in the middle of the nineteenth century, when medical journals claimed that senescence was a distinct, vulnerable stage in life. By the turn of the century, the institutionalization of pensions reified that age norm. Carole Haber (1983: 108–9) describes how the quick adoption of pensions by corporation and government bureaucracies created a barrier between the elderly and the labor market. In her view, pensions had an ambiguous legacy, both responding to "growing awareness of the plight of the elderly" but also making forced retirement seem "natural and correct":

By accepting a pension, the worker would at least be able to avoid ending his life amid the squalor of the almshouse. Yet, in their eventual adoption, these plans also reflected the widely shared conviction that old persons could in general be characterized as "over the hill" and, for their own sake and that of society's, should be forced to retire.

Haber places the bureaucratization of old age in the context of burgeoning age classifications at the turn of the century; the concept of pensioners became common at the same time as the popularization of other age-related concepts such as adolescence. From a long-term perspective, dropping out has become one more term Americans use to classify expectations by age.

The most direct parallel to dropping out, as a social construction, is the relatively recent hysteria over teenage pregnancy. Like dropping out, teenage pregnancy became visible despite demographic changes to the contrary. As Frank Furstenberg (1991: 128) asks, "Why was teenage childbearing discovered in the late 1960s when fertility rates among teenagers had actually been declining for almost a decade?" Broadly speaking, concerns about both dropping out and teenage pregnancy demonstrate an unusual focus on adolescents in the midst of larger social changes. The job market and fertility behavior changed for adults of many ages after World War II. Yet, despite this intergenerational nature of change, anxieties about social disorder have concentrated on adolescents. In part, that is because the high school was unusually visible after the war, having become the dominant institution of adolescence. In addition, however, the focus on teenagers has simply maintained a deep-rooted obsession about transitions between dependence and independence in American society. Growing high school attendance in the first half of the twentieth century matched the simultaneous reduction in child labor, and the new mission of comprehensive secondary education made that exclusion from labor seem appropriate. Teenagers should go to school, people agreed, so that they could be productive as adults. The recent development of this belief, and the guaranteed dependency of teen students, went largely unnoticed by educators and their critics.

AGE NORMS, VOLUNTARY ATTENDANCE, AND THE PURPOSES OF SCHOOLS

Surprisingly, the 1960s concern over dropouts did not provoke states into raising compulsory attendance ages to eighteen. Such proposals have been around since the early twentieth century, yet attendance for older teenagers remains largely voluntary in the United States. Dropping out has penalties, but they have usually been more economic and social than legal. This makes the social construction of dropping out different from that of truancy. Fiona Paterson (1989) has traced the development of compulsory schooling and the concept of truancy in nineteenth-century Scotland. She argues that the development of truancy as a recognized problem went hand-in-hand with a coercive purpose of schools. Paterson is correct to note the connection between the development of a social construct like truancy to institutional developments such as compulsory attendance. One cannot have truants without schools.

However, at least two differences separate Scottish educational history from the dropout problem of the 1960s. First is the loose, decentralized nature of consensus in the 1960s United States. The dropout problem was not a creation of federal policies (though federal officials participated in the stereotyping rhetoric). Rather, it represented similar statements and actions by hundreds of educators and school critics across the country. Because the United States is fragmented into small jurisdictions, educational policies represent something less than the legislation of a unitary government like the United Kingdom, even considering separate policies for Scotland. However, that relatively noncoercive nature (of both policies and attendance) suggests the power of normative expectations in the formation of the dropout stereotype. The dropout problem appeared despite the decentralized nature of educational politics in the United States and despite the voluntary nature of school attendance. That suggests that it held some common persuasive pull, primarily consisting of fears of dependency and criminality. The rough consensus suggested that high schools were responsible for taking care of adolescents before they entered work.

In addition to the voluntary nature of teenage attendance, the United States "dropout problem" is different from the construction of truancy in the United Kingdom because of popular support of schooling in the United States. As Ira Katznelson and Margaret Weir have written (1985), the working class in the United States did not oppose education in the same way that European working classes did. Rather, because of the early spread of the franchise for white males, education became something sought as part of citizenship. That difference offers considerable hope for public education in the United States. We are not bound by the common view that dropping out is a problem because of its social costs. We can, instead, turn to the alternative view that education is a right of citizenship, and differential graduation by race, sex, and economic circumstances is evidence of inequities to be rooted out because we are a democracy.

The hope for a democratic education is important. Without it, education is little more than a tool for ameliorating social chaos, one that obscures larger economic problems. As I was beginning research that led to this book, historian Robert Engs asked my opinion of education in general. Was it liberating or repressive? This was no idle question; Engs' own research into the history of Hampton, Virginia, in the nineteenth century suggested the ambivalence rooted in educational politics. Hampton Institute, led by Samuel Chapman Armstrong, helped create the late nineteenth-century educational program of industrial education for African American Southerners. The advocates of industrial education stated openly that black Southerners could never aspire to equality with whites. The actions of Hampton officials, in concert with Tuskegee Institute Principal Booker T. Washington and white philanthropists, suppressed dissenting views (Anderson 1988; Harlan 1972). If one looked at the influence of Hampton Institute nationally, one might well conclude that it was nothing more than a tool of social control.

Yet Engs documented that Hampton Institute was a valuable resource to African Americans in and around Hampton. Graduates became politicians, merchants, landowners, and the core of a diversified economy. The relative independence of the African American community in Hampton lasted until nearly the end of the nineteenth century, despite growing political and economic restrictions by race in the late nineteenth-century South. Community survival came in part because of the aid that Hampton provided as school, employer, and resource (Engs 1979: Chap. 8). Thus, Hampton Institute represented the multivalent possibilities of education. Nationally, it disseminated the philosophy of industrial education. Locally, however, it empowered African Americans in many of the aspects of citizenship to which they aspired after the Civil War, even when that empowerment explicitly contradicted the philosophy of industrial education.

The United States has the opportunity to choose from various historical purposes of schools. One is a variety of social control. There is a strain of thought, rooted deeply in American history, that sees schools as an appropriate way to socialize the next generation of children, before they are old enough to create unacceptable social chaos or become dependent on society as poor adults. Another use of schooling has been as a credentialing, or sorting, institution. High schools have had the most prestige historically when they have had restricted or selective enrollment and have provided diplomas that are rare and (in part because of that rarity) valuable. Both of these missions—socialization and credentialing—are conservative, yet in some sense they conflict with one another. In addition, more democratic views of schooling have usually existed alongside the instrumentalist missions of education. Shaping education as a democratic institution is messy, as anyone who has read John Dewey can attest. Yet it is the best way out of the current trap high schools have created.

One can have little doubt that high schools have trapped themselves inside the contradiction between credentialing and socializing purposes. Ultimately, dropout policies had little effect because high schools are organized to sort rather than socialize. The notion of a high school serving all adolescents is relatively recent, and demands for effective socialization of every teenager ran counter to the history of secondary schools. High school education has only recently become a mass phenomenon, for urban high schools began their existence as selective institutions. While they usually maintained claims of meritocratic selection and evaluation of students, high schools never attempted to serve more than a small minority of elementary students in the nineteenth century. Only in the twentieth century have they begun to share with elementary schools an obligation to teach the majority of potential students.

The common perception of a dropout problem in the 1960s represented the most vocal articulation of that change. Within a few years, hundreds of educators and others were arguing that high schools should graduate most, if not all, teenagers. The common socialization of adolescents, not sorting, became the explicit goal of high school for many on the front lines of the dropout problem. Those attempting to solve the dropout problem in part formed a crusade to complete a long-term change in the mission of high schools, from selective to comprehensive education. Those attempts did little to change demographic patterns in part because schools have been impervious to changes in habitual practices.

Both of those tasks—getting schools to socialize all teenagers and be responsible for reducing dropping out—remain today. As Lawrence Cremin wrote, the growing comprehensive nature of secondary institutions has saddled high schools with the expectation of universal education. Only the success of high schools in becoming mass institutions has made the idea of a "dropout problem" possible, yet it still suggests that high schools have failed in some basic task (Cremin 1990: 12–15, 19–20). High schools can remove themselves from this trap when public schooling takes on more than instrumentalist missions.

1

Long-Term Demographic Patterns

High school graduation in North America has become an important ritual. The attendance of graduates' relatives, the careful order of events, the invocation of secular and sacred symbols of power, and the passage of students from one state (student) to another (graduate) suggests the importance of the commencement in recognizing graduates as adults (Fasick 1988). It also suggests, to the historian, the ways in which graduation has become invested with multiple meanings over time, from completion of a curriculum of studies to economic credential to rite of passage. None of these meanings are inherent in graduation. Certainly, graduation from high school was not an expectation of adolescents 100 years ago. At the turn of the twentieth century, only a minority of students in North America ever attended high school, let alone graduated. The increasing proportion of teenagers earning diplomas has made it possible for us to expect children today to graduate. That change was a necessary condition for the development of a new expectation, or norm.

With the joint development of increasing graduation and the expectation of graduation, demographic trends and the social construction of adolescence have woven together and reinforced each other. Thus, demographic changes are an important component of the story of dropping out as a social problem. Several general conclusions emerge from the analysis of 1940–90 trends below. First, high school graduation has become common among all population groups. This broad trend is the foundation for the development of new expectations for graduation among adolescents. Second, the gap in graduation between racial minorities (especially African Americans) and whites has narrowed, particularly between African Americans and others of similar income and other family characteristics. This turnaround in the relative educational experiences of African Americans and other minorities came from changes in labor markets and opportunities that accelerated during and after World War II.

This chapter also presents evidence of other factors related to graduation. Females and children from wealthier families have had a consistent advantage in earning diplomas. Furthermore, having parents who graduated from high school gave children advantages relative to their peers. The disadvantage of living in the South (for everyone, not just African Americans) had largely disappeared by 1980, after accounting for other information. Nativity, though, has been important recently, with U. S. natives having a sizable advantage in 1990. Lastly, young adults from large families are at a educational disadvantage compared with peers equal in other respects. This information is largely consistent with what other historians and social scientists have described for attendance in school and graduation, though my analysis relies on a long-term set of nationally drawn data, rather than local or single-cohort data sources.

This chapter also presents evidence that no major demographic trend in high school graduation started in the 1960s. The general increase in educational attainment, narrowing of racial differences, and narrowing of regional differences all began before 1960. Almost every other relationship of importance remained consistent through half a century of schooling. If the concern of dropping out described in later chapters had any impact, it was not on the trends presented here. This is important evidence of the general impotence of dropout prevention in the 1960s. After a brief discussion of the censuses that are the source of the analysis, I turn to each of the major conclusions one can draw from the census samples.

CENSUS PUBLIC USE SAMPLES

In the analysis below, I use samples drawn from decennial censuses from 1940 to 1990, known collectively as public use microdata samples. These samples draw randomly from households surveyed in each census. The wealth of household as well as individual records provides information for tabular and multivariate analyses of graduation over the past half-century. The first two tables, in the following section, present simple percentages. Table 1 presents a rough look at high school credentials reported by twenty- to twenty-four-year-old natives in each census from 1940 through 1990. Table 2 presents the proportion of fifteen-year-old Southerners from 1940 through 1970 with at least a ninth-grade education. This chapter also includes a multivariate analysis of reported graduation for young adults living with relatives in the 1940 census and in each census from 1960 through 1990. In each of those five censuses, the public use sample allows one to gather information about household heads (where teens were living as dependents of a relative). The information used here—race, sex, nativity, region, household income, renter/owner status, household head employment, head self-employment, head's high school graduation status, and the number of persons in the household—is comparable across census years.

I have chosen to examine the associations between these traits and the likelihood of being a high school graduate at the age of eighteen for each census year. The analysis using these samples is a snapshot rather than a longitudinal analysis of graduation. Nonetheless, it provides important evidence about the relative importance of an individual's background in assisting or hindering graduation, at least by the spring when one was age eighteen. Not everyone who would graduate had done so by the age of eighteen (especially for the last several census years), but using eighteen-year-olds maximizes the likelihood of their living with older relatives and of having a reasonable proportion attained graduation. Over 85 percent of eighteen-year-olds in the 1960 census sample were living as dependents of relatives, and over 90 percent of the samples in 1940, 1970, 1980, and 1990 were doing so. In each census sample, over 30 percent had graduated.

The multivariate analysis uses odds ratios from logistic regression, with claiming a high school credential as the dependent variable. Logistic regression associates characteristics (for example, race) with the answers to a yes or no question, here being whether the person graduated from high school. Unlike ordinary linear regression, logistic regression assumes effects are multiplicative, expressed here as odds ratios, representing the relative odds of a person changing one characteristic. The odds ratios shown in Table 3 are calculated for the characteristic in combination with all the other information available. For example, the odds ratio associated with being African American in 1940 is 0.34, representing the estimate that an African American dependent eighteen years old in 1940 had odds of being a graduate only 34 percent the odds of other dependent Americans of the same sex, household economic circumstances, family education background, region, nativity, and household size. An odds ratio greater than 1 means that being in that category (or the change indicated) corresponds to a relative advantage in education. An odds ratio less than 1 indicates a relative disadvantage.

The analysis here has its limitations, as do all historical sources. First, the 1940 census figures overstate graduation. The way enumerators asked about educational attainment may have confused respondents, because they asked for the highest grade completed. Respondents may have claimed that an eighteen-year-old had graduated from high school (i.e., had completed the twelfth grade) when he or she was still attending twelfth grade (U. S. Bureau of the Census 1953: 6). This does not change the figures in Table 1 (for those twenty to twenty-four years old) more than 1.3 percent for any group listed, largely because few people graduate from high school after their twentieth birthday. Analyzing graduation at eighteen with a more strict definition (i.e., those claiming exactly twelve years of schooling completed are counted as a graduate only if they are not attending school) is different. Far fewer eighteen-year-olds would count as graduates under a stricter definition (21 percent as opposed to 30 percent), because more eighteen-year-olds were still attending school. However, logistic regression using the strict definition results in almost identical odds ratio estimates. The one exception is the effect of home ownership, which is somewhat less for the stricter definition of graduation. Thus, the question of graduation's definition for the 1940 census does not dramatically change the conclusions presented here.

The second limitation is the use of only those eighteen-year-olds who were dependent on relatives. Between 7 percent and 15 percent of eighteen-year-olds in each public use sample lived away from relatives, and that selection is certainly biased by income, race, region, and education. One way of gauging the effect of the selection bias is to analyze sixteen-year-olds using a loose proxy for future graduation: whether they were attending at least tenth grade. Fewer than 3 percent of sixteen-year-olds in each census year were living away from relatives. More sixteen-year-olds were theoretically on target toward graduation than ever graduated, so one should not interpret odds ratios from the analysis of sixteen year olds as directly representing an analysis of graduation (some left school before graduation). Still, an analysis of being on target toward graduation at sixteen arrives at the same general trends as in Table 3, with two minor exceptions. It appears that, for the sixteen-year-olds, being in the Northeast and living in the house of a self-employed adult did not have the same magnitude of relationship as for eighteen-year-olds, though the direction of association was the same. For the most important trends, however, the analysis of sixteen-year-olds who were attending tenth or higher grades confirms the analysis of graduation at eighteen. To gauge the effect of analyzing graduation at eighteen, when the majority of graduates had not yet completed school in the last three censuses, I also conducted analyzed graduation at nineteen. The results are substantially the same. The one important exception is the odds ratio for being African American in 1990, discussed in the relevant section below.

Finally, censuses are limited by the extent to which they accurately cover the population. There are three types of noncoverage that are particularly relevant here. One is the failure of enumerators to reach an individual—the case of census undercounting. Estimates of undercounting ranged from 5.4 percent in 1940 to 1.8 percent in 1990, though a disproportionate number of racial and ethnic minorities were subject to undercounting (U. S. Department of Commerce 1994: 1). A logical supposition would be that poor, transient families and individuals would be more likely to be undercounted than others. This would lead an analysis to underestimate the effects of family economic circumstances on the odds of graduating, if one also assumes that transient families are less likely to have children graduating from high school. The addition of poorer, disproporately nongraduate individuals to the samples analyzed would tend to increase the estimated association of economic circumstances with graduation. Second, the census typically does not cover individuals who were overseas with the military. The small proportion of individuals overseas should not bias the estimates much, except perhaps in 1970 during the Vietnam War. Ultimately, though, there is no way to confirm the potential influence of census undercoverage on the analysis here.

The last type of coverage problem is the lack of answers to specific questions. Respondents may not give information on every item, leaving missing values for a range of census questions. The public use samples have imputed data where information is missing, and the public use samples for 1960–1990 typically have about 5 percent of individuals with imputed educational information. The information in the tables exclude individuals with imputed educational information. Because the public use samples imputed data from individuals similar in age, sex, and ethnicity, imputation should not affect the simple proportions reported in Tables 1 and 2. Multivariate analysis that includes the imputed cases does not change the results of Table 3 substantively.

INCREASING PREVALENCE OF GRADUATION

High school graduation credentials have become more common since 1940. The first trend, generally increasing proportions with diplomas, is evident from the simple statistics presented in Table 1. These show the relative proportion of U. S. natives twenty to twenty-four years old in each census year who claimed to have completed high school. In 1940, less than 50 percent of U. S. native-born residents twenty to twenty-four years old had high school diplomas. In 1980, that national figure was over 80 percent. And, with one statistically insignificant exception, the proportion of high school graduates increased between any two censuses for all the population groups identified in Table 1. One should note, however, the relative stagnation between 1970 and 1990. For whites, at least, improvement slowed to a creep, though the gap between whites and nonwhites narrowed between 1970 and 1980. Thus, while the census does

Table 1
Percent of Natives Twenty to Twenty-Four Years Old with High School Diplomas, by Ethnicity

	1940 %	1950 %	1960 %	1970 %	1980 %	1990 %
All U.S. natives	44.2	49.9	64.0	79.0	83.7	84.8
White	47.9	54.1	67.3	81.6	85.7	87.3
All nonwhite	13.9	23.1	41.5	60.5	72.9	74.4
Racial difference	34.0	31.0	25.8	21.1	12.8	12.9
African American	12.9	22.3	40.1	59.1	73.1	75.0
Hispanic	a	a	a	56.1	72.1	71.4
Spanish surnamed	18.1	22.5	39.7	60.0	72.5	a

Sources: Census public use samples.

a Category did not exist for this census.

not distinguish among the different types of diplomas, the years between 1940 and 1970 show a steady increase in the high school credentials that U. S. natives twenty to twenty-four years old have claimed.

Increasing graduation is consistent with enrollment trends for secondary education. Between the late nineteenth century and the middle twentieth century, enrollment in secondary education grew rapidly (Snyder 1993: Fig. 6–7). It is not surprising that as more children attended high schools, more also graduated. Historians David Angus, Jeffrey Mirel, and Maris Vinovskis (1988) argue that school officials made promotion easier in the decades after 1900 and that high schools adopted social promotion in the 1930s. Little change in the curriculum or course enrollment occurred, though, in the next several decades. Therefore, the rise in graduation between 1940 and 1970 did not come from school becoming easier; it came from higher attendance of teenagers.

Yet this explanation begs the question: What drew children first to attend high schools and then to graduate from them? Some form of elementary schooling had been popular for more than a century before high school enrollment swelled. As the next chapter details, even the existence of high schools was controversial through the nineteenth century. In the late nineteenth century, though, parents began sending their children to high schools in unprecedented numbers, and within seventy years the high school (rather than the labor market) became the dominant institution in which children spent their teenage years. To some extent, one can divide these explanations into changes in family strategies and changes in access. At some point, parents and their children began to decide that schools were more valuable for adolescents to attend. Also, high schools became more available to adolescents. These developments came in tandem. Demand from parents led educators to build more high schools, and the opening of a new high school probably stimulated enrollment in many towns or cities.

The changing labor market both pulled teenagers into longer school enrollment and also pushed them out of steady employment. In the late nineteenth century, growing corporations created specialized jobs for handling paperwork, helping to divide the labor market into specific, segmented areas (Chandler 1977; Gordon, Edwards, and Reich 1982). As some economists have described, the economy has structured occupations and jobs so that they often have unique characteristics. A corporate career ladder is very different from part-time work in a fast-food franchise or a unionized manufacturing job. Stability, pay, and benefits distinguish some jobs from others. Control over work environment or collective bargaining authority are other factors that differentiate segments of the labor market. The growing office workforce at the turn of the century encouraged older girls (and a smaller number of boys) to remain in school for one or two additional years before trying to find a job. Thus, high school enrollment became predominantly female in the late nineteenth and early twentieth centuries, as incentives for remaining in high school grew (Rury 1991; Tyack and Hansot 1990: Chaps. 7–8). One may describe this role as the credential value of an education, as adolescents traded attendance and graduation for some value in the labor market.

At the same time, fewer jobs remained for adolescents. Child labor persisted for several decades (especially in the South), but it slowly became more difficult for teenagers to acquire jobs. Technological changes in work, the availability of adult immigrant labor, growing child-labor law enforcement, the Fair Labor Standards Act of 1938, and seniority rules slowly circumscribed the work available to adolescents (Osterman 1980: Chap. 4). Without much prospect for jobs, a growing proportion of teenagers turned to school as an alternative. Both of these factors—the pull of the credential value of schooling and the push of scarcer jobs—led to growing high school enrollment. The only time between 1900 and 1950 that high school enrollment dropped was during World War II, when the labor shortage strongly encouraged early entry into work (Snyder 1993: Fig. 6). This exception to growing enrollment suggests the power the labor market has had in shaping adolescent school enrollment.

The historical curiosity is the way in which high schools have come to dominate the lives of adolescents in this century. Harry Braverman (1974: 278–81) noted how social institutions like high schools tend to absorb those who are tangential to labor markets. Warehousing institutions largely sprouted in North America in the nineteenth century, at the beginnings of the modern wage-labor market (Katz, Doucet, and Stern 1982: 364–69). Yet the dramatic growth of high schools came well after the creation of many institutions for youth. In the late nineteenth and early twentieth centuries, high schools as a group became more successful than any other adolescent-based institution. Other institutions, including those created around the turn of the century (Kett 1977), were much less successful in warehousing unemployed adolescents. As Robert and Helen Lynd observed about 1920s extracurricular groups in the Midwestern city "Middletown," private youth associations were on "the periphery of this high school activity. . . . All these organizations frankly admit that the fifteen to twenty-one-year person is their hardest problem" (Lynd and Lynd 1928: 216). By contrast, the high school became the dominant institution of adolescence during the early twentieth century. The growing supremacy of the high school among competing institutions for adolescents is the hidden story behind the growth of high school enrollment and graduation.

The potential value of further education was the advantage high schools had over other institutions. While staying out of the labor market, high school students were accumulating more value as workers. Those who remained until graduation gained the most value from education through a concrete credential. Few other institutions could claim such a tangible consequence of membership for adolescents. One exception was commercial education, whose functions schools quickly mimicked (Kantor 1988). At the same time, the growing presence of high school graduation made it possible for employers to use graduation to screen candidates for jobs, as education increased beyond the strict requirements of occupations (Rawlins and Ulman 1974). The growing use of graduation as a credential by businesses increased the draw of high schools and solidified its dominance over competing institutions. The power of high school attendance and a diploma as credentials in labor markets created an incentive for graduation from high schools.

The expansion of high school attendance consolidated two uses of secondary education—to provide credentials and to hold places for nonworking youth. This combination established the conditions for several sets of contradictory expectations for high schools. First was a tension between increasing and limiting access to credentials. The draw of credentials had created pressures to expand access to urban high schools since the nineteenth century. Yet the prestige of credentials meant that schools and programs had the most autonomy and status inside school systems when they remained selective (Labaree 1988). On top of the strain inherent in a public credential-granting institution came the added expectation that high schools were the appropriate institution for all adolescents. The incremental exclusion of teens from labor markets and the advance of high school enrollment made high schools seem the natural place for teenagers. Demography thus encouraged—but did not determine—the rationalization of universal secondary education.

NARROWING RACIAL DISPARITIES

In addition to the general trend of increasing graduation, over the past half-century the gap between the proportion of whites with high school credentials and those in minority groups has narrowed. If one examines graduation proportions in Table 1 for those twenty to twenty-four years old, the gap between whites and others mostly closed between 1940 and 1980, though no improvement occurred between 1980 and 1990. (The tabulation is for U. S. natives only. Including immigrants changes the statistics for Hispanics dramati-

Table 2
Percent of Southern Fifteen-Year-Olds with High School
Experience, by Race

Year	African Americans	Others	Difference
	%	%	%
1940	21	54	33
1950	34	72	38
1960	61	76	15
1970	75	84	9

Source: Census public use samples. The census question on educational attainment in 1940 asked for the highest grade completed and may underestimate the proportion who ever attended ninth grade.

cally.) In addition, the proportions of young adult African Americans and Hispanic natives (identified by surname or self-identified ethnically) are very similar to each other in each census year. Superficially, it appears that schools have treated these racial minorities in similar ways. This is a tentative hypothesis; these are only crude proportions, without any analysis to adjust for family background or immigration. Nonetheless, the similarity across half a century suggests that something may be operating to treat educational access for some minority groups in similar ways, with a generally narrowing disparity among races.

The dramatic narrowing between 1970 and 1980 in the racial gap in graduation in Table 1 masks long-term trends. Consider the prerequisite for graduation: high school attendance. Table 2 shows racial disparities in the proportion of 15 year olds who had ever attended ninth grade in the South from 1940 through 1970. All Southerners improved attendance at high school, yet the most dramatic gain was for African Americans between 1950 and 1960. In

Table 3
Graduation Odds Ratios for Eighteen-Year-Olds (Dependents Only)

Category	1940	1960	1970	1980	1990
African American	0.34*	0.79	1.08	0.98	0.96
Female	1.76**	1.99**	1.40**	1.51**	1.51*
Living in owned home	1.47**	1.19	1.50**	1.26*	1.10*
Doubling house income	1.03**	1.22**	1.12**	1.11**	1.11*
Employed head	1.50**	1.35	1.49**	1.04	0.98
Self-employed head	1.66**	1.23	0.97	1.07	1.07
Graduate head	3.12**	1.36*	1.38**	1.35**	1.48**
Living in the Northeast[a]	1.03	1.43**	1.23*	1.23	1.31**
Living in the South[a]	0.59**	0.62**	0.74**	0.97	1.05
Being a U.S. native	1.09	4.65*	1.27	1.03	1.21**
One more person in house	0.84**	0.84**	0.91**	0.94*	0.93**
Proportion graduate	0.33	0.37	0.41	0.40	0.38
Unweighted N[b]	11,010	1,694	2,398	2,619	25,216

Sources: Census public use samples. Odds ratios compare individuals who are different only in the relevant category. For example, the odds ratio for having a graduate head of household in 1940 meant that someone dependent on a high school graduate had 3.12 times the odds of graduating as someone living with a nongraduate, given everything else equal.

[a] Omitted category is living in the West or Midwest regions.

[b] Sample for 1990 is weighted; 1940 individuals were selected using the self-weighting variable; other samples are unweighted.

* $p < 0.05$. ** $p < 0.01$.

addition, the effects of race, after accounting for other information, shows a long term improvement ending in 1970 (see Table 3). The narrowing in the gap between 1970 and 1980 occurred largely because high school graduation stagnated for whites. Improvement in the education of racial minorities more broadly was long-term.

Since 1970, it appears that being African American has no longer been the dramatic penalty that it was earlier in the century. African Americans are still less likely to be high school graduates today, but differences in family characteristics account for virtually all of that difference. This is consistent with a report of the National Research Council in 1989, *A Common Destiny*. The report concluded that racial disparities narrowed in both academic experiences and achievement between 1940 and the 1970s, though some signs of a decline in the fortunes of African Americans in higher education appeared in the 1980s (Jaynes and Williams 1989: Chap. 7). The analysis in Table 3 is also consistent with Featherman and Hauser's (1976) analysis of education for men born in the first half of this century.

One important exception is the odds ratio for African Americans nineteen years old in 1990. A separate analysis of nineteen-year-olds (not presented here) confirms all of the long-term trends discussed in this chapter, with one anomaly. The odds ratio for African Americans nineteen years old rises between 1940 and 1970 to 1.02 in 1970. After 1970, however, the odds ratio dips to 0.84 in 1980 ($p = 0.23$) and 0.69 in 1990 ($p < 0.001$). Changes in the proportion of nineteen-year-olds dependent on relatives cannot account for the drop; a higher proportion was dependent in 1980 (86 percent) than in 1970 or 1980 (80 and 81 percent, respectively). If anything, 1990 should reflect relationships in the general population more accurately than the two prior censuses.

The odds ratios for nineteen-year-olds suggest instead that the narrowing racial gap in education represents two different patterns: increasing equality in the likelihood of graduating young, but an increasing reliance on alternative credentials to narrow racial gaps at older ages. Most eighteen-year-olds enumerated in the spring of the census year were seventeen the prior year at graduation. Thus, the patterns depicted in Table 3 represent greater equality for African Americans' likelihood of graduating slightly young. Table 1, as well as other evidence (Jaynes and Williams 1989; McMillen, Kaufman, and Whitner 1994), provides convincing evidence of narrowing racial gaps in credentials by the time people are in their mid-twenties. However, the relative position of African Americans nineteen years old deteriorated between 1970 and 1990, *after* achieving relative parity. This coincided with the increase in the proportion of graduates with General Educational Development (GED) credentials rather than regular diplomas (see Chapter 7). Recent African American graduates have been more likely to hold GED credentials than other graduates (Cameron and Heckman 1993). This suggests that the narrowing racial gap after 1970 in the proportions of young adults holding diplomas has relied partly on the increase in alternative credentials. This is applicable only to those who do not receive diplomas at early ages; African Americans are still as likely to have received diplomas before eighteen as others with similar background characteristics.

The same factors operating for other Americans—mostly, the push-pull relationship between the labor market and school attendance—also led African American adolescents to increased high school graduation in the twentieth century. Attendance at school for Southern African American teenage males climbed steadily from 1900 through 1950, and labor force participation deteriorated at the same time (Margo and Finegan 1993). Growing adolescent attendance came in part from the incentive of joining the Great Migration of African Americans out of the rural South, which started early in the twentieth century and drew disproportionately those who had more education (Grossman 1989; Margo 1990). One should keep in mind, however, that these were relative improvements in attendance; Southern blacks still lagged behind whites in adolescent school attendance, in large part because of widespread peonage and the low funding of black schools in the South. White planters had no interest in children being in school during peak periods of labor needs during the year, and their antipathy toward black schooling only grew as the more educated African Americans fled northward (Grossman 1989: 249–50; Wright 1986: 79, 177). The growth in black schooling came largely despite, not because of, planter attitudes toward schooling.

The long-term trend toward adolescent schooling of African Americans accelerated after 1950. First came high school attendance, then the equalization of graduation odds for people of the same economic and family circumstances, and finally the narrowing racial gap in actual graduation proportions. Two related sets of events pushed African American teenagers out of the labor market after 1950 and pulled them into schools. One was growing opportunities for adults in occupations that did not encourage child labor, coupled with the loss of agricultural opportunities from the mechanization of Southern agriculture. Intertwined with changing labor markets was the determination of African Americans to make a better life for themselves and their children after World War II.

Labor opportunities formed one major influence on education. Black migration to cities and the depopulation of the rural South changed the nature of labor markets for African Americans, with farm labor (for men) and domestic service (for women) decreasing in importance between 1940 and 1960 (Jaynes and Williams 1989: 272–73). The dwindling of sharecropping began with crop-reduction farm subsidies in the New Deal, as landowners were paid to decrease acreage in cultivation and ignored nominal requirements to keep tenants on the land. What the New Deal started, cotton mechanization and the growth of cotton in California rapidly completed. By the 1950s, hired workers outnumbered farm tenants in the South, and the total number of workers on Southern farms declined by 1960. In addition, the extension of federal minimum-wage laws to more occupations, including those in agriculture, completed the exclusion of teenagers from primary labor markets. These developments affected African

Americans in the South disproportionately, and the rise in secondary schooling was one consequence (Kirby 1987: Chap. 2; Wright 1986: 241–57).

With few options available in the first half of the century, most African Americans could not have afforded to send their children to high school. Both farming and domestic service provided opportunities for child labor that families could scarcely give up. For Essie Favrot, born in 1910, high school was not a conscious option: "I finished out of the eighth grade in the country. But by then my very oldest sister had come to stay with my aunt, and she decided it was time I came, too. The onliest thing then was for a black girl to do was to get domestic work. So, I worked" (Tucker 1988: 118). For Favrot and her aunt, high school was not part of their expectation for growing up. Instead, going to work was normal. This does not mean that education was unimportant for African Americans in general, but this evidence suggests how economic opportunities shaped the individual decisions made when children became teenagers.

With the decline of sharecropping and domestic service came the end of child labor and the push toward extended schooling for many families. The opening of some other job opportunities, with the obvious credential value of schooling, provided a pull toward schooling, and adults shifted the priorities they had for adolescents. Martha Calvert, born in 1953, had a dramatically different set of opportunities from Essie Favrot. Seventeen years old in 1970, she was at the end of the long sweep of improvement documented in Table 3. As the youngest of fifteen children, she described in vivid terms how her mother, a domestic worker, had changed expectations by the time she was growing up: "I was the first one to go to college. . . . [S]he had this idea about what I was going to be, and one thing I wasn't going to be was a domestic. I came along at a time where, yeah, it looked like it could be possible that a black woman could be more. She worked for me with that in mind" (Tucker 1988: 40). For Calvert's mother, changing opportunities made advanced education for her youngest child feasible and sensible.

In addition to changing labor markets, a new assertiveness by African Americans after World War II changed their opportunities for high school graduation. To some extent, civil rights efforts and labor market opportunities overlapped, as activists opened some defense-related employment to African Americans during World War II. Civilians employed in defense-related industries and returning veterans helped spark the civil rights movement in Southern cities (Norrell 1985). Their search for equal rights as individuals brought African Americans into high schools. To put it bluntly, African Americans were much less willing after the war to accept second-class citizenship and worked to improve their own lives and the lives of their children.

As in other postwar periods, civil rights activism in the 1940s through 1960s took a two-pronged approach, including both collective action and individual choices. After the 1954 Supreme Court *Brown v. Board of Education* decision ruling school segregation unconstitutional, civil rights workers filed desegregation lawsuits across the South and eventually in the North. Change was slow, though. Few Southern schools desegregated until after the Civil Rights Act of 1964 threatened to cut off federal aid to segregated systems (Orfield 1993). This slow pace is perhaps one of the reasons why the final equalization of graduation odds for African Americans and for others of similar circumstances came between 1960 and 1970.

Yet the acceleration of secondary education for African Americans came well before the federal government took action. The dramatic change in Southern enrollments in high school between 1950 and 1960, shown in Table 2, suggests a dramatic shift in family strategies that began with a new generation of children, those born during and after World War II. Millions of African Americans were unwilling to tolerate second-class citizenship after the war and acted individually in various ways—fleeing the rural South, working for civil rights, or deciding that their children should attend high school or college. It comes as no surprise that they were unwilling to see their children as tenant farmers for white planters or domestic servants in white households. As opportunities for child labor shrank and opportunities in industrial jobs appeared on the horizon, African American families began to send their children to high schools in overwhelming numbers.

Did white politicians in the South respond to the migration of African Americans out of the region after World War II by opening up access to high schools for African Americans? Economist Gavin Wright has written, "Concern for the loss of labor led Southerners to upgrade the level of spending on black schools" after the war (Wright 1986: 245). Wright is correct that the ratio of spending on black to white schools (relative to population or attendance) improved between early in the century, when black schools received about 35 percent of what white schools received, and the 1950s, when even rural black schools received 62 percent of what white schools did (Lieberson 1980: Table 6.6). In part, higher spending for black schools was a last-ditch effort of white politicians to avoid the judicial overthrow of segregation laws. However, the improvement after World War II was for both white and black schools during the baby boom, and most capital spending was for elementary schools. In 1951, only 23 percent of secondary schools in the Census Bureau's South region were open to African Americans (U. S. Office of Education 1952: Tables 16, 39). Rural areas had the fewest high schools. For example, the 1950 biennial report of the Georgia Department of Education reported that thirty-three counties had no black high schools, while only three had no white high schools (Georgia Department of Education annual reports).

Improvement between 1950 and 1960 was scant. A comparison of the high schools available to whites and blacks in Tennessee shows the limited impact of spending on the availability of secondary education. In 1950, high schools were widely available to whites. There were 350 schools with a twelfth grade, and only four rural county systems were without a twelfth grade being available at all. By contrast, only sixty-nine black high schools with a twelfth grade existed in the entire state, and African Americans in fifty-one rural county systems had no high school available to them (Tennessee Department of Education 1950: 52–55). In 1960, the comparative situation was little better. Whites had gained ten high schools, and only one rural county system was without a twelfth grade available to whites. African Americans, however, had only gained fourteen high schools, and forty-seven county systems still had no black high school in 1960 (Tennessee Department of Education 1960: 82–85). This suggests that high schools were not much more widely available to AfricanAmericans in 1960 than in 1950. Yet, as Table 2 shows, a far higher proportion of teenagers attended high school by 1960. The change in high school attendance in the South came, once again, despite and not because of the decisions of white politicians.

Finally, one must keep in mind that the amelioration of differences in graduation appears only after accounting for family circumstances. Minorities still have a distinct disadvantage in graduating from high school. Furthermore, evidence of racial discrimination in labor markets abounds. Even with equivalent educational experiences, racial minorities have less income and wealth than whites, and some evidence exists of widening disparities among college graduates (Freeman 1980; Freeman and Holzer 1986; Harrison and Gorham 1992; Jaynes and Williams 1989; Moss and Tilly 1991). The evidence presented here suggests that racial minorities, and African Americans in particular, are as motivated to achieve in schooling as others when the opportunities exist, not that racial inequality has disappeared.

PERSISTENT GENDER DIFFERENCES

Males have persistently been at a disadvantage in graduating from high school for almost a century. This was true at the turn of the century (Tyack and Hansot 1990: Chap. 7), and the evidence since 1940 is consistent with that information. According to Table 3, being female was an advantage for the fifty years between 1940 and 1990. This is notably different from college, where men have consistently been the majority enrolled until the late 1970s (Solomon 1985: Table 2). While private academies in colonial times were predominantly male (as were grammar schools and colleges), coeducation quickly became the norm in most schools. This extended to high schools, despite the few, such as in Boston, that maintained single-sex restrictions. Gender differences in attending high school were more like those in primary grades than in college because coeducation was the historical norm in high schools as well as in elementary schools.

Females have outnumbered males in high schools and in graduating classes because males have consistently been more likely to go into the labor market as teenagers. Whether this was because more jobs have usually been available to teenage boys than girls or because families expected boys to earn income is difficult to discern; probably both factors were important until recently. In addition, occupational segregation gave an incentive for girls to remain in school longer than boys: A higher proportion of jobs for women required education than jobs for men. In the late nineteenth and early twentieth centuries, the best jobs available for women were teaching and clerical positions, and that probably encouraged high school enrollments (Licht 1992: 91, 94–95; Rury 1991). This effect of occupational segregation has probably continued to the present.

The continuing advantage of females through the present is also consistent with evidence that males have been less successful in advancing through the grades. Documentation of this trend also existed early in this century (Ayres 1909). In the last decade, nonpromotion has been common, especially in elementary grades, for a variety of reasons (Shepard and Smith 1988). Again, one cannot unambiguously know whether this is because school routines are more hostile toward the way boys are socialized, or whether boys in this society are more likely to act in ways less acceptable to teachers than girls. One must contrast this advantage of girls in continuing through and completing elementary and secondary schools, however, with the disadvantage girls have in other areas of schooling (Wellesley College Center 1992). The advantage females have in graduating from high school may represent schools' accepting them more often as conforming as well as the occupational segregation which may provide differential incentives for high school graduation.

PARENTS' ECONOMIC CIRCUMSTANCES

Sorting out the influences of family economic circumstances on graduation is difficult, for several reasons. Nonetheless, Table 3 suggests the continuing importance of wealth in determining who graduates. Four economic variables were comparable across all census years: whether the person lived in an owned (as opposed to rented) residence, household income relative to other households in the census (represented by the logarithm of household income), whether the household head worked, and whether the household head was self-employed. These are rough indices of economic circumstances. Still, they encompass three dimensions of economics. Household ownership tests whether a family has reached a certain minimum threshold of wealth. Household income and head employment suggests how desperate a family might be for alternative income sources. Household head self-employment indicates some independence from the wage-labor market and has been important in other studies of economics and school attendance (e.g., Katz, Doucet, and Stern 1982).

Economic circumstances that have had the most consistent associations with graduation are home ownership and household income. Table 3 suggests that, all other circumstances being equal, home ownership has made high school graduation consistently more likely since 1940. Additional income has also made graduation more likely. By contrast, employment and self-employment have diminished in importance since 1940 (though the direction of association suggests that families in more secure circumstances are still better able to afford, in some sense, to send their children to high school). Household income and home ownership, as well as parental education, may have captured the effects of working and self-employment. In addition, with growing segmentation of the labor market, self-employment is no longer as important an indicator of economic power. This is consistent with other historical evidence about the importance of labor market segmentation in the development of a white-collar class (Stern 1989).

There is a large difference between the odds of graduating for children of parents who have property or sizable income and for those who have little income or no house. This is independent of the obvious measure one might claim as a proxy for parental persistence or intelligence, household head graduation. Instead, the influences of home ownership and income suggest a different dynamic: Those who are well-off are able to use education to help pass on economic advantages to their children. This is consistent with other information about the influence of education on intergenerational mobility (e.g., Bowles and Gintis 1974; Jencks et al. 1972). The choice of school attendance for adolescents at some point comes down to whether parents can afford to pay the living costs of a child during schooling. Those who own homes or have more income are more able to afford that cost, despite (or perhaps more emphatically so) in difficult circumstances.

Home equity, in particular, is a valuable buffer in hard times that renters do not have. One can borrow against the value of a home, enabling one to meet household expenses and, in effect, substituting debt for the income of a working teenager. Renters usually have no substitute source of collateral for debt. Since World War II, a college diploma has replaced high school graduation as the credential that only a minority of adults have, and the use of home equity to buffer families from the costs of attendance has shifted to a different level of schooling. A study of students enrolled in college in 1986 found that over 7 percent of contributing parents took out a second mortgage to support their children in college (Churaman 1992: Table 4a). Nonetheless, the relationship among wealth, income, and schooling can still exist for younger adolescents. The continuing relationships among home ownership, income, and high school graduation suggest that some unaffordable cost to high school attendance still exists for some families who, because they are renting, have little cushion against economic vagaries.

PARENTS' EDUCATION

Like the advantage of home ownership and greater income, the advantage of living in the house of a high school graduate has remained since 1940. High school graduation is an advantage one can successfully transmit to children. Whether through sharing ways of negotiating school routines, teaching or modeling useful skills, or simply being a role model, high school graduates make it much easier for children under their care to graduate from high school. Others may attribute the influence of parental education to inherited intelligence or character traits like persistence. Some of this is certainly true.

In addition, the anomalous influence in 1940 (when the dependent of a high school graduate had odds of graduating more than three times better than odds for others) suggests, once again, the ways in which education can serve as an instrument of intergenerational security and a buffer against downward mobility. One should be somewhat cautious in interpreting the odds ratio for 1940, as the advantage shrinks if one uses a stricter definition of graduation. Nonetheless, even with a stricter definition, the advantage in 1940 is greater than in other years with a statistically significant difference ($p < 0.05$). When the Great Depression struck in the 1930s, many otherwise comfortable families found themselves in difficult straits. The credential value of a high school diploma was one perceived way to give children an advantage in the labor market. Whatever was the advantage in being the child of a high school graduate, these families must have encouraged in a way unique to the 1930s. The logical interpretation is that economic depression gave families an incentive to use every means to safeguard their children from economic ruin. The education of one's parents or guardians has remained important through 1990, if less dominating.

OTHER CHARACTERISTICS

The remaining information in Table 3 suggests the relative influences of region, nativity, and household size on the odds of being an eighteen-year-old high school graduate in each census. With one exception, there is little surprise in the direction or magnitude of influence. In the case of region, the association with living in the South or Northeast are in contrast to that with living in the Midwest or West census regions. Living in the Northeast appears, after all else, to have conferred some advantage throughout the fifty years between 1940 and 1990, though the influence was stronger in some census years than others. Living in the South was a distinct disadvantage until 1980 and 1990, when it appeared to have no net influence compared with living in the Midwest or West. This change came because of the growing urbanization and industrialization of the South and the slow growth in school expenditures. One should keep in mind that this amelioration of net disadvantage exists after accounting for other information, such as economic circumstances of families. In addition, the influence of the region as a whole may mask substantial educational disadvantages in specific states.

As one might expect, having been born in the United States confers a distinct advantage in the odds of being a high school graduate in the last census (with growing immigration since 1965), and Table 3 confirms that. The estimated effect of nativity in 1960, when being born in the United States appears to confer relative odds almost five times as great as for immigrants, is anomalous.

Fewer than thirty out of 1,700 cases in 1960, however, were immigrants; the estimate is probably unreliable. More reliable are the figures for 1980 and 1990, when approximately 5 percent and 10 percent of records, respectively, represented immigrants. The 1990 odds ratio still shows an advantage in being a high school graduate, though a less substantial one than one might guess from the 1960 estimate alone.

Finally, living in a large household has been a consistent disadvantage in education. In most large families, an eighteen-year-old is one of the oldest children in a house and among the most likely to get a job if household circumstances require additional income (or had required it in the recent past). Teenagers may also be called upon to help families in other emergencies, such as with child care or elder care during a health crisis of a parent (Fine 1987: 96–97). Older children can serve as supports in a society where social services do not give parents any reliable safety net. This is consistent with what historians know about family consumption patterns and the use of teenagers' income as part of family strategies (Goldin 1981; Hareven 1982; Modell, Furstenberg, and Hershberg 1978).

The cost of relying on teenagers, seen here, is that older children in larger families are less likely to graduate from high school; they are more likely to be relied on for household income. The disadvantage of large families has decreased in the past fifty years, demonstrating the importance of a welfare system in buffering children from crises affecting their parents. Because logistic regression calculates the logarithm of odds, the disadvantage of living in a large family is estimated as multiplicative: *Each* additional family member incurs the disadvantage listed in Table 3. Small changes in the relative odds for one additional family member may translate into substantial changes in the relative disadvantage for large families. To the present, some disadvantage still accrues from living in a large family.

OTHER RESEARCH

The evidence presented in Table 3 and the explanations above connect what historians know about school attendance of teenagers to contemporary research into attendance and graduation. Most social science research into high school graduation and dropping out uses recent data or, in the case of longitudinal studies, analyses of one or two cohorts' experiences. Contemporary research, therefore, does not provide evidence of historical trends. Many historians have carefully reconstructed attendance patterns through examinations of census manuscripts in specific places like Hamilton, Ontario, in the mid-nineteenth century or Providence, Rhode Island, in the early twentieth century (Katz, Doucet, and Stern 1982; Perlmann 1988). Because of the lag time (seventy-two years in the United States) between a census and the manuscripts' becoming available to the public, however, historians have only examined individual-level data linked to school records through the early twentieth century. The recent availability of public use samples from the 1940, 1950, and 1990 censuses now provides a fifty-year record of high school graduation in the United States that links what historians know about the nineteenth and early twentieth centuries to the present.

In general, the information I present here confirms what other researchers have claimed. Even if one includes only multivariate analyses, the literature on attendance and graduation is rich. Historians have discussed most of the relationships described here, with the exception of the influences of region and parental education (Kaestle and Vinovskis 1980: Chap. 4; Katz, Doucet, and Stern 1982: 252–54, 264–74; Perlmann 1988). Economists, sociologists, and educational researchers have also explored graduation, acknowledging the importance of economic circumstances, sex, parents' experiences with education, nativity, and the presence and number of other dependents in the household in educational attainment and graduation more specifically (Ekstrom et al. 1987; Featherman and Hauser 1976; Mare 1980, 1981; Natriello, Pallas, and McDill 1987; Rumberger 1987; Walters and Briggs 1993).

The primary discovery for historians in this analysis is how the racial gap in educational experiences narrowed for African Americans. The timing of the change suggests that the civil rights movement by itself was not responsible for the improvement in the odds of graduation. This is consistent with Featherman and Hauser's (1976) analysis of changes in educational attainment across generations, which also provides evidence of the equalization of educational opportunities after accounting for family circumstances. A combination of changing labor markets, individual action, and collective activism best explains the relative improvement in graduation for African Americans at the same time as graduation for everyone was becoming more common. One must be cautious in generalizing from these results, for they say nothing about the success of civil rights activists in other areas of education. High school graduation is, after all, a very small part of educational experiences and achievement.

AGE NORMS, INSTITUTIONS, AND DEPENDENCY

Most of this chapter discusses the influences of various social and economic circumstances on the odds of being a high school graduate at age eighteen. Certainly, the analysis does not discuss the internal workings of schools or the situations of specific communities, which have been important in shaping attendance. For succeeding chapters, one should keep in mind the importance of the general trend for expectations of graduation. It is unlikely that high school graduation would have become a widespread expectation when a small minority of children earned diplomas early in this century. Having a majority of teenagers earn diplomas made the expectation reasonable. At the same time, however, graduation became an expectation—and dropping out an apparent crisis—while a sizable minority still were without diplomas. Demography did not entirely deter-mine the timing (and certainly not the manner) of changing age norms. What was required, in addition to majority graduation, was a change in expectations for high schools.

This chapter also underscores the relationship between schooling and labor markets. As succeeding generations of adolescents withdrew from and were pushed out of full-time labor, a higher proportion attended school longer and more consistently. Schooling thus came to dominate adolescence by the mid-twentieth century. In the long run, it is perhaps not surprising that schooling extended further as the population aged. Both lower mortality and fertility made children a smaller proportion of the population after the middle of the nineteenth century. In 1850, almost half of the population was under eighteen; 52 percent was under twenty (U. S. Bureau of the Census 1975, 15). In 1900, 40 percent of the population was under eighteen; in 1950, 31 percent; in 1990, 26 percent (U. S. Bureau of the Census 1975: 8, 10; U. S. Bureau of the Census 1992: 20). With more of the population in adulthood, a society can (theoretically) afford to send children to school longer.

Demographic changes are not enough, though, to explain growing graduation, for the rise in high school attendance and graduation continued well after the demographic transition to lower mortality and fertility in the United States. In addition, growing high school graduation between 1950 and 1970 went *against* an increasing proportion of the population under eighteen with the baby boom; 34 percent of the population was under 18 in 1970 (U. S. Bureau of the Census 1975: 8, 10). Intertwined with demography were important changes in labor markets and the role of institutions. As described earlier, teenagers and their families met with growing restrictions on child labor, while school became increasingly visible as a source of credentials usable in adult labor markets. Pushed and pulled into school, teenagers were more likely to graduate each decade.

At the same time that the dynamics of child labor markets were beginning to change, institutional reformers were devising more intentional means of socializing teenagers (Cravens 1993; Kett 1977; Rothman 1980; Zelizer 1985). The publication of G. Stanley Hall's *Adolescence* in 1904 popularized the term because it resonated with existing concerns about youth and dependency. As in the middle of the nineteenth century, Progressive Era reformers were concerned about children growing up in poverty, especially with how they would behave as adults. The transition between childhood and adulthood—and the potential for idleness in between—worried reformers, and Hall's idea that adolescence was a time with the potential for extreme behavior matched those concerns. Thus, reformers devised or modified voluntary and coercive mechanisms to socialize youth.

The use of adolescence as a justification for institutional reformers accommo-dated growing age-consciousness in the United States. Howard Chudacoff (1989) describes the growing age stratification after the middle of the nineteenth century.

The wage-labor market linked this age consciousness, as Chudacoff terms it, to growing fears of dependency. Most of the age-segregated institutions created in the late nineteenth and early twentieth centuries had, as a core part of their aim, the prevention or amelioration of dependency. Programs for children and youth were to prevent or stop delinquency and poverty in young adults. Pensions and retirement rationalized the exclusion of older people from the labor market.

The high school became, by the middle twentieth century, the dominant institution for youth. This created dilemmas for educators because the high school then acquired all the baggage of age norms for teenagers, including the prevention of dependency. High schools were not created originally as a means of preventing poverty or delinquency, nor as a means of general education. Yet, by the middle of the twentieth century, educators actively rationalized universal attendance of teenagers as a means of socializing the next generation. This shift in missions came from the changed role of secondary education and its success in dominating adolescence. Few anticipated the dilemmas this created for educators when high school graduation became expected of everyone.

2

The Changing Mission
of High Schools

The increased likelihood of graduating from high school was the demographic foundation for our current expectation of universal (or near universal) graduation. It is unlikely that graduation could have become a widespread expectation of adolescents when only a small fraction graduated. In addition to demographic changes, though, the definition of dropping out as a serious problem required the belief that everyone should attend high schools. Dropping out is a concern precisely because of deeply held views that the high school is an essential part of formal education. This role for high schools is an historical artifact. The common view of high schools as comprehensive was not inevitable in North America and became entrenched only after World War II. Until then, high schools were selective institutions, enrolling and graduating only a portion of adolescents.

Some suggested, early in the century, that high schools be universal, yet no consensus existed about the proper extent of high school attendance for several decades. Slowly, high schools evolved into mass institutions. As they did so, the presumed purpose changed. Over the first half of this century, high schools became community institutions in many towns, perhaps more known for their sports than their graduates. During the Great Depression, school officials added custodianship of youth to the mission of high schools. By the end of World War II, educators had expanded the mission of high schools to include the vague goal that schools should help students adjust to adult life. Here, then, was a mission that fit universal attendance, though it landed administrators in hot water in the 1950s.

This shift in goals was by no means uncontested. In every decade, cynics questioned the propriety of broader high school attendance as school officials and their critics fought over the appropriateness of high school expansion (Angus 1965). Yet the opponents of universal high school attendance were fighting a losing battle. In the end, it was not the conscious decision of educators that made high schools a mass institution, but growing attendance by teenagers. Educators matched the goal of high schools to what they saw as changing educational demographics. Nonetheless, while they were rationalizing a *fait accompli*, they chose how to justify growing high school attendance.

The belief in high schools as the capstone of public education developed in rough tandem with growing attendance, but public debate and demography were only loosely linked. Certainly, the rhetoric of educators did not always reflect the reality of secondary schools. The growing network of school administrators created a national culture of professional educators that bridged regional and local differences (Tyack and Hansot 1982). Similar justifications by educators for secondary education across the continent obscured important regional differences in the development and availability of high schools. Conversely, demographic developments sometimes led public opinion. Attendance at high school increased dramatically between the turn of the century and World War II. However, it was only in the 1930s and 1940s that high schools became an unquestioned place where adolescents should spend their teenage years. The rise in high school attendance may have encouraged the belief that high schools should be universal, but demographic patterns did not determine the timing or intellectual basis for that tenet.

Over the long term, the acceptance of high schools as comprehensive was a dramatic change in how North Americans have used and described schools. For almost three centuries, some form of secondary education has existed on this continent, yet for most of that time advanced schooling was limited. In retrospect, the fact that high schools are now unquestioned as the appropriate place for teenagers is nothing short of astounding. However, this apparent democratization has come at a price: the end to meritocratic ideals of the older urban high schools. When enrollment started to expand in the late nineteenth century, a debate ensued over the purpose of high schools and their curriculum. Were high schools to remain primarily academic, with curriculum focused on an academic education, or would several curricula exist to differentiate among students? In the twentieth century, differentiated education won out in high schools (as it dominated elsewhere). This differentiation allowed the expansion of high school enrollment while retaining an internal elitism for secondary schools, through tracking or the occasional selective high school.

This one-chapter sketch of high school history cannot substitute for the more general accounts of Robert Hampel (1986), Edward Krug (1964, 1972), or William Reese (1995), or the case study of David Labaree (1988). My purpose here is to emphasize, first, the growing pains of high schools as a set of institutions and, second, the role of educators in shaping the consensus by mid-century that high schools had a clear purpose in educating all adolescents. The legacy of this history is a longstanding tension between the platitudes of universal secondary education and the sorting and credentialing functions of high schools. Sensitive observers of schools have noticed this tension and explained it in various ways.

Some have hoped high schools could serve both purposes, to socialize and to sort. Successfully balancing both objectives of high schools implied truly universal attendance, and this suggested that those who left high school (or dropouts, as they became known in the 1960s) were a sign of failure for the comprehensive high school. The unquestioned primacy of public high schools at mid-century was thus the intellectual foundation for the definition of dropping out as a pressing social problem.

SELECTIVE EDUCATION WITH A PUBLIC PURPOSE

For most of the history of English-language settlement in North America, advanced schooling was the privilege of a minority. Few attended the loose configuration of private academies and seminaries, grammar schools, high schools, and colleges that made up secondary and higher education. Nonetheless, advanced schooling had more than a private purpose. From the beginnings of English settlement, colonial leaders crafted rationales for the public support of higher education. The Massachusetts Bay colony and most of New England nominally required towns of a certain size to maintain a grammar school or some way of educating older boys who were beyond the basics of learning their letters. While these mandates for towns were typically part of larger prescriptions for education, the requirements for establishing grammar schools were distinct from those for general education. According to colonial leaders, everyone was to learn something in order to be able to read the Bible and obey civil authority. But the towns were also to maintain some schooling for boys who might aspire to leadership (Cohen 1974: 1:394, 399–400).

As formal schooling developed more extensively in British North America, the distinction between elementary and higher education continued. As early as the eighteenth century, primary education was available to most of the population in many areas (Cremin 1970: 544). Schools also consistently became coeducational as they became widespread (Tyack and Hansot 1990). Yet few students advanced beyond the primary grades. Many grammar schools and academies were glorified primary schools, as they either had students unprepared for more difficult work or unprepared teachers. The lines between primary grades, grammar schools, academies, and colleges were not necessarily based on what the schools actually taught (Cremin 1970: 187, 192–93). What was undoubtedly true, however, was the limited access to advanced education. It was who attended schools, not what they learned, that made higher education selective.

In the nineteenth century, a new form of advanced education evolved in the towns of the Northern United States. Called public high schools, they competed with private academies and colleges for attendance of the few students who advanced beyond elementary schooling. Again, this new form of higher education commanded a public purpose, despite the limited entry. For common school reformers, high schools were to be the pinnacle of public schooling. They would educate in a classical or more modern curriculum those boys who went beyond the primary and grammar schools, providing democratic access to higher education. Whether working-class children attended high schools was not the concern; access was sufficient (Reese 1995: 46–49). The advocates of high schools consistently defended them not for their coverage but their fairness. Thus, high schools had a different public purpose from elementary schools. While free public schooling was to be common for younger children, it was important for high schools to be available, not necessarily widespread (Katz 1968: Part I; Labaree 1988). This difference provided a critical wedge that separated the politics of elementary schooling from secondary education. Debates about secondary education in the nineteenth century consistently revolved around fairness and access because of their selective nature.

In addition, common-school reformers hoped the existence of high schools would improve education in the lower grades (Reese 1995: 56–57). Students would gain entrance through competitive examinations, providing an incentive for the lower grades to teach students the prerequisite skills for gaining admission to high school. Primary schools would, theoretically, have to run their classrooms and schools to satisfy the high school's requirements. Henry Barnard hoped that high schools would "operate as a powerful and abiding stimulus to exertion throughout all the lower schools" (Barnard 1865: 283). Thus, selectivity was an essential part of high schools' purposes, according to common-school reformers.

High schools, however, were not accepted immediately as valuable community institutions. The unpopularity of publicly supported antebellum high schools has been the subject of much debate among historians, but there is no doubt about its controversial nature. Michael Katz (1968) argued, from a vote of residents to abolish the high school of Beverly, Massachusetts, in 1860, that the unpopularity of high schools represented class-oriented reactions to antebellum school reform. Laborers were unconvinced of the benefits of high schools, Katz claimed, while urban professionals and property owners agreed with the basic tenets of antebellum common-school reform. Vinovskis (1985), on the other hand, argued that partisan and geographic, not class, interests dominated the vote in Beverly. (In other words, Katz showed that laborers and unpropertied artisans were more likely to vote to abolish the high school than town professionals. Using multivariate analysis, Vinovskis argued that those living in the outlying parts of the town were more likely to vote to abolish than were those living in the town center, and that geography was more important than occupation in determining the vote.) Yet what is controversial about the vote for historians is not *whether* high schools were unpopular but *why* (and Katz's class interpretation of the vote). The 1860 vote was one of many over several decades in Beverly in which town residents repeatedly demonstrated opposition to the high school. They tolerated the existence of a high school only when the state required it.

What the vote of Beverly shows is that high schools quickly became embroiled in political controversy about their essential purposes. Were they to cement a system of education or to provide some avenue of upward mobility? Town residents in Beverly and elsewhere seemed largely unpersuaded by the original justifications for high schools. A state mandate, not popular consensus, drove the creation of high schools in Massachusetts. (In Beverly, a lawsuit against the town finally convinced residents to reopen another high school after the 1860 vote.) Vinovskis argued that class was not the fundamental difference between supporters and opponents of the high school in Beverly, Massachusetts. Yet his evidence suggests that the limited access to high schools was one of the most controversial aspects. Why should most town residents support a high school that few of their children would ever attend? Initially, high schools had little broad support because they did not seem to have much connection with the lives of town residents. The later growth of high schools suggests that the credential value of high school attendance brought one kind of popular support, although with pressures to increase access to secondary education. In the beginning, though, high schools did not have much democratic appeal to citizens in the nineteenth century.

The unpopularity of high schools was dramatically different from the support lower grades received. Approval for elementary schools was widespread, including that of workingmen's associations of the early nineteenth century (Katznelson and Weir 1985: Chap. 2). By the Civil War, most white children in the Northern United States spent some time in elementary schools. The consistency and amount of time may have varied dramatically by place and circumstance, but almost everyone had some elementary schooling. Such was not the case for high schools. Maris Vinovskis (1988) has argued that a substantial minority attended high schools in one Massachusetts county in the middle nineteenth century. Vinovskis' account underscores the importance of access to high schools in the growth of secondary attendance: Where high schools existed, many attended, yet that access was spotty. Massachusetts had a state mandate for town high schools that few other states matched for many decades. Few attended high schools in most areas, and one does not wonder at the vote to abolish the high school in Beverly when the high school served only a few dozen students in 1858 and 1859 (Vinovskis 1985: 81–82). Thus, early high schools experienced a tension between their selective nature and public skepticism about access to them (see also Reese 1995: 59–79).

As high schools developed, attendance acquired a credential value. Attendance at high schools was limited, and that rarity by itself, in addition to what high schools presumably taught, made attendance and graduation valuable in nineteenth-century labor markets. Credentialism vied with the inherently selective origins of high schools. David Labaree (1988) has argued that the credentialing function of Central High School in nineteenth-century Philadelphia created tension between its singular status in the city and demands for increased access to high schools in Philadelphia. The prestige of the school and the autonomy of its faculty depended on its holding a monopoly on a rare credential in the city. Yet the obvious power of that credential led to demands for increased access to secondary education. Through most of the nineteenth century, the school tried to satisfy political pressures by claiming that access was fair and equitable and that fairness was enough. Thus, Central High School experienced directly the tension between credentialing and the political demands for access. Supporters of the school claimed that blindly graded examinations eliminated the privilege of wealth. Every boy had the option of attending Central High School, if only he could pass the entrance examination. To advocates of a limited credential in the nineteenth century, the possibility of access was sufficient to meet democratic obligations.

The history of high schools in the nineteenth century shows one element of the later contradictions of high school expansion: the strain between its selective nature and the egalitarian assumptions of public support. From their origins, high schools were controversial because few attended them. Later in the nineteenth century, high schools had to balance the high status of limited access against the demands of parents. City residents demanded wider access to high schools, and these political pressures reinforced the meritocratic rhetoric of high school supporters. Their defenders justified high schools not by acknowledging a need for increased access but by claiming instead that access was fair. Politics of the high school in the nineteenth century revolved around the nature of access, not the proportion of children who attended. For most of the nineteenth century, the limited access to high schools held. Slowly, more high schools opened and competed for students with private academies, yet few in the total population attended.

HIGH SCHOOL GROWTH AND CURRICULUM DIFFERENTIATION

In the early twentieth century, the focus of high school politics shifted in two ways. First, the expansion of high school enrollment led to changing ideas about the coverage of high schools and the new idea that secondary education should be universal. Closely linked to the rationalization of high school expansion was the changing nature of the high school curriculum and the structure of urban high schools. These new dimensions supplemented, rather than replaced, the earlier tension between selectiveness and public support. Left intact was the contradiction implied in public support of limited education. The apparent resolution of the conflict, differentiation of the high school curriculum, allowed selectiveness within a comprehensive institution by creating internal sorting within public schools. Only a limited proportion of students would enroll in the academic track in the early twentieth century, preserving the status and power of an elite curriculum.

One rationalization of differentiation and tracking was the presumed needs of working-class students. Not only were wealthy students disproportionately represented in the higher tracks, but many educators explicitly argued for tracking based on class. This rationalization fed the desire of Progressive Era administrators to coordinate schools with an industrial economy (Krug 1964; Tyack 1974). As Raymond Callahan (1962) noted, school officials borrowed freely from business metaphors of efficiency. The effect, however, was to justify inequities in urban schools that paralleled the social structure of the economy. Educators argued that schools should help students accommodate to an industrial world and their presumed place in it. One should be cautious in interpreting curriculum changes in terms of social efficiency and the social ordering of schools. Educators had a loose set of ideas rather than a coherent philosophy, and schools carried the burden of reforming the poor well before the turn of the twentieth century. In addition, the evolution of high school structure was not entirely a story of top-down imposition. Conflict shaped the structure of high schools and the secondary curriculum in local systems across the country. Nonetheless, differentiation of the curriculum formed the core of changed basic assumptions about high schools. Whereas nineteenth-century debates focused on the fairness of access and the problems in public support of selective institutions, twentieth-century high schools became known as mass institutions with the mission of socializing a growing proportion of teenagers. This shifted the focus of secondary education from the question of democratic support to that of utilitarian purpose, and the differentiated curriculum made the change seem natural.

The key factor in the change was enrollment. At the turn of the century, high school attendance exploded. Immigration, in particular, facilitated the exclusion of teenagers from work, as employers could turn to adult immigrants for cheap labor. The result, in part caused by the exclusion of teenagers from labor markets, was a ninefold increase in students attending public high schools, from just over 200,000 in 1890 to over 1.8 million in 1920. The number of high schools also mushroomed in the same period from about 2,500 to over 14,000 (Krug 1964: 5, 11, 439). This growth led to redefinition of the scope of high schools, such to lead the National Education Association (NEA) Commission on the Reorganization of Secondary Education, author of *Cardinal Principles of Secondary Education* in 1918, to declare that secondary education was "essential to all youth" (29).

Despite growing attendance, however, most acknowledged that high schools were the realm of relatively few students. This was not inconsistent with the claim that high schools were a fundamentally democratic institution. Educators considered the availability of secondary education advanced compared with that of other countries. School officials thus still relied on the nineteenth-century concept of democratic access to explain why limited attendance was sufficient. The statement of Columbia University Teachers College professors George Strayer and Edward Thorndike (1913: 69) on the subject was probably typical:

This country's great contribution to educational practice is the public high school, providing boys and girls from thirteen to nineteen with free education and free preparation for professional schools, technical schools and colleges. That a fifth to a third of all children go to high school for at least a time is a sign of the economic prosperity of the country which permits so many children to be freed from productive labor for so long.

Strayer and Thorndike celebrated the growth of secondary education, yet they acknowledged what educators knew, even in the midst of this growth: High schools were not universal institutions for adolescents in the early twentieth century.

Some were not persuaded that the growing popularity of high schools demonstrated an opportunity available on a democratic basis. George Counts (1922), just a few years after publication of the *Cardinal Principles of Secondary Education* report, argued vociferously that high schools were elitist institutions. Family economic background, race, and sex were important influences not only in determining who attended high schools but also (among attendees) in the curriculum taken and whether students graduated. Class considerations were the focus of his analysis. Children of wealthy parents were more likely to attend high school, take an academic curriculum, and graduate, according to Counts. Thus, high school was not a democratic opportunity: "Secondary education is not education for adolescence, as elementary education is education for childhood, but rather education for a select group of adolescents" (141). Counts recognized the tension between the continuing selectivity of high schools and the notion of universal access, and he reiterated the older arguments against the high school. One of the evils of the selectivity of high schools, according to Counts, was the public support of an elite education: "The poor are contributing to provide secondary education for the children of the rich, but are either too poor or too ignorant to avail themselves of the opportunities which they help to provide" (152). Yet Counts' solution to eliminate the advantage of the wealthy also derived from the nineteenth century: "Either open the doors of the high school to all children, and take care that all enter without favor, or frankly close its doors to all but a select group, adopt objective methods or selection, and teach to this selected group the meaning of social obligation" (156). The latter had been the claim of Central High School in Philadelphia, but it was no longer plausible with the expansion of high schools.

Thus, the growth of high schools did not eliminate older arguments about access and selectivity. In addition to the concerns critics had about access to high schools, though, their growth created another issue, a debate about the curriculum of secondary education. Were high schools to continue to have primarily academic aspirations, or were they to have other, more utilitarian goals? To some extent, this debate about "traditional" versus "practical" subjects had been a recurring theme for more than a century. Benjamin Franklin had proposed an English academy for the colony of Pennsylvania in the mid-eighteenth century (Cremin 1970: 375–78), and ninteenth century high schools struggled to define an appropriate curriculum (Reese 1995: 80–102). In addition, the nature of the curriculum has no intrinsic "practical" value in labor markets. Attendance at nineteenth-century high schools was extremely practical for young men in search of jobs, even though the curriculum for some schools was firmly grounded in classical education.

Yet in the three decades after 1890, the debate about the nature of high schools shifted from how the high school could fulfill some democratic purpose to how it would help students adjust to their likely economic status as adults. The center of discussion moved as educators struggled to accommodate growing high school attendance. They responded with the language of business efficiency and social order. Earlier educators and social critics had also hoped schools would shape the next generation, but discussion in the two decades before World War I took on particularly Darwinist tones. Advocates of the new utilitarian curricula hoped that schools would help individuals adjust to the new, industrial labor market (Krug 1964: 251–55). This was a far cry from the defense in Philadelphia of a meritocratic high school. In the nineteenth century, credentialism could be compatible with the belief that high schools provided an opportunity for upward mobility. In the early twentieth century, however, a utilitarian mission began to overshadow the older justification for a selective high school.

Two reports sponsored by the NEA provided intellectual bookends for this period and suggest the change in the purpose of high schools that their writers advocated. In 1893, the Committee of Ten, chaired by Harvard President Charles Eliot, produced a report recommending identical teaching methods for students regardless of whether the student was attending high school in preparation for college. The report concluded that high schools did not, on the whole, exist as college preparatory institutions:

Their main function is to prepare for the duties of life that small proportion of all the children in the country—a proportion small in number, but very important to the welfare of the nation—who show themselves able to profit by an education prolonged to the eighteenth year, and whose parents are able to support them while they remain so long at school. (National Education Association 1893/1894: 51)

Thus, the report argued, "every subject . . . should be taught in the same way and to the same extent to every pupil so long as he pursues it, no matter what the probable destination of the pupil may be, or at what point his education is to cease" (17). Eliot and his colleagues were not arguing for universal high school attendance, as the above quotation makes clear. Neither were they arguing against any differentiation of curricula: The report included four sets of model curricula, from "Classical" to "English" (46–47). Rather, they were staking a claim to standardization of coursework within each subject and, implicitly, to academic rigor in any curriculum.

By contrast, the report of the Commission on the Reorganization of Secondary Education (1918) on the *Cardinal Principles of Secondary Education* suggested an emphasis not on academics but on adjustment to modern life. In this report, at least, the social efficiency philosophy won. The main objectives of education, according to the commission, were health, "command of fundamental processes," "worthy home-membership," vocation, citizenship, leisure, and ethics (10–11). Thus, the commission recommended reorganization of high school subjects and, especially, the creation of different curricula for different students guided by "a system of educational supervision or guidance" (21) as to which curriculum to enter, based on the presumed future station in life: "The basis of differentiation should be, in the broad sense of the term, vocational" (22). Only as an aside did the commission acknowledge academics: "Provision should be made also for those having distinctively academic interests and needs" (22). It recommended that the comprehensive high school include all aspects of the differentiated curricula, because these would allow the variety of courses the commission believed was necessary for "a wise choice of curriculum" for each student (25). On this basis, then, the commission claimed that "an extended education for every boy and girl is essential to the welfare, and even to the existence, of democratic society" (29) and recommended the extension of compulsory attendance to eighteen, at least for part-time attendance at school (30–31).

The reports were dramatically different in both the supposed purposes of high school and its ideal enrollment. The Committee of Ten advocated standardization of academic subjects and equal treatment of all students in the context of limited high school enrollment. The Commission on the Reorganization of Secondary Education advocated a differentiated curriculum, but for everyone. To what extent was the abandonment of academic focus a trade for the dream of universal enrollment (Lazerson and Grubb 1974: 39)? In truth, both reports were idyllic statements, rhetoric that vaguely resembled contemporary reality. As the *Cardinal Principles* report acknowledged, few who attended high school in the early twentieth century finished (8). In addition, differentiated curricula were a prominent addition to schools across levels in the early twentieth century, and not just for high schools. It was not, therefore, an explicit exchange.

Nonetheless, the forces behind differentiation of the curriculum at both elementary and secondary levels had at least one critical element in common: Dramatically increased attendance put pressures on inadequate school organizations. For elementary grades in cities, the increased immigration from Europe meant overcrowded schools, double shifts, and a wide gap between the largely native, middle-class teaching force and the cultures and conditions of immigrants. Educators were also facing increasing numbers of students who demanded access to high schools. At both levels, the increase in attendance was an unexpected, and at least partly unwelcome, intrusion on the administration of schools. School officials struggled to respond in a way to expand and maintain professional autonomy.

Differentiation of the curriculum served the purpose of social efficiency advocates and school administrators well. The *Cardinal Principles* report justified it as responsive to the practical needs of the new high school enrollees. "The character of the secondary-school population," it claimed, "has been modified by the entrance of large numbers of pupils of widely varying capacities, aptitudes, social heredity, and destinies in life." Because of the change in students, the schools must change: "The needs of these pupils can not be neglected, nor can we expect in the near future that all pupils will be able to complete the secondary school as full-time students" (8).

Behind this facade of utilitarianism, however, lay the ideals of social efficiency; the children of laborers would become laborers and thus deserved a "useful"—and nonacademic—education. That a large plurality of high school students enrolled in Latin in 1890, and a majority in 1900, was a disturbing state for many concerned about the "proper" education of youth (Krug 1964: 176–77). The fact that Latin was no more of daily use for middle-class clerks than for the children of the working class was lost in the concern over the proper guidance of adolescents and, therefore, the consigning of laborers' children to a nonacademic curriculum. Academic disciplines faced an onslaught of criticism with the slow triumph of efficiency advocates (Krug 1964).

In the operation of schools, though, the results of differentiated education were more a consequence of accommodation than of the straightforward implementation of social efficiency ideals. The expansion of secondary education threatened the position of existing high schools, which had traded on the exclusiveness of their enrollment and curriculum. Still, accommodation for the specialized, prestigious high school remained an option in the long term. Central High School in Philadelphia lost much of its prestige and autonomy as the school system created other high schools, centralized, and pressured the Central High School faculty to reduce its exclusiveness. The school faculty had practiced collective governance of the school for decades, but by the turn of the twentieth century the school system exerted more bureaucratic control over the school. Nonetheless, the school's faculty and supporters fought this demotion at every turn. It retained enough of an identity to be reborn as a selective high school at the end of the 1930s (Labaree 1988: Chaps. 4–5).

The fate of vocational schooling in high schools was also the result of conflict and negotiation over the meaning of schools. Across the country, educators, businessmen, laborers, and others debated whether the proper location of vocational education was in separate vocational schools or as part of comprehensive high schools. Perhaps the most famous conflict was in Chicago. There, a number of businessmen proposed a system of vocational schooling in the early twentieth century, in a separate set of schools. That system never came into being because of the opposition of Chicago's unions. The unions were not opposed to vocational education in principle. They objected to the tracking of poorer children into the separate schools and the possibility that Chicago businesses would use these schools as a place to socialize a nonunion workforce.

Because members of Chicago's working class banded together in their concern over workplace issues, they were able to defeat the plan for separate vocational schools (Katznelson and Weir 1985). In some places, the results of local politics were different.

Yet the result in most areas was some form of differentiated education with nonacademic tracks. The high schools of one Midwestern town, labeled "Middletown" by sociologists Robert and Helen Lynd, show one example of differentiation. In 1890, Middletown's high school students had only two choices for curriculum, Latin and English. By 1924, however, the high school had twelve tracks, including college preparation and a "general" track as well as shorthand, bookkeeping, applied electricity, mechanical drafting, printing, machine shop, manual arts, and home economics. Students took somewhat more than one-half of their coursework in common classes such as English and the rest in electives aligned with the student's curriculum. Latin still had a prominent place, with more than 10 percent of student hours in Latin during the 1923–24 school year. However, the other, new tracks dominated academic electives. Commercial, home economics, manual arts, and vocational courses occupied 18 percent of student hours, with commercial courses alone taking up 9 percent. Differentiation came to Middletown's high school with a vengeance, as the high school grew from 170 students in 1890 to 1,849 in 1924 (Lynd and Lynd 1928: 183, 194–96, 525).

This differentiated curriculum, one should clearly note, was part of a repertoire of differences in education by social class, race, and gender, and not the only mechanism for inequality. Consider, for example, the history of education of Southern African Americans after the Civil War. The fundamental fact of segregated education was the dramatically inferior education available to African Americans. This included limited access to high schools. As James Anderson (1988) has argued, Southern states built high schools for whites early in the twentieth century. Most African Americans, however, lived in counties where there was no high school they could legally attend, even when they did complete elementary schooling. If they were able to attend secondary schools, they frequently faced a vocational curriculum different from the vocational schooling whites experienced and focused on the jobs assumed appropriate for them (Anderson 1982: 197–214). Differential education was thus one of many barriers to a decent education. Only a small minority of teenagers completed high school in the early twentieth century. If differentiation was in exchange for universal secondary education, it was for universality only in rhetoric.

"CARELESSLY WASTED"

The legacy of the Progressive Era debates was the combination of broad access to comprehensive high schools outside the South, limited but expanding enrollment, and differentiation within comprehensive high schools. Left unresolved were tensions among the competing values of meritocracy, universality, and the dynamics of credentialism. The call for universal secondary education continued in the Great Depression. Educators used the continuing growth in high school enrollment and the vast unemployment of both young and older workers to create another reason for universal high school attendance: custodianship outside the labor market. For some, custodianship was a crude tool to prevent teenagers from competing with adults. For others, custodianship of all youth would simply ensure the best possible education for life as adults (Krug 1972: 311–14). One should note that this new rhetoric did not reflect a dramatic change in enrollment patterns. The Depression did not speed up what had been a long-term trend toward increasing high school enrollments (Tyack, Lowe, and Hansot 1984: 144–48). What was new was the notion of the high school as a place for unwanted laborers. This warehousing function was not new for schools; it has existed since the nineteenth century. But in the Depression, it appeared as a naked purpose for extended compulsory schooling and universal secondary education.

Several circumstances in the Great Depression suggested a need for extended education (Kett 1995: 275–77). First, the sheer magnitude of unemployment suggested the futility of teenagers' working. In addition, some argued that frustrated youth would create problems, either through simple demoralization or as fodder for fascist movements. Finally, some educators argued that schools could serve a legitimate purpose in training students for a future technology-based economy. Against this, though, was the realistic understanding that economic circumstances accounted for most attrition from school, as well as questions as to whether increased vocational training might itself lead to the excessive ambitions and frustrations schooling was supposed to ameliorate (Angus 1965: 84). As historian Joseph Kett wrote, "even progressive justifications of prolonging education were still hedged by reservations" at the end of the Depression (Kett 1995: 277).

Again, Midwestern towns provide an illustration of the tensions inherent in expanding high school education and the limitations of universal education. Robert and Helen Lynd reported that Middletown parents accepted and wanted prolonged education for their children. Yet at the same time, poor parents knew that their children might not complete high school. The president of the local school board acknowledged the shift in high school purpose from training leadership to providing credentials to vocationalism: "For a long time all boys were trained to be President. Then for a while we trained them all to be professional men. Now we are training boys to get jobs" (Lynd and Lynd 1928: 194). When August Hollingshead described the life of adolescents in "Elmtown" almost two decades later, however, he found the businessmen who ran the school board much more ambivalent about the expansion of high school than in Middletown:

The members of the Board were of the opinion that not everyone had the ability to justify a high school education. They believed that many boys and girls who were in high school would have been better off on the farm or at the Mill. They were interested, however, in seeing that everyone who could profit by a high school education was provided with the necessary facilities, . . . No Board member was found who at any time believed that it was the responsibility of the community to provide educational facilities for *all* high-school-aged adolescents. (Hollingshead 1949: 125)

In Elmtown, nineteenth-century notions of access remained: School board members thought it sufficient to provide the opportunity to attend high school. One should note, however, that World War II may have affected the views Hollingshead heard in 1941–42 (Elder, Modell, and Parke 1993: 7). Employers faced a labor shortage, and women only partially filled the gap. Businessmen may well have wanted some teenagers to leave school and work instead. In both towns, however, the expansion of high school vied with its limits for poor children.

World War II forced a re-examination of the purposes of secondary schooling, at least for a few years. Increased child labor and decreased high school attendance put professional educators and child labor activists on the defensive in a sudden reversal of a decades-long trend. Conflicting and ambivalent statements by the federal government, sometimes suggesting that teenagers would be important to the war effort, did little to alleviate the conflict between employment in wartime and schooling. The response, by the end of the war, was another call for universal education. This time, educators used the specter of depression and riots after World War II to call for extended education. One result of concern over postwar society was the Servicemen's Readjustment Act of 1944, also known as the GI Bill. Another was the renewed assertion that all adolescents belonged in high school (Angus 1965: Chap. 4; Kett 1995: 278–79).

A commission sponsored by the NEA advocated universal attendance–and now high school graduation–the same year that the GI Bill passed. The Educational Policies Commission, supported by the NEA and the American Association of School Administrators, wrote several volumes of educational policy proposals in the middle 1940s about postwar education. The volume on secondary education was appropriately titled *Education for All American Youth* (1944). The commission members hoped that local school systems and states would aggressively reform schools after the war and promote school guidance and occupational training. Key to their prescription was the extension of education to age eighteen and beyond, including compulsory attendance until eighteen or high school graduation (Educational Policies Commission 1944: 48, 189, 226–27). In its imaginary history of education policy in the fictional state of Columbia, the extension of compulsory attendance was explicitly to withdraw teenagers from the job market:

With the approach of the end of the war, the employment of sixteen- and seventeen-year-old boys and girls fell off sharply. . . . It was thought better by far, for both youth and society, to have young people in attendance at schools in which they could secure occupational training, work experience, and a well-rounded general education than to have them enter an already oversupplied labor market without training, experience, or adequate educational background. (350)

Thus, the commission recommended compulsory attendance until eighteen and the extension of secondary education to thirteenth and fourteenth grades for willing students. Now, truly, high schools were assumed to be for all adolescents. "When we write confidently and inclusively about education for *all* American youth, we mean just that," the commission wrote. "Not one of them is to be carelessly wasted. *All* of them are to be given equal opportunities to live and learn" (Educational Policies Commission 1944: 17–18; emphasis in the original).

The Educational Policies Commission's recommendation for extended secondary education came in the context of educators' concerns about rivalry from federal agencies (Angus 1965: 103–5). Educators worried that the federal government might re-create federal youth programs after the war. While the Civilian Conservation Corps and National Youth Administration had reached only a small fraction of teenagers during the Great Depression, they represented the first new institutions appealing to adolescents since the Progressive Era, and their potential threatened educators (Krug 1972: 319–27). The worst possible outcome of peace, according to the Educational Policies Commission, would be if the federal government re-created national youth programs after the war. Thus, it offered secondary schools, operated by education professionals at the local level, as the logical alternative. Local schools, the commission argued, could perform all of the functions necessary to enhance the lives of adolescents. It proposed that schools "extend their services so as to meet all the educational needs of youth" broadly defined (Educational Policies Commission 1944: 18). In truth, schools had little to fear from the federal government; conservative Congress members in the late 1940s ensured that few extensive domestic programs, certainly none that threatened local control of education, would become law.

Yet this assertion of universal utility for high schools, extended by the Life Adjustment movement, brought educators under harsh scrutiny. As Lawrence Cremin (1961) described it, the Life Adjustment movement brought together educators who believed that schools should teach a broad set of life skills. Its critics argued that the Life Adjustment philosophy removed academics from the focus of schooling. The Educational Policies Commission report, and the views of professional educators more generally, came under vicious attack several years later by critics of public schools. Historian Arthur Bestor, in his 1953 *Educational Wastelands*, lambasted educators for what he saw as their anti-intellectual bent. Bestor's attack was part of the general criticism of progressive education in the 1950s (Cremin 1961: 343–47). While he addressed all levels of schooling, his criticism of curriculum, including the program laid out by the Educational Policies Commission (Bestor 1953: 74, 213 n.5), was largely aimed at secondary schooling, which he accused of abdicating its responsibility to teach students within academic disciplines. Yet for all his criticisms of schools, he did not question their broad reach. On the contrary, he accused leading educators of elitist impulses, of assuming the incapability of students to become liberally educated. He argued that the expansion of education could not excuse such snobbery:

There is no reason whatever for assuming that the schools of today have a smaller proportion of students of high innate ability merely because they are drawing more students from families low on the income scale. To assert that intellectual capacity decreases as one reaches down into lower economic levels of the population is to deny, point-blank, the basic assumptions of democratic equalitarianism. (Bestor 1953: 36)

Bestor thought the remedy required a choice between returning to limited education or emphasizing academics for everyone: "We can accept the situation as it is and attempt to discover a means of providing intellectual training for a select few somewhere in the interstices of the system [or] . . . [w]e can reaffirm, before it is too late, our own and our nation's belief in the value of intellectual training to all men" (78–79). For Bestor, the universal reach of education, including high schools, was unquestioned. It was, in fact, a critical underpinning of his argument for schooling focused on academic disciplines.

Some critics of schools did question the appropriateness of universal high school attendance (Angus 1965: 126–29, 146). Yet the focus of critics' ire was curriculum, not the reach of high schools. In the end, the most widely read prescription for high schools in the 1950s tried to satisfy both the urge to select and the urge to socialize. James Bryant Conant, former Harvard University president and advocate of specialized training of a technical elite for the Cold War, thought high schools could perform both functions. The ideal high school should be comprehensive, he wrote in *The American High School Today* (1959), so that everyone would be socialized in a common setting. Yet high schools also had the duty to identify outstanding students and encourage them to enter science and mathematics. The key question, he wrote, was the capacity to balance two competing goals:

Can a school at one and the same time provide a good general education for all the pupils as future citizens of a democracy, provide elective programs for the majority to develop useful skills, and educate adequately those with a talent for handling advanced academic subjects–particularly foreign languages and advanced mathematics? (Conant 1959: 15)

Conant recognized the philosophical problem in advocating specialized training in a putatively egalitarian society. His solution—the extensive use of guidance counselors to identify the potential academic elite—mirrored the National Defense Education Act (NDEA) of 1958. Title V of the NDEA authorized federal funding of local counselors and testing programs (Public Law 85–864, sections 501–504). With counseling, Conant hoped, a high school could simultaneously educate everyone while choosing a few to encourage further.

Conant's approval of counseling matched the prescriptions of educators well, despite his other criticisms. Since the early twentieth century, school officials had advocated the use of extensive guidance to select which curriculum students would take. Conant's conception of the comprehensive high school was therefore not a substantial deviation from what educators had proposed for decades. His starting assumptions—that everyone should attend a comprehensive high school, that some should take an academic curriculum but most would not, and that the schools had the responsibility to guide students into the proper curriculum— were, in outline, what the *Cardinal Principles* report had described. Conant wanted to augment the academic, college preparatory curriculum, but that was a change in emphasis. Advocates of a differentiated, universal high school had won the fight over the purpose of high schools. Even a school critic like Conant would not disagree.

In the end, though, Conant could not resolve the conflict between the need to restrict credentials for their value and the goals of comprehensive education. In part, by assuming ubiquitous attendance at and graduation from high schools, educators of the late 1940s and their critics were in front of demographics. By 1950, fewer than half of the nation's twenty- to twenty-four-year-olds had high school credentials. Yet the dominance of high schools in public education was unquestioned. Nowhere in the Educational Policy Commission report or in Bestor's criticism was the type of acknowledgment one saw from the Committee of Ten or the Commission on the Reorganization of Secondary Education, that not everyone attended high schools and that universal graduation was but a dream. For postwar educators and their critics—despite their disagreements over the purposes of schooling—high schools had become a place most adolescents attended and, presumably, graduated from. Ethel Percy Andrus, the director of the Ojai, California, National Residence for Retired Teachers, summed up the changed assumptions about secondary education in 1951: "For the average pupil, a half century of educational progress has transformed the formal college-preparatory school of the privileged few . . . to the democratic comprehensive secondary school of today" (57). What Andus did not mention was the vast number of students who did not complete high school. Those "early school leavers" provoked comment by educators in the first half of the twentieth century, but they became a problem of crisis proportions only when high schools were supposed to be teaching everyone.

3

Early Attitudes Toward Attrition

Despite growing arguments that the high school should be the primary institution for adolescents, concerns about those who left without diplomas did not become a well-recognized, cohesive issue until the 1960s. Instead, discussion of the problems of early school leavers or elimination from school (as dropping out was sometimes called) was idiosyncratic and unfocused. What was new in the 1960s was not concern over school leaving by itself but the definition of a discrete social problem with a clear sense of why the problem was important and what caused it. Educators and others may have been worried about attrition before 1960, but few defined it as a crisis.

Thus, the concerns that later became part of the common description of the dropout problem were not inevitably part of that definition. These issues were, instead, part of a very loose set of discussions about the purposes and problems of formal schooling. Slowly, the debate over the purposes of schooling, and especially high schools, became more coherent. At first, educators and their critics applied these concerns to elementary schools, which the vast majority of students in the nineteenth century attended. Slowly, though, secondary schools came to occupy a larger place in the debate over what schools should do and how they should function. At mid-century, discussion about school leavers began to snowball.

Since the early days of the republic, social critics in the United States have worried about the consequences of poor school attendance. Proponents of public schools in the early nineteenth century thought that too few children of poor parents were in urban schools. They argued that free primary education would help remove the stigma from what had been called pauper or charity schools, thus raising attendance. School officials in mid-nineteenth-century factory towns constantly worried about fluctuating enrollments and truancy, which made planning impossible (in their view) as well as letting immigrant children elude the influence of public schools (Katz 1968: 101–3; Vinovskis 1988: 555, 561–62). The rationale for compulsory attendance laws, enacted in most states between 1880 and 1920, was to enforce a standard of attendance in school between certain ages. The strict enforcement of compulsory attendance laws usually followed rather than preceded attendance of the relevant age groups in school (Tyack 1974: 66–71). Compulsory attendance laws were thus early markers of school attendance age norms. Until the twentieth century, however, most of these concerns (especially those about attendance) focused on younger children, not teenagers, and on attendance in the elementary grades.

Between 1900 and 1960, some educators wrote about student attrition from high school. Those explorations, however, lacked the cohesion and stereotypes that marked 1960s writings. Widespread concern over a "dropout problem" as such appeared only in the late 1950s and early 1960s. Dropout, student elimination, withdrawal, and early school leaver were interchangeable terms in the first half of this century, whereas "dropout" dominated captions, titles, and epithets in the 1960s. This does not mean that no one worried about school attendance or high school graduation. For example, the verb "to drop out" appeared in American writings at the turn of the century. In the decades after 1900, a few fretted about dropouts, or student elimination as they more often called attrition. These early writings on school withdrawal or dropping out did not, however, constitute a large or coherent body of literature on high school dropouts. Worries about withdrawals fit into larger patterns of concern about the relationship between school and work or appropriate sex roles for adolescents, issues that underlay the widespread debates in the Progressive Era about the nature and purpose of vocational education.

Two major issues, however, did presage the discovery of dropping out as a problem: debates over vocational education and child labor. Discussion about vocationalism easily overshadowed all writings about graduation per se in the early twentieth century. Reformers had many different reasons for supporting vocational education. Although the lines between "manual," "industrial," and "vocational" schooling were hazy, advocates all agreed that some vocational schooling would shift the schools from a narrow-minded academic focus to a more practical bent. As historian Harvey Kantor (1982: 15) describes,

Beginning in the 1880s, schools were charged with being irrelevant to the economy, with failing to teach the skills needed for occupational mobility, and with ignoring the social consequences of modern industrial life. Groups from outside and inside the educational system . . . [argued that] it was the job of the school . . . to train youth for work and to integrate them smoothly into the occupational structure.

Vocational proponents permanently changed the focus of educational politics with the assumption that schools should be attuned to the labor market. However, the closest connection between vocationalism and attendance concerns was the claim (by advocates of vocational education) that these programs would improve attendance (Lazerson 1971: 138). Graduation, in itself, was not the focus.

Child labor, in addition to vocationalism, was a lens through which social critics saw school attrition. Child labor activists were explicitly concerned with the relationship between attendance and child labor. In particular, officials at the Children's Bureau of the federal Department of Labor and the National Child Labor Committee consistently saw attrition from school as a problem of child labor and school attendance as essential to eliminate child labor. Child labor activism thus helped keep the issues of school attendance and truancy alive throughout the first half of this century. It is important, however, to note that while they were concerned with attendance, child labor activists did not focus on graduation as such. They occasionally noted the rewards to an education, but always within the context of increasing school attendance and preventing early entrance into labor.

Thus, antecedents to the dropout debate of the 1960s existed, in some form. However, they were not focused on graduation so much as mere attendance. As a result, the rhetoric before 1960 emphasized general increases in educational experiences. As Joseph Kett noted, "educators devoted much more attention to increasing the average educational attainment . . . than to the prevention of dropping out" (Kett 1995: 265). The concerns that some raised about the act of leaving school left little permanent mark upon education or educational debates until the 1960s.

FROM STUDENT ELIMINATION TO NONPROMOTION

The first swell of concern over students who left high school came in the first decade of the twentieth century. As happened in the 1960s, educators used attrition as a lens for their current concerns. Unlike later, however, there was little agreement on why attrition was a problem or what the proper solutions were. The only agreement among educators was in the need for more information. In the early twentieth century, with the Progressive penchant for gathering statistics, this became one of the first issues addressed by the new school survey movement. The first few surveys, though, shifted focus from student attrition to the issue of promotion through the grades.

W. L. Steele, superintendent in Galesburg, Illinois, told his audience at the 1899 National Education Association meeting of switching to an elective system of courses in the high school. It began, he asserted, because of concerns of the local board: "The few graduating from the high school, compared with the many entering it, has long been the subject of comment by the members of the board of education." An examination of records showed that the average number of students entering the school annually was eighty, but the average number graduating was thirty-six. Steele had inquired into the causes: "A closer examination revealed the fact that thirty-two of these forty-four pupils dropped out during the first year ... [T]he cause was found to be the failure of the pupils to do the work in one or more branches required to complete the course." Because most of the failures were in Latin or algebra, Steele recommended electives as the solution (Steele 1899: 331).

Kansas City, Missouri, Superintendent James Greenwood disagreed with Steele's interpretation at the next year's meeting: "I am not aware that, with the slightly changing conditions [i.e., electives] better and more persistent attendance has been secured. Instead of one or two factors operating, there are many causes operating" (Greenwood 1900: 341). Greenwood had conducted his own examination of records in Kansas City, as well as sending questionnaires to superintendents across the country. He noted that the putative causes of leaving ranged from illness to employment to the "inability to do the [academic] work." In one tabulation of reasons why students left, however, more than a third of students left for unknown reasons (343). The strongest conclusion he could reach, at the end of his paper, was that students who were young when entering high school were the least likely to leave, whereas "the older pupils ... were most likely to fail or leave" (350).

Others had yet more explanations of cause, but most noted a multiciplicity of causes, like Greenwood. University of Illinois professor Stratton Brooks tried to explain the relative risks of leaving for students of various temperament, from "nervous" to "stolid," but he acknowledged that these were only descriptions of probabilities. Ultimately, the art of teaching was most important; any teacher "may know all this [about temperament] and yet continue to drive pupils from school. It is the sympathetic attitude that counts. ... Any boy may desire to leave school for any of a hundred causes" (Brooks 1902: 455). Clark University fellow William Book collected the opinions of 961 high school students on the reasons that students leave school, and he sorted their answers into three general categories: commercial opportunities outside school, individual reasons (like illness), and problems schools create (Book 1904).

Educators typically used attrition to justify their own views about the high school. Superintendent Steele used attrition to explain the advantages of electives. William Book collapsed the various reasons into a justification for the "practical" high school curriculum: "On one side is the modern, strenuous, unattractive, college-serving high school. Over against it are arrayed the alluring attractions and pressing interests of the world. In this country the boys are largely left to take their choice between the two" (Book 1904: 231-32). University of Texas education professor A. Caswell Ellis held a similar view. All attempts at retaining students would fail, he said, "unless the subject-matter and discipline of the school meet the inner and outer needs of adolescent's nature better than do the shops and factories" (Ellis 1903: 793).

Opinions differed among educators, however, over how important this problem was. Ellis thought that attrition was a crisis: "The slaughter of the Light Brigade at Balaklava pales into insignificance, then, beside the slaughter of the educational hopes and possibilities of our children by the present school system" (Ellis 1903: 793). Thomas Balliet, responding to Ellis, was more sanguine. School leaving would be a problem if everyone entered high school in order to graduate. However, Balliet pointed out, "some pupils enter simply to get one or two years more of school training, knowing beforehand that they will not be able to graduate" (Balliet 1903: 800). Anderson, Illinois, Superintendent J. W. Carr showed what was probably a typical response by administrators to Ellis' charges. He acknowledged that attrition was a problem but noted that the Anderson high school had graduated 131 in the prior ten years, about one-third of its entering students. In comparison with the cities Ellis had statistics for, Carr claimed, "this is not a bad showing" (Carr 1903: 798). F. D. Boynton, the superintendent of Ithaca, New York, expressed similar feelings (Boynton 1902). School leaving was a misfortune but not an indictment of schools. For educators of the time, as in the nineteenth century, access to high schools seemed sufficient.

Much debate centered on the correct statistics for attrition. Figures on those students remaining to enter high school ranged from 5 percent to about a third (e.g., Boynton 1902; Ellis 1903; Greenwood 1900). Columbia University Teachers College psychologist Edward Thorndike stepped into this fray in 1907. His report, *The Elimination of Pupils from School*, appeared as a bulletin of the U. S. Office of Education. After examining records of more than two dozen cities, he claimed that two-thirds of white students failed to finish elementary school, and fewer than 10 percent graduated from high school (Thorndike 1907: 9–10). If school systems were unable to advance students through the grades very well, they were guilty of waste. Yet Thorndike did not claim that schools should graduate everyone. On the contrary, he accepted attrition for appropriate reasons, and the judgment was a matter of comparison: "A system in which laziness and stupidity eliminate pupils is better than one in which they are eliminated by poverty" (7). Like many others, he thought the high school curriculum (that is, an academic focus) was to blame for attrition in the first year of high school: "A large share of the fault lies with the kind of education given in the high schools" (21). Despite these pronouncements, though, Thorndike was largely uninterested in the social meaning of graduation or attrition.

Instead, most of his report consisted of statistical analysis. Thorndike discovered, like many since him, that official school statistics do not lend themselves well to analysis of student attrition. Schools generally report figures by grade (that is, first grade, second grade, etc.). However, students do not progress neatly through grades. (Thorndike ignored other complications, such as transfers between public and private schools and migration into and out of cities.) At the turn of the century, many students stayed in first grade in urban schools for well over a year. Table 4 shows the clear disparities between first and other grades in Baltimore, Maryland, and Trenton, New Jersey. First grade enrollment, therefore, did not represent those students entering the first grade that year. How, then, to estimate the proportion of entering students that schools lost? Thorndike simply averaged the enrollment figures for the first three grades and called the average the "correct representation" of entering students (Thorndike 1907: 46). From that base, he made his analysis of attrition. He also commented on this as evidence of widespread failure to promote students (24–25).

Responding to the Thorndike report, the Russell Sage Foundation sponsored a study by Leonard Ayres (1909) on grade retardation (or promotion failure). Grade retardation, as Ayres termed it, was a problem because it was inefficient. He claimed that in the fifty-five city school systems he studied, grade repetition cost the systems $13 million, or about 15 percent of the total costs of the system (96–97). Overcrowded schools, he suggested, were the result of inefficiency, and grade repeaters were a sign of waste in school systems (89–90). He discussed various causes of nonpromotion, and many of his conclusions about the proportion of students failing to advance in school were roughly similar to Thorndike's.

One other statistical survey existed on elimination. Joseph Van Denburg (1911) examined the records of 1,002 high school students in New York City. When he received his degree from Teachers College and published his study in 1911, it came after the main flurry of reports. Nonetheless, it is interesting for Van Denburg's repudiation of the goal of universal graduation. As with the other statistical efforts, Van Denburg concluded that few who entered high school graduated within four years (approximately 12 percent in his group of children), that white children of natives did not necessarily have an advantage over the children of immigrants, and that both sex and the occupational status of the father made some difference in continuation through school.

However, rather than decrying the inefficiency of the school system for failing to advance students, Van Denburg criticized the injustice of retaining students beyond the time when he thought they should leave. He noted the tension between the ideal of high schools as mass institutions for the "general intelligence of the growing members of a community" and the older "selection . . . of future leaders":

Table 4

Students in Beginning Grades: Baltimore, Maryland, and Trenton, New Jersey (c. 1900)

	Baltimore	Trenton
First grade	54,097	7,361
Second grade	35,328	3,348
Third grade	29,284	3,329
Fourth grade	25,373	2,985

Source: Edward L. Thorndike (1907): *The Elimination of Pupils from School.* U. S. Bureau of Education Bulletin No. 4, Whole No. 379. Washington, D. C.: Government Printing Office.

To a certain extent these two purposes of the high school as a social institution are antagonistic. In the first case, elimination is a fault to be seriously studied and so decreased to the lowest possible amount; while in the second case, elimination is no fault at all, but rather evidence of the successful progress of the process of selection which is one purpose of the high school to advance. (Van Denburg 1911: 136)

Van Denburg did not approve of universal education, but he did think the schools were inefficient. The problem, he believed, was inefficient sorting. He thought, therefore, that high schools should deliberately select those students whom they thought would graduate. He came to this conclusion from his claim that teachers could predict who would do well in high school. In his longitudinal study, he had followed one entering group of high school students. He received ratings of the ability, industry, and results of entering students from seventy-nine teachers. He claimed that these judgments predicted the probabilities of graduating. Of the highest third judged on results, 28.4 percent graduated; of the lowest third rated by teachers on academic results, 3.0 percent graduated. The futures of poorly-judged girls was worse than boys; of the bottom third rated by teachers, only 1.1 percent had graduated by the end of four years. It was the enrollment of these girls at all, not their elimination, that was the crime: "It is a serious question . . . whether it is really wise, and just to the taxpayer, to carry along over ninety girls of inferior Results so that one may graduate. The saving which could be effected by excluding at once all girls of inferior Results would be obviously very great" (Van Denburg 1911: 167–68). For Van Denburg, student elimination was not the problem; *inefficient* attrition was the disgrace.

Some disagreement existed about statistics. Ayres and others criticized some details of Thorndike's analysis, especially his averaging the enrollment figures of the first three grades as an estimate of entering students. Ayres and Thorndike agreed, however, on one essential: Nonpromotion through the grades was inefficient. School officials responded over the next decade by some manipulation of student statistics and by making it easier for students to progress through grades (Angus, Mirel, and Vinovskis 1990: 220–25). Yet the impetus had shifted from school-leaving to nonpromotion through the grades. While Thorndike had discussed both, Ayres discussed nonpromotion almost entirely. After the first decade of the twentieth century, interest in student elimination (as Thorndike and Van Denburg had called it) had mutated.

Thorndike had focused on the passage through school and noted the problem of nonpromotion; Ayres had focused entirely on nonpromotion. That was what later researchers remembered. In the Great Depression, Hollis Caswell of George Peabody College for Teachers analyzed nonpromotion once again. His conclusions were similar to those of Ayres a generation earlier. For Caswell, as with Ayres, the inefficiency of nonpromotion was one of its chief problems. Specifically, Caswell argued that those schools with slower rates of promotion did not have more homogeneous achievement than schools with relatively high rates of promotion; thus, nonpromotion was not justified as a way to make teaching easier (Caswell 1933: 66). Caswell was also concerned with the psychological effects of failure on children and, especially, on the intrinsic value of schoolwork to children: "It is practically impossible for an elementary school child to discover relationships between his activities during a semester or year of school work and his failure to be promoted" (73). In the end, according to Caswell, "nonpromotion is a type of failure that tends to deaden, disillusion, and defeat the child" (81). The solution, according to Caswell, was to eliminate nonpromotion in schools. Any explicit recognition of school leaving as a problem in itself, though, had disappeared. Educators discussing early school leavers at mid-century had to begin the debate anew.

Illustrative of the disappearance of attrition as an issue was the casual indifference toward adolescents out of school in Middletown and Elmtown. School officials, lay and professional, largely ignored teenagers out of school. Middletown did not keep any record of student attrition (Lynd and Lynd 1928: 182). Elmtown's school officials told Hollingshead that he would only find "some" city youth out of school; most non-attending adolescents were children of farmers, they insisted (Hollingshead 1949: 329). (The school officials were wrong; country adolescents were not disproportionately represented among those Hollingshead found out of school.) In both cases, educators in local settings excluded nonattenders from their primary concerns. Perhaps this came from the growing identity of high schools as centers of athletics, which the Lynds argued facilitated a sense of community cohesion (Hollingshead 1949: 193–94; Lynd and Lynd 1928: 212–14, 485–87). The identification of schools as places for adults to attend basketball games (especially in Middletown) may have distracted educators and city residents from educational problems (Kett 1995: 273–74). More important, however, is that the absence of explicit concern towards school attrition in these towns was probably representative of public opinion in the United States.

CHILD LABOR AND LEAVING SCHOOL

The most sustained interest in school attrition in the early twentieth century came not from educators but from child labor activists. As the first flurry of concern over attrition was mutating into the debate over nonpromotion and the school survey movement, child labor activists were having their first successes in effective legislation restricting child labor. Supported by industries that had access to adult immigrant labor (and thus did not need children), activists persuaded several state legislatures to enact laws restricting the hours of child workers and prohibiting work in certain hazardous industries (Osterman 1980: Chap. 4). In addition, Congress authorized a Children's Bureau within the federal Department of Labor. From its founding in 1912, the Children's Bureau was a focus of child labor activism and an advocate of increased restrictions on child labor.

One critical component of this strategy was the use of school attendance to reduce child employment. Officials cf the new Children's Bureau and the National Child Labor Committee understood the reciprocal relationship between work and schooling, and increased teenage schooling was one of their key hopes for eliminating child labor (Trattner 1970: 156–57). (What they did not understand was that reduced child labor would be more important to increasing high school attendance than the reverse.) In both world wars, the Children's Bureau went so far as to develop publicity campaigns to encourage children to remain in school. In each case, child labor activists were responding to real concerns about the expansion of child labor during wartime labor shortages. The Back-to-School campaign of 1918 was an effort to entice children to remain in school voluntarily, in large part because the Supreme Court had ruled that year that the first federal legislation restricting child labor was unconstitutional. Left with no enforceable tool to reduce child labor, federal officials turned to publicity. The Back-to-School drive, however, produced little change in enrollment, despite the war's end and the return of veterans to the labor force (Angus 1965: 34–38).

Child labor activists continued to research and report on child labor conditions through the Great Depression, and school attendance continued to be a minor theme. For example, the White House Conference on Child Health and Protection published a volume on child labor in 1932 written by two Children's Bureau officials, Ellen Nathalie Matthews and Nettie Pauline McGill. In it, the officials argued, "School attendance laws, if properly enforced, may be expected automatically to prevent employment during school hours" (454). They proposed the professionalization of truant officers, adequate censuses of children, and prompt response to excessive absences. They noted that a majority of states required working minors to attend some special classes (typically called continuation school) and pressed for enforcement of attendance at continuation schools and a strictly enforced return to regular school upon unemployment (454–69). Yet it is notable that, while they advocated schooling as a remedy for child labor and a reason to oppose it, they did not mention graduation as such. School attendance was the primary goal of child labor activists.

Again in World War II, officials of the Children's Bureau and private child labor activists were concerned with increased child labor during a labor shortage. In 1943–46, the Children's Bureau and Office of Education jointly sponsored national "Go-to-School" drives during the summers. As in the earlier crusade, these publicity campaigns produced few results, and even officials of the National Child Labor Committee admitted that they were empty gestures when contrasted with the power of the labor market during war (Angus 1965: 92–98). After the war, the National Child Labor Committee sponsored two studies of employment and school leaving by Connecticut school official Harold Dillon (Trattner 1970: 220–22). The first volume, on work-experience programs, advocated part-time schooling as a way to ease older teenagers into work without putting them in dangerous work situations. Dillon argued that work experience encouraged students to remain in school (Dillon 1946: Chap. 14). The second volume, *Early School Leavers* (1949), more directly addressed school attrition. Dillon argued that children left school both because of work and because of disinterest in schooling. In these studies, Dillon expressed some interest in graduation as such. However, the primary aim, especially in the first booklet, was to explore the increase of school attainment in general and the delay of entry into full-time work.

Child labor activists, through the federal Children's Bureau and the National Child Labor Committee, were the primary alternative to educators in discussions of school attrition during the first half of the twentieth century. They were explicitly aware of the role of labor markets in school attendance, and they were concerned with preventing damage to children as individuals. This was in marked contrast to educators' concerns with social efficiency and the education of children for future roles as adults. Nonetheless, one must remember that graduation did not appear at all as a goal in activists' writings until after World War II, and the primary aim, above all else, was prevention of child labor. Growing concern about graduation came after the National Child Labor Committee had accomplished most of its goals.

A NEW DEBATE BEGINS

In the fifteen years after World War II, interest in the problems of student attrition arose again among educators and others. None, however, referred to the earlier discussion of student elimination at the turn of the century. Gone also, for the most part, was concern over promotion of students that Thorndike had provoked. Another idiosyncratic, unfocused debate on attrition began. The renewed discussion about dropouts after the war was dappled with singular ideas, isolated explanations for attrition that appeared in the 1950s and vanished almost entirely when the dropout problem became more visible.

One example of an idiosyncratic view was August Hollingshead's (1949) study of social class influence on a Corn Belt community's teenagers, which included "leaving school" as one of the results of low social status. In 1941 and 1942, Hollingshead had moved to a Midwestern town and studied the lives of 735 adolescents. Using preliminary interviews about the status of a small group of those adolescents, he divided the group into five classes, in order of relative status in the community. Throughout the study, *Elmtown's Youth*, Hollingshead claimed that social class greatly influenced the lives of adolescents, and his chapter about attrition from school was no different. Of the bottom class of adolescents, 88 percent were out of school, and Hollingshead concluded that social status greatly affected attendance: "The out-of-school adolescents are products, in large measure, of the impact of the Elmtown social system on them" (375). Intertwined with class, Hollingshead thought, were the ways in which family survival strategies shaped educational options. For the poorest adolescents, their childrearing revolved around the need for income and jobs. "An essential conditioning factor in his childhood," Hollingshead wrote of teenagers in the lowest class, "is the desire to grow up and get a job; this means for all practical purposes withdrawal from school" (358).

One strand of concern came from the shrinking high school enrollments of wartime. Teenagers left school in the early 1940s in the major exception to the decades-long trend of increasing teenage school attendance. Labor Department officials were still concerned with child labor and thus addressed poverty, school attrition, and the labor market from a perspective different from Hollingshead. In 1948, the director of the U. S. Labor Department's Child Labor Branch, Elizabeth Johnson, worried that Americans were "reluctant . . . to admit any large number are leaving school" too early, though she thought that labor trends pointed to severe employment problems for adolescents out of school. Her primary concern was "to facilitate the transition of young people from school to work and increase the vocational satisfactions they will receive through their work" (Johnson 1948: 55). She thought that the draw of a job was a temptation to leave school, a conclusion she believed was bolstered by the rise of teen employment during World War II and the slump in high school enrollment (also see Snyder 1993: Fig. 6; Tyack, Lowe, and Hansot 1984: 144–48). The consequences she foresaw were grave: unemployment or dead-end and unsatisfying jobs.

Not all worried about the outcomes of the children as individuals, though, and the concerns of child labor activists were only a small part of discussion in the 1950s. When the Cold War brought attention to concerns over skilled manpower (a gendered term, but the one used), attrition became a threat to national security, according to some. For example, Daniel Snepp, a guidance counselor in Evansville, Indiana, thought that the nation's security depended on universal high school graduation. In the Cold War, he argued, the country depended upon "wise use and efficient development of our natural and human resources . . . If we would train everyone to the limit of his capabilities, we must adopt a policy of attracting and holding every student in school for as long as he has the abilities to achieve and the willingness to co-operate" (Snepp 1956: 49). The counselor was echoing (albeit inaccurately) the contemporary discussion of military manpower needs. In the late 1940s and throughout the 1950s, critics like Admiral Hyman Rickover argued that high schools were failing to train the technical elite that could keep America secure from the Soviet threat. Among the earliest of those criticisms came from the president of Harvard University, James Bryan Conant. He told a congressional panel in 1947 that he wanted the National Science Foundation to foster the training of talented high school students (Spring 1989: Chap. 2).

Snepp's statement turned the manpower argument away from its emphasis on skilled training and argued instead that manpower needs required training everyone. The application of this rhetoric to comprehensive schooling was thus ironic. The strain between egalitarianism and manpower concerns was not lost on Conant, who wrote in 1959 that high schools should seek to train everyone and also select out the brightest. Nonetheless, the use of a manpower argument to justify concern over dropouts removed manpower concerns from their original context. Rickover and Conant wanted to emphasize training the elite, not everyone, as the educational solution to the Cold War. The guidance counselor quoted above turned the original manpower argument on its head, arguing for training everyone.

A different writer mirrored Conant's concerns more accurately. Joseph Bledsoe, a faculty member at the University of Georgia, wrote in 1959 that more students should graduate, despite differing abilities. He was especially concerned about academically talented leavers:

The age of automation and atomic energy requires a better educated populace . . . It is obviously too optimistic to expect everyone to attain this level since not everyone has the necessary mental aptitude. Far too many able students, however, withdraw from high school prior to graduation. (Bledsoe 1959: 3)

This compromise between skilled training and comprehensive education was fraught with tension between seeing schools as a place to identify the gifted and seeing schools primarily as a place to socialize young citizens. The dropout problem could conceivably have served as a floating metaphor for this conflict between sorting and socializing. Joseph Bledsoe saw the problem as evidence of unbalanced school priorities. However, his application of manpower rhetoric to dropping out (and that of Snepp) was ignored by later writers. This visible concern over manpower disappeared in the widespread discussion of dropouts in the 1960s.

Other interpretations in the 1950s focused on the causes of dropping out. One California teacher thought that car ownership might account for differences in academic achievement and tried to design a statistical test to compare "the number of dropouts between the frequent drivers and the nondrivers" at his school. He reasoned, "[T]he relatively unrestricted use of automobiles by our secondary-school students . . . has never heretofore been considered as a factor of school adjustment" (Sharp 1957: 83). Car use never became a major issue in the 1960s discussions of dropping out. Another teacher thought in 1950 that the return of veterans to school after the war should be a model for public schools: "It proves that many drop-outs are educable. It proves that maturation factors and experience do change attitudes towards education. It may prove that army discipline has had a beneficial effect in this respect" (Goff 1950: 332). Ten years later, the discussion of the dropout problem scarcely mentioned the experience of veterans.

Thus, no clear agreement about dropouts existed in the 1940s or 1950s. The cautious conclusions of Elizabeth Johnson and another Labor Department specialist represent the lack of any strong consensus about a problem: "The findings of this study show that the problems of young people in connection with school leaving are many and varied and are inextricably interwoven with their own personal needs, with existing educational programs, and with opportunities in the employment field" (Johnson and Legg 1948: 24). The authors did not follow any conventional wisdom because none existed about dropouts. Most of those who wrote about dropping out in the 1950s had little influence over later writings. They show, however, alternative ways of exploring the issue and the range of discussion that was possible. Authors could have framed the dropout problem in the 1960s as a parallel to GI policy, as a concern of national security, or even of teenage car use. The narrowness of debate in the 1960s, evident below, was not inevitable.

WAVES OF CONCERN ABOUT ATTRITION

Approximately fifty years apart, two generations of writers became concerned about adolescents who left school. In both cases, discussion began as idiosyncratic and unfocused. No clear understandings about the reason for concern or causes of the problem existed at first. The trickle of concern became a torrent of writing after 1960, with a rough consensus developing about the nature and importance of dropping out. The tale of that development is in the following chapter. Yet the question remains: Why did the discussion among educators at the turn of the century *not* become a well-defined social problem?

In part, other topics diverted discussion of attrition in the Progressive Era. First, discussion of student elimination was motivated by concern over the teaching of boys. With recurrent concerns about the proper socialization of male adolescents, the fact that most high school students were female concerned educators (Kett 1977: 221–28; Tyack and Hansot 1990: Chap. 7). Thus, articles on high school attendance had such titles as "The percentage of boys who leave the high school" (Ellis 1903), and their focus was frequently on the proper gender socialization in schools and the need for differentiated curriculum planning.

The development of high school surveys and the focus on statistical research also diverted attention from attrition as a topic. Some of Edward Thorndike's most enthusiastic students in statistics courses at Columbia University Teachers College were school officials, not academic researchers, and survey methodology was of interest as a professional tool (Joncich 1968: 296–300). (See Tyack and Hansot 1982 regarding school surveys and professionalization.) When George Strayer and Thorndike published a textbook in 1913 on statistics for administrative purposes (called *Educational Administration*), attrition became a small topic in one section on "studies of the students." Gone was even the minimal debate on whether, or why, to be concerned at all about attrition. The statistical methodology was the focus. The treatment of Joseph Van Denburg's study demonstrates the elimination of intellectual discussion. While discussing Van Denburg's research in some detail, absent was the vivid argument about efficient sorting and the need to rid high schools of poorly performing students. Replacing this was the bland assertion of the need for student guidance: "Such educational probabilities should be used to determine both the advice and the treatment given to individuals" (Strayer and Thorndike 1913: 53). Strayer and Thorndike failed to mention that Van Denburg had proposed dismissal from high school as his preferred "treatment."

The key difference between the Progressive Era discussion of attrition and the debate after World War II, though, was in the expectation of high school graduation in the 1960s. Distracting issues and professional concerns of administrators existed in the 1960s, yet the dropout debate merely absorbed or ignored them in the definition of the problem. What was truly different was the combination of demographic reality and expectation. In the Progressive Era, universal attendance was a dream, a hope expressed by the *Cardinal Principles* report. Attrition was lamented but accepted as common. By the 1960s, though, widespread attendance at some point in high school existed, and educators and their critics alike argued about the purposes of high schools as comprehensive, not selective, institutions. The definition of a new social problem was imminent.

4

"Social Dynamite"

In the spring of 1962, National Education Association (NEA) employee Daniel Schreiber spoke about dropouts at a panel of the annual convention of the National Association of Secondary-School Principals. Portraying dropouts as "running away from work half-done, from school half-completed," he declared: "How American education solves the problem of school dropouts . . . may well determine America's future" (Schreiber 1962b: 234). Schreiber was one of the primary crusaders who made a headline issue of high school dropouts, and his speech evoked many of the themes that 1960s writers echoed in discussing the "dropout problem." Dropping out was a serious problem for several reasons, Schreiber explained. First, the population expansion of the 1950s increased the absolute numbers of dropouts, even if the proportion of students graduating from high school stayed constant or increased slightly. Second, technological improvements were rapidly making unskilled work obsolete. As unskilled work disappeared, Schreiber thought, workers would have to know more to get a job, a fact confirmed (he thought) by the companies who "require a high-school diploma" for employment. Although the proportion graduating from high school had increased dramatically, dropping out was becoming more of a problem. Because "we live in a viable, dynamic, and fecund country," Schreiber said, the decreasing proportion of dropouts was becoming a larger dilemma (Schreiber 1962b: 235–36).

In 1962, Daniel Schreiber had been the director of the NEA Project on School Dropouts for less than a year. He was, at the convention of principals, speaking to his professional peers. Schreiber had been a junior high school principal in New York City and the head of Higher Horizons, the city's first cultural enrichment program (Dan Schreiber, 71, educator 1981). The NEA chose him to head the research project when it received a grant from the Ford Foundation to establish a center for research and information on dropping out.

According to Schreiber, the research project was "designed to arouse greater public interest and discussion in order to uncover its [dropping out's] causes, dangers, and evils, and possible preventive and corrective measures" (Schreiber 1962b: 241). Schreiber proceeded to do his best to "arouse public interest and discussion" of dropping out. During the grant period, he visited scores of school districts, wrote dozens of articles, and spoke to many groups. In addition, the NEA Project on School Dropouts conducted five conferences and filled more than 15,000 orders for free literature (NEA Project on School Dropouts Papers, section 3).

Spurred in part by the NEA Project on School Dropouts, a 1961 book by former Harvard University President James Bryant Conant, and other publicity, the word "dropout" quickly became the dominant description of those without high school diplomas. Popular magazines began to publish articles on the dropout problem before Conant or Schreiber called attention to the issue, but recognition of it snowballed afterward. *Life* was the first popular magazine to describe dropping out as a national problem: "Leaving school is usually one more step on a treadmill of discouragement, failure and escape. But the individual tragedy is also a national waste" (Dropout tragedies 1960: 106A). Health, Education, and Welfare Department Secretary Abraham Ribicoff declared in 1961: "Our high school dropout rate has reached fantastic proportions . . . This is a national problem of frightening implication representing a terrible waste of our youth" (14). Shortly, popular periodicals were filled with laments about the dropout problem. Mary Conway Kohler and André Fontaine wrote in the *Saturday Evening Post* in 1962, "We waste more than a million kids a year. As we once wasted natural gas and forests and topsoil, today we waste our most valuable natural resource—the productive power of young brains and muscles, the creative power of young imaginations and emotions" (16).

By 1965, popular journals and education magazines had regular articles on the dropout problem. Even those who ridiculed the concern acknowledged the visibility of the issue. As junior high school principal Walter Burke lamented (1965: 44), "The current hue and cry, the newest fuss and furor, the latest of the perennial problems which plague the educational scene is concentrated on the public school dropout. . . . [A]ll become misty-eyed and choked with emotion when the public school dropout is mentioned." The dropout problem thus had become part of the national discussion of social problems by the mid-1960s.

The ubiquitous usage of the term "dropout" today belies its relative novelty, for the socially recognized category of high school dropouts did not exist until thirty or forty years ago. In a few years after 1960, though, dozens of people wrote articles and books about why dropping out was a problem, who dropped out, and what could be done about it. Of all materials indexed in *Education Index* and *Reader's Guide to Periodical Literature* between World War II and 1970 on the subject, the number of titles not only increased, but also used the word "dropout" far more regularly, between 1960 and 1965 (see Table 5). The drop in articles after 1965, in particular, suggests that explicit interest in the subject was higher in the early 1960s than later. Table 5 is only a rough gauge but still illustrative of how "dropout" became a visible social issue in the 1960s. What was new in the 1960s that made dropping out a headline issue?

The spreading concern over high school dropouts in the 1960s reflected the completion of a long-term exclusion of teenagers from labor markets and the acceptance of a new mission for secondary education. As more adolescents graduated from high school, graduation slowly became an expectation. As the cultures of teenagers came to revolve around public high schools, anxieties grew about the role of schools. Not surprisingly, adults focused much of their postwar anxieties on this rapidly expanding set of institutions. Conflict over school segregation, teacher loyalty oaths, and youth culture arose in part from the growing importance of high schools, and worries over high school dropouts grew from the same milieu. Once it arrived, the dropout stereotype remained in our cultural parlance. The creation of the dropout problem also signaled a new mission of high schools, the prevention of urban chaos. Whereas concerns about attrition early in the century had focused on efficiency, crusaders against dropping out in the 1960s were concerned with the potential for dropouts to become poor, maladjusted, and delinquent.

COMPONENTS OF A STEREOTYPE

Much space within the dropout literature was devoted to five motifs, all of which were to some extent explicit. Completely classifying and labeling the arguments within an emerging literature is futile, in part because it is still

Table 5
Titles on Dropping Out or Equivalent Subjects

Years	All titles	"Dropout" in title[a]	Proportion with "dropout"
1945–49	21	7	33%
1950–54	72	23	32%
1955–59	69	31	45%
1960–61	36	24	67%
1962–63	140	115	82%
1964–65	166	86	52%
1966–67	96	53	55%
1968–69	76	20	26%

Sources: Education Index and *Reader's Guide to Periodical Literature*, 1945–70. Note that the first three lines cover five years each, but the last five cover two years each.

[a] These titles include variants such as "drop out," "drop-out," "dropping out," and plurals.

unformed. Several hundred articles in education journals alone in the 1960s mentioned dropping out in their titles. Nonetheless, several variants of a dropout stereotype, as well as explanations of the importance and causes of the problem, had coalesced by 1965. These themes included the following: equating the dropout problem with unemployment, linking it with urban poverty, using the language of juvenile delinquency, assuming that dropouts were male, or asserting that psychological defects were a primary distinction between dropouts and graduates. Many authors focused on one or two themes, but very few writings on the dropout problem omitted all of the five motifs listed above. Identifying the more common concerns and explanations demonstrates two aspects of the dropout literature. First, by 1965 it was no longer the amorphous set of articles and studies that had existed before 1960. A set of issues dominated debate, even if it did not do so completely. Second, the 1960s literature has had a long-lasting impact on popular definitions and explanations of the dropout problem. Many of the themes dominant in the 1960s persist today in public debate.

Most authors of dropout-problem articles mentioned, at least in passing, concerns about labor market changes, especially the consequences of new technologies. In their view, automation was soon going to eliminate most unskilled jobs, removing all possible employment for future dropouts. A short blurb in *U. S. News and World Report* explained the reasoning: "A high-school education is becoming more important. Each year, it becomes harder for a young person without a high-school diploma to get a job. And unemployment among the young is growing" (The facts about school "dropouts" 1963: 11). As Bert Greene (1966: 8) described, "The time when an unskilled laborer could easily obtain employment is rapidly disappearing." Unemployment problems, Daniel Schreiber argued, came directly from lack of training for skilled jobs: "The inexcusable tragedy of unemployment lies in the fact that the number of available, but unfilled, skilled jobs in the United States is generally equal to the number of those unemployed because they possess no skills" (Schreiber 1962a: 52).

U. S. Labor Secretary Arthur Goldberg (1961: 9) agreed that dropouts faced a much worse time in the labor market and reasoned that prospects for dropouts were slim because of the numerical competition: "The youth of our nation will have to compete more keenly than ever before for the better jobs because there will be so many of them looking for work." The majority of articles and books on the emerging dropout problem assumed that growing workforce automation made a high school diploma a requirement for most future jobs. Advocates of this argument claimed (and many continue to say today) that the future of our economy depends on skilled workers whom only the schools can train. Dropout articles also followed concerns in the 1950s about the labor market. Starting in the middle 1950s, the Labor Department published a series of articles about the consequences of automation and the existence of an earnings gap between high school graduates and nongraduates in its *Monthly Labor Review* (e.g., Riches 1957). Articles and books on the dropout problem used these reports to argue that the problem of unemployed dropouts was the natural consequence of technology.

Another major concern surrounding the issue of high school dropouts was the extent (and threatened expansion) of urban poverty. A large proportion of authors referred to or quoted James Bryan Conant's 1961 book *Slums and Suburbs*, in which he wrote that America was "allowing social dynamite to accumulate in [its] large cities" (2). As Daniel Schreiber wrote for *NEA Journal*, "The recent national concern about school dropouts is largely a response to the situation among out-of-school, unemployed youth in our great city slum areas, which Dr. Conant, in a now famous phrase, has described as 'social dynamite'" (Schreiber 1962a: 51). An *Ebony* editorial said, "The drop-out is a waste of human resources and a drain on the welfare budget" (The tragedy of drop-outs 1961: 48).

Ebony's writers, like many others, were as concerned with the potential for delinquency as with the apparent human tragedy: "The existence of thousands of frustrated youth roaming the streets foreshadows a rise in juvenile delinquency" (48). Again, they (like others) were following James Conant's lead. Without skills to get a job, Conant thought, a dropout was "not likely to become a constructive citizen of his community." Instead, "as a frustrated individual he is likely to be anti-social and rebellious, and may well become a juvenile delinquent. The adverse influence of the street is largely a consequence of gangs of such youths, out of school and unemployed" (Conant 1961: 35). John O'Neill (1963: 157) thought that "the reasons for drop-outs are practically the same as the cause for delinquency." And Lucius Cervantes was sure that dropouts would be "gangsters, hoodlums, drug addicted, government-dependent-prone, irresponsible and illegitimate parents of tomorrow" (Cervantes 1965: 197).

Some were more concerned than O'Neill and Cervantes with the economic conditions that presumably fed delinquent psychological profiles. Alfred Simons, a counselor in an elementary school, and Nelson Burke, an official of the local Youth Center, made a more compassionate link between delinquency and the plight of dropouts in the nation's capital. They thought that for a number of dropouts, the school experiences that "contribute to [their] desire to leave" also create "negative attitudes, truancy, low achievement, and frustration," leading to "a delinquency orientation." They concluded, "When the dropout factor is coupled with employment possibilities for youth in Washington, D.C., serious portents for crime become apparent. These twin frustrations are especially damaging to Negro youth" (Simons and Burke 1966: 27).

As the examples above show, worries over juvenile delinquency appeared in many contexts. "Delinquency" was a very flexible term, and it paved the way for the universal use of "dropout" by social critics. Both conservative and liberal authors wrote about the problems of delinquency and the need to prevent students from dropping out, although they phrased their concerns differently. In addition, the language of delinquency often served as a substitute for race in the dropout debate. In some cases, as in the Washington, D.C., study quoted immediately above or in Conant's *Slums and Suburbs*, race was explicitly mentioned. For others, like Lucius Cervantes, "delinquency" might have been a code word for young male African Americans.

One would be wrong, however, to view the dropout solely as a race- or class-based category. Authors in the 1960s did not necessarily offer a uniform class or race typology of the dropout problem. In some articles, authors argued that the typical dropout was white, while others thought that dropouts were usually a racial minority. Some articles (described below) thought that the real moral crisis was the existence of so-called "high ability" dropouts. Others, quoted above, were clearly concerned about working-class dropouts. What is striking about the dropout debate is its flexibility, the way in which the same issue could provoke some authors into moral outrage at evidence of middle-class dropouts, while others felt threatened by the existence of dropouts from poor families. A significant proportion of articles may have assumed that the dropping out of poor African-Americans was more dangerous to the rest of society (and hence more important to prevent) than other dropouts, but the existence of the dropout literature was not inherently class- or race-based. It was, however, flexible enough to let contemporary preconceptions and prejudices seep in.

Racial assumptions of dropout articles had their origins in concerns about juvenile delinquency. The language of the dropout-delinquency connection in turn grew out of the public concern over juvenile delinquency during and after World War II (Gilbert 1986). Juvenile delinquency returned to the public vocabulary in the 1940s when FBI Director J. Edgar Hoover claimed that a youth crime wave was sweeping the nation. Congressional hearings in the mid-1950s focused on a supposed link between mass media and crime committed by youth. Despite the paucity of solid evidence about a wave of violence, critics charged that crime comic books and films like *The Wild One* glamorized crime and encouraged male adolescents to rob, mug, and murder. This concern prompted many schools and other local authorities to intervene in youth culture in attempts to prevent working-class (especially African-American working-class) culture from permeating middle-class teenage life (Graebner 1989). Many who wrote about dropouts were using a stereotype that already existed for deviant teenagers: Deviant male adolescents are delinquent.

Females, however, were conspicuously absent from the dropout stereotype. Only a few articles discussed women who were dropouts. Articles usually assumed or explicitly said that most dropouts—and the most dangerous dropouts—were male. Although contemporary surveys showed that a substantial minority of dropouts were female, the stereotype of the dropout was overwhelmingly male (Dropout tragedies 1960). For example, *Life* magazine's eight-page spread in 1961 pictured only one woman. In large part, authors believed that male dropouts posed more of a threat than females. James Conant (1961: 50–51) believed that "Boys in this group [dropouts] have much more difficulty finding a job than girls." A study sponsored by the Scholarship and Guidance Association (1962: 250) claimed that male dropouts were more likely to have psychoses than female dropouts:

To the inhibited boys, seeking competence in any of these areas [like sports] unconsciously represented becoming better than their fathers and carried the threat of castration. They were consciously afraid that they could not be successful and would get hurt in the process of trying to achieve. Much more security and safety lay . . . in being nonachievers.

This gendered definition of dropout psychology followed a long legacy in educators' writings. U. S. anxieties about adolescents have often been framed as the dangerous behavior of men. At the turn of the century, educators thought that male teenagers were much more dangerous out of school than were females, and they articulated that concern as the "boy problem" (Tyack and Hansot 1990: 174–75). The stereotype of the postwar juvenile delinquent was also male. And again, in the 1960s, writers framed the dropout issue primarily as a problem of male dropouts.

One exception to this pattern was an unusual article that argued that Americans should pay more attention to the problem of women dropping out of school. The impact of automation was not what worried Bernice Milburn Moore in 1965; rather, she thought that dropping out prevented schools from fulfilling their responsibility "for preparing young women for the strenuous demands of [the] combination of homemaking, child rearing, and earning" (Moore 1965: 22). She thought that among "the primary causes for the high rate of dropouts among women is undoubtedly early marriage," which was counterproductive because women worked "during some part of their adult years" and needed to contribute to household income (Moore 1965: 23). In Moore's eyes, the dropout problem for women was not only a labor market issue but one of fulfilling family responsibilities. Her article demonstrates that the gendered stereotype of the high school dropout was not inevitable but a choice among alternative views. That choice derived in part from the psychological assumptions of many dropout article authors.

The psychological arguments about the dropout debate took several forms. Many articles tried to sort dropouts (or reasons for dropping out) by personal characteristics of the individual student. For example, researchers at San Diego State College thought that one could distinguish "three major types of dropouts": "1) the involuntary dropouts [those who leave school out of a personal crisis], 2) the retarded dropouts, and 3) the intellectually capable dropouts" (Voss, Wendling, and Elliott 1966: 366). Junior high school Vice Principal Michael Rovello (who thought the media were too sympathetic with dropouts) thought that he could divide dropouts into those whom the school had failed, those who "come to school totally unmoved by the idea of learning," and those "who are morally corrupt and who in turn corrupt others" (Rovello 1965: 402–3). Penn State University psychologist Joseph French (1969) argued that the difference between "high ability" dropouts and students was "their perception of parental attitude. Persisters feel that their parents force them to stay in school, but dropouts feel that their parents . . . did not force them to do so" (77).

While some authors tried to sort dropouts by psychological causes, other authors wrote a real or composite biography of what they thought were poignant examples of dropouts. *Life* magazine spent most of its first article describing one dropout: "The story of dropouts and their personal anguish is reflected in the story of Charlie Amitrano told on this and the following pages. Two weeks after his 16th birthday Charlie signed himself out of the 10th grade at Brooklyn's John Jay High School. As he slouched alone across the bleak, wet playground, he bravely told himself, 'Bein' out in the world don't bother me'" (Dropout tragedies 1960: 108). The titles of some articles demonstrate their focus on describing a modal dropout. A teacher at a New York City vocational high school titled his short biography, "Dropout Case No. 22" (Newman 1965). Two education professors at Marquette University collapsed all the information they had gathered from other articles into a dense stereotype:

The average school leaver is about 16 years old; frequently he merely marks time until he can legally leave school; most likely he will leave around the tenth grade; generally, avoids participation in extracurricular activities; and usually does not identify with any social group within the school setting. He lacks social skills for interpersonal relationships with teachers and peers by being tense, suspicious, and under strain. . . . The typical school leaver's parents tend to be indifferent to the value of education. (Topetzes and Ivanoff 1962: 36)

These capsule portraits of a "typical dropout" demonstrate the way in which the social construction of a dropout problem gelled in the early 1960s. Instead of the complex description of dropping out that Labor Department officials presented in the 1950s, these mini-biographies implied that potential dropouts were clearly identifiable and distinct from other students, and that the phenomenon of dropping out was easily explainable. What separated dropouts from graduates, the stereotype suggested, were character flaws, personal traits of a man who could not adjust to high school and who was too ignorant to understand the consequences of leaving school. The studies that looked for personality explanations for dropping out reinforced the tendency to see dropouts themselves as a problem.

Not everyone agreed, however, that dropping out was much of a problem. Junior high school principals Walter Burke (1965) and Michael Rovello (1965) thought that the mass media made too much of the problem. Some students, Rovello thought, should drop out. Sociologist Paul Goodman also dissented from the dominant debate, though from a different perspective. To Goodman, the existence of dropouts showed the failures of compulsory education. He responded primarily to one proposal by U. S. Labor Secretary Arthur Goldberg to raise the upper limit of compulsory schooling to eighteen:

Twist it and turn it how you will, there is no logic to the proposal to extend compulsory schooling *except* as a device to keep the unemployed off the streets by putting them into concentration camps called schools. . . . As an academic, I am appalled by this motivation for schooling. As a citizen and human being, I am appalled by this waste of youthful vitality. (Goodman 1964: 54-55; emphasis in the original)

Adolescents had tremendous energy, to Goodman, and they should have the opportunity to educate themselves, but the mission of universal education was a mistake. Goodman and a few others, however, were iconoclasts in the dropout debate. Most authors assumed the importance of the problem and agreed that dropouts threatened to become delinquents and dependents.

Lost in the 1960s dropout debate was any sense that the economy produced unemployment. In most writers' views, dropouts and their characteristics were the problem; lack of skills produced unemployment. Also, in few cases did the structure of schools come under fire, except where people proposed additional programs to raise graduation rates. As two critics of dropout studies argued:

Clinically oriented researchers tend to find character disorders . . . Sociologically oriented researchers tend to find disorganized families and associated evidence of poor early socialization. These emphases draw our attention away from the school, its program, and its staff and direct us toward developmental failures. (Dentler and Warshauer 1965: 5)

This pattern was in notable contrast to the concerns of Thorndike, Ayres, or Caswell earlier in the century and their confident belief that efficient school management could eliminate grade retardation. In a period when schools had become the institution where the most adolescents spent several years, writers claimed that dropouts, and by extension their families, deserved most of the blame for the failure of two social institutions, schools and labor markets. The economy and schools largely escaped criticism in the social construction of the dropout problem.

"DROPOUT RATES"

An important part of the dropout discussion was a focus on statistics. As with previous incarnations of concern over attrition (such as Edward Thorndike's), people wanted to illustrate their opinions about attrition with numbers. One consequence was the rapid acceptance of "dropout rate" as a meaningful term. Junior high school Principal Walter Burke wrote in 1965, "The average citizen in any city, town, village, or hamlet in the United States can quote with varying degrees of accuracy the percentage of students who do not finish high school" (44). Articles in popular journals consistently used the NEA Project on School Dropouts' estimates of dropout rates and income figures from the Census Bureau's Current Population Survey. School officials regularly used dropout numbers to justify new programs or, conversely, to claim success with specific projects. Philadelphia's public school guidance newsletter repeatedly wrote articles on "why the nation's high drop out rate is a tragedy" (National stay in school campaign 1960). In a press release dated February 4, 1960, praising the Demonstration Guidance Project for success across a broad range of measures, New York City schools Superintendent John Theobald noted that one of the benefits of the program was greater persistence through school: "We have been heartened by the fact that there have been fewer drop-outs and transfers from the project classes than from the non-project classes" (New York City School Office of Public Relations Records, box 16, folder 2).

While school officials used numbers for their own purposes, some local activists used dropout statistics as well. Philadelphia civil rights activists used statistics published by the NEA Project on School Dropouts to criticize school policies. Kelly Miller, the chair of Philadelphia's Citizens Against Segregated Schools, spoke before the Board of Public Education on August 8, 1966, in part because "the system is plagued with one of the highest dropout rates in the nation" (Citizens Committee on Public Education in Philadelphia Papers, box 6). In a statement April 20, 1966, the West Philadelphia Schools Committee criticized the board on similar grounds: "In *1961* our system had the highest rate in the nation, *27%*; in *1965*, it had risen to *32.7%*" (Citizens Committee on Public Education in Philadelphia Papers, box 6; emphasis in the original). Thus, a variety of people, including those who regularly fought over public school politics, tacitly agreed that some objective measure of the dropout problem was necessary, feasible, and easily defined.

How does one measure a dropout rate? In the early 1960s, the most common approach was the grade cohort method, comparing a graduating class with the size of the tenth-grade class three years earlier (or ninth-graders four years before, or eighth-graders five years earlier, and so forth). The proportion staying in school was often called the "holding power" of schools, and the unaccounted proportion was called the dropout rate. The NEA Project on School Dropouts used this technique when estimating dropout rates for large cities (Schreiber 1964a). The grade cohort method (following a grade through school) was also the most common description of what a dropout rate was. Leonard Coplein, coordinator of curriculum and instruction in the Camden, New Jersey, schools, thought that grade cohort measures were the natural measure (Coplein 1962: 526). In presenting the official statistics from six high schools in Los Angeles (with whose policies the authors disagreed), two UCLA researchers wrote, "The dropout rate refers, *of course*, to the proportion of school enrollees who have left school without indicating any intention of entering another" (Singleton and Bullock 1963: 138; emphasis added). By the mid-1960s, very few authors explained what they meant by dropout rates. They usually cited numbers casually, as though it were obvious what a dropout rate was.

The practice of following a grade cohort through school as the way to calculate dropout or graduation rates rested on several assumptions. One is that the grade cohort measure will capture only the difference between those who graduate and those who drop out. Several types of events, though, can change a person's enrollment status. Dropping out and graduating are only two. Students can also transfer in or out of the school (or school system) or in a few cases die. Finally, students can be retained in the same grade for several years. This last possibility is critical to understanding the limitations of grade-based data: The age-and-grade distribution of students depends not only on population age distribution in a school but also on grade promotion practices. These promotion practices can change rapidly, making comparisons across years worthless. For all these reasons, the group graduating from high school may bear little relationship to the group in ninth grade four years earlier and almost none to those in first grade twelve years earlier. In combination, inward migration, outward migration, and changing grade promotion practices make tracking students by grade statistics difficult and largely useless.

The second assumption of grade cohort measures is that an easy, objective dropout measure exists. No single, definitive measure of any demographic processes exist. Some are easy to calculate; others require professional training. Some are comparable across time, while others are not. Some have a more intuitive rationale than others. One has to choose which statistic to calculate and use. Implicit in the 1960s debate over the dropout problem was the idea that defining a dropout was the primary quantification problem. Agreeing on a definition was presumed a logistical problem because school systems calculated dropout rates differently: Leonard Coplein thought that "some standardized procedure of reporting and summarizing should be adopted which allows for comparisons with local, state, and national findings" (Coplein 1962: 529). Nominal agreement on a definition was possible. Several conferences concluded that a dropout was anyone who left a school without graduating or enrolling in a different school (National Education Association Research Division 1963). No solid records exist as to how many school systems followed through on the common definition of a dropout. The existence of another debate over proper definitions in the 1980s suggests little acceptance of the uniform definition of a dropout drafted in the 1960s.

THE "DROPOUT PROBLEM" AND UNEMPLOYMENT

Daniel Schreiber was not without some historical perspective on concern over dropping out. He was very aware of the difference in attitude from prior years. He explained it as reflecting the growing economic importance of a diploma:

[I]n 1950, only 13 years ago, for the first time in American educational history, more students graduated from high school than dropped out. Yet, so far as I know, there was no dropout problem 14 years ago as we know it today. There was, however, a large demand for unskilled labor; and we might hazard the guess that the winnowing involved in the educational process . . . was even encouraged as a natural reinforcement of the division of labor. (Schreiber 1964b: 2)

Schreiber was partly correct. Writers about the dropout problem, Schreiber among them, focused on the labor market as their concern. However, labor market changes cannot explain the sudden visibility of the dropout problem. Teenagers and young adults had been increasingly excluded from full-time work since the turn of the century. Moreover, Schreiber's language borrowed from much older concerns about the link between schooling and the labor market. Worries about school attendance have existed since the early days of public schooling. Advocates of vocational education early in this century claimed, like the writers discussed in this chapter, that the future need for skilled labor demanded changes in school curricula.

Important differences exist between the turn-of-the-century debate over vocational education and the debate over high school dropouts. Nonetheless, arguments about the economic utility of education far preceded the dropout problem. Twentieth-century schools have always had critics who thought they do not adequately prepare students for work. Comprehensive high schools, in fact, have rarely provided the directly relevant skills or personal contacts needed in labor markets (Licht 1992: Chap. 3). Yet the recurrent criticisms of high school's relevance to labor markets have usually oversimplified the consequences of technological change. Warnings about automation were no more accurate in the 1950s and 1960s than they were four and five decades earlier. Computerization has made more cashiers' jobs—as well as engineering jobs— possible. Technological advances have never forced uniform changes in labor markets. They often lead to greater skill requirements in some positions and deskilling in other occupations, and sometimes shifts in the gender associated with an occupation (Braverman 1974; Davies 1982). Nothing happened in the 1950s that pointed to an inherent need for new training. American industry passed no magic threshold in the 1950s that suddenly made high school graduation a *production-related* requirement for employment.

The second fallacy in Schreiber's explanation is the male-oriented stereotype of the dropout. If they had truly been prescient observers of labor markets, writers on the dropout problem would have focused their concerns more on women. The fastest-growing segment of workers in the 1950s and 1960s was that of women entering (or re-entering) the labor force (Kessler-Harris 1982: 300–303; Oppenheimer 1970: 8–9). The National Manpower Council recognized that "women [had] accounted for most of the growth of the nation's working population" in the postwar period (National Manpower Council 1957: 17). Competition for jobs grew faster for women than for men. Yet the argument about growing scarcity of jobs for the unskilled often assumed that men were the relevant objects of study and concern. Those writing about dropouts in the 1960s were responding more to prejudices of the day—primary among them, concerns about dependency—than to labor market changes.

No one can dispute, however, that a high school diploma is now a requirement for most jobs and that an economic stigma follows anyone without a degree. Changes in the skills required for steady employment are hard to pin down. However, the widespread use of a degree as a credential has obscured its artificiality. Those arguing that high school diplomas were a necessary condition of future work in the 1960s and since have conflated the credential value of a high school diploma with the skills supposedly learned while completing a high school program. David Labaree (1988: 178) has explained that the skills and the credentials acquired in school are not necessarily identical:

Education is a use value which involves the acquisition of knowledge and skill; it is difficult to imagine having too much of it. Credentials are exchange values, which are desirable only as long as they can be traded for something useful, like social position and money. The two forms of educational value can vary quite independently of each other.

In the labor market, a high school diploma functions both by conveying skills and as a credential that employers can use to screen applicants. The first urban high schools in the nineteenth century recognized this value and maintained their prestige by keeping high school diplomas a rare commodity. Because a high school diploma was rare until the turn of the century, it had a high market value for young adults looking for jobs. The increase in graduation, and the use of credentials, encouraged expectations that teenagers would attend high school.

Expectations obscure and mislead almost as much as they reveal. High school graduation became the norm in public writings while a significant minority of students remained dropouts. Dropping out has persisted in some areas more strongly than in others. In addition, not everyone agreed on the causes or consequences of the dropout problem. The articles on the dropout problem in popular and education journals reflected the views of the authors, which others did not necessarily share. Nonetheless, the modal description of the dropout problem drew upon a set of common assumptions. Many writers thought that dropping out was a new problem because men (not women) would find employment difficult. Studies tried to identify attributes that dropouts shared. Most writings argued that the act of dropping out, not the schools or the economy, was the fundamental problem. For many, the dropout problem was a floating metaphor that touched upon racial prejudices or fears about adolescent males.

REFLECTION OF AN AGE NORM

The common motifs do not completely classify the dropout literature of the 1960s. Idiosyncratic explanations of dropping out still existed after 1965. Nonetheless, a handful of themes had begun to dominate debate. The specific way that themes were articulated was more often a variant of old worries than an entirely new one. For example, the concerns about dropouts and automation were a reformulation of older arguments about education and labor markets that run throughout the extensive writings on vocational education around the turn of the century. The dropout debate of the 1960s also borrowed the language of 1950s hysteria over juvenile delinquency, especially when it assumed that dropouts were the near-certain "hoodlums" of the future. The focus on personality flaws of dropouts continued the long history of educators' attributing character defects to some (or many) Americans. The themes in themselves were not what was new in the 1960s concern over high school dropouts.

However, those old concerns were not combined with an age norm until the 1960s. Progressive Era educators did not view early school leavers as varying from some expected behavior. The existence of school withdrawals was lamented, certainly, and school officials worried about the relationship between education and the labor force. In those respects, as well as in the obsession about proper statistics, real continuity exists between Progressive concerns and those voiced in the 1960s dropout debate. However, only a small minority of public school students graduated from high school at the turn of the century. No one writing then defined the problem as those few who did not meet an expected goal. Half a century later, the sense that graduation was expected and normal made dropping out a much more urgent issue.

What was new in the 1960s was the notion that a high school dropout was varying from a social norm. Educators writing about early school leavers at the beginning of the century did not think that the vast majority of adolescents would graduate from high school. On the contrary, they assumed that leaving school without a diploma was the usual, if regrettable, experience. That presumption of selective secondary education changed by mid-century. Most who wrote about education after World War II, including both critics and defenders of public schools, assumed the opposite of Progressive Era writers. Many educators and school critics since 1960 have implied that high school attendance and graduation are the normal and expected experiences of teenagers.

The headline status of the "dropout problem" in the 1960s thus marked a turning point in the perceived role of high schools, from an elite to a comprehensive institution. For the first urban high schools, the primary problem was maintaining public support (or, often enough, tolerance) for an elite institution. By 1965, one of the primary questions for high schools was how to fulfill the role of a universal institution. The comprehensive mission of high schools is relatively new. It is, for such a new idea, almost unquestioned. One way we can date the acceptance of a universal need for a high school education is when the lack of a high school diploma became a significant social issue. Graduating was less common in the early 1960s than it is today. Nonetheless, dropping out had already become an action that many defined as unusual and troublesome.

We can best understand concern over high school dropouts by seeing it as a label for variation from this age-specific norm of high school graduation as a teenager. Expectations like these are usually hidden. We go about daily life without examining why we went to school at a certain age or why retirement rules persist. Nonetheless, these implicit rules are often a powerful influence on our lives. Age expectations usually have two key characteristics. First, new norms create and require new words. When we think most people should behave in a certain way, we coin terms to describe those who fit or fail those standards. The creation of the word "dropout" thus shadowed the developing norm of high school graduation. The second trait of age norms is their development in rough coordination with specific social institutions. Expectations about age-specific behavior reflect changing relationships between families and other social institutions. Without Social Security, many elderly would rely entirely on younger relatives for survival. The norm of universal retirement required some way to provide for the dependent elderly, and Social Security shifted much of the burden away from individual families and onto the workforce as a whole (Graebner 1980; Haber 1983). Even the language we use to describe norms implies the existence of organizations or authorities. One cannot define a pensioner without a pension fund or dropouts without schools.

In the case of dropping out, age norms reflected institutional developments in response to major economic changes. High schools grew as a warehousing institution as teenagers withdrew from full-time labor. The age norm of graduation, and the language of the dropout problem in the 1960s, showed evident anxiety about the assumed dependency of dropouts. When President John Kennedy wrote Congress about the needs of education in January 1963, he presumed that schools were the appropriate place to respond to the problems of dependency.

Ignorance and illiteracy, unskilled workers and school dropouts—these and other failures of our educational system breed failures in our social and economic system: delinquency, unemployment, chronic dependence, a waste of human resources, a loss of productive power and an increase in tax-supported benefits. (Kennedy 1964: 105–6)

Key among the failures of schools, according to Kennedy, was dropping out. Concern about dropouts has been one variant of a recurring obsession with post-puberty years whenever the nature of work has shifted. The first concerns about juvenile delinquency came from the early factory towns in the nineteenth-century North, as growing wage labor markets attracted teenagers from rural communities. Public schools and factories absorbed some of those abandoned by a decaying domestic economy in the early nineteenth century. Adolescence became a common term around the turn of the century as child labor slowly became obsolete in a standardizing, industrializing economy. The expansion of high schools and private youth organizations accompanied the Progressive Era recognition of adolescence as a separate stage in life (Kett 1977: 189–98, 222–28, 248–54). Juvenile delinquency again became a focus of concern during and after World War II as labor market segmentation increased. Not surprisingly, the United States has built prisons and colleges to take custodial care of young adults who do not fit neatly in postindustrial labor markets. Institutions that have served teenagers and young adults have grown, in large part, from these worries.

Yet dropping out in itself was not a primary concern of educators until the mid-twentieth century. Many of the issues we think of today as connected with dropping out—the need to socialize children, the response of schools to urban poverty, the economic promise of education, and the problems of children who have academic difficulties in school—have appeared frequently without being part of an explicit discussion about dropping out. Only after 1960 did they become commonly identified as part of a specific problem called "dropping out." Concerns about dependency, the belief in schools' ability to improve the poor, and the expectation that all teenagers would be in school gelled in the dropout debate. Then, educators struggled to respond to the "new" issue of dropping out.

5

The Limits of Dropout Programs

Programs for school dropouts ... are mushrooming at a hurried pace, close to the point of overlapping in large urban centers.

—Charles Savitzky, "Job Guidance and the Disadvantaged"

By 1965, many school districts were operating programs they called "dropout prevention." The NEA, the U. S. Office of Education, and other organizations published several bibliographies on the subject in the mid-1960s, lists that included surveys of programs supposedly designed to attack the dropout problem (L. Miller 1965; Miller, Saleem, and Bryce 1964; Varner 1967). Dropout programs, which followed the rise in concern over the dropout problem, shared several traits with the conventional wisdom about dropping out. While recommendations, proposals, and operating programs rarely matched precisely, most programs shared at least a few assumptions with the national literature on high school dropouts. Job-training programs implied that anyone with skills could get a job. Counseling programs assumed that the problem with potential dropouts was their inability to adjust to school. Public relations campaigns implied that if dropouts returned to school, the dropout problem would largely disappear. As well as reflecting the naiveté of dropout stereotypes, the dropout programs of the 1960s reflected the institutional structures within which they operated. The programs rarely fulfilled their advocates' wishes, either in scope or in the nature of programs. Constrained by budget limits, informal protocol, and often contradictory demands of sponsors and clients, programs failed to eliminate dropping out.

Dropout prevention programs were far too small to counter other policies that encouraged or coerced students to leave school. To be blunt, dropout projects did not eliminate the phenomenon. As one *Saturday Review* article in 1966 put it, "What schools are doing about [the dropout problem]—while often irrelevant—covers a wide range of approaches . . . The list goes on and on, but what does it add up to? Frequently, nothing" (Bard 1966: 78–79). Superintendents could (and did) announce dropout prevention programs to serve a few dozen students while public school principals or counselors told thousands of students each year to leave school because they were discipline problems, were pregnant, or had poor academic records and had turned sixteen or seventeen (Binzen 1964b). In other cases, school districts turned away adults who wanted to return to school. New York City's school superintendent stated in a circular dated June 29, 1965, that dropouts had no right to public schooling if they had been gone for more than a year (New York City Schools Superintendent Circulars, box 36). Dropout prevention was a puny effort against an enormous flow of bodies out of schools, part of which school policies encouraged or created. The conflict of scale made dropout prevention largely irrelevant. Few people at the time, though, pointed out the inconsistency in policies.

Finally, public school bureaucracies made dropout programs irrelevant through isolation from or within school systems. Programs arose sporadically, without long-term financial or organizational commitments from school districts or local governments. Dropout prevention programs shared, in that sense, one critical trait with other attempts to reform schools in the 1960s. Many pilot programs coped with awkward administrative positions, peculiar funding status, and uncertain commitment by schools to the programs' future. Unable to fit easily within a complex bureaucratic framework, most pilot programs (dropout prevention among them) died within a few years. Most of those that survived either created their own constituency, had some statutory backing (perhaps required by federal law), or eventually fought their way into bureaucratic security. Dropout programs, on the other hand, developed no permanent constituency, had no statute requiring their existence, and had mixed success in resolving problems within school systems. Dropout prevention was therefore a transient phenomenon with no lasting impact on school policies.

This larger failure to eliminate dropping out should not obscure the fact that some programs succeeded in getting a few individuals back into school or into jobs. Work-experience plans occasionally provided short-term aid to poor families, gave young men and women some exposure to community advocacy, or stimulated political activism. These achievements are notable in themselves, and clients appreciated them. The accomplishments of programs were more in line with their actual scope than with the grandiose goal of eliminating the phenomenon of high school dropouts.

PROPOSED SOLUTIONS

The solutions to the dropout problem proposed by writers in the 1960s generally matched their assumptions about its origins. Those who believed that some form of maladjustment was the root of dropping out often proposed intensified counseling programs. Those concerned about the economic consequences of dropping out usually argued for work-experience programs. Counseling and work experience programs existed well before dropping out acquired headline status in the 1960s. Tucson, Arizona, public schools began their counseling program in 1947, and within a decade its coordinator was claiming a reduction of dropout rates because of it (Young 1955). Some forms of manual, industrial, or vocational programs have existed in most urban school systems since the late nineteenth and early twentieth century. The Smith-Hughes Act in the early twentieth century put federal support behind vocational programs, and they were the only type of educational program that Congress supported even through the Great Depression (Tyack, Lowe, and Hansot 1984: 110–11). Older civil rights organizations like the Urban League allied with local business leaders, the public schools, and city governments after World War II to support job-training programs. For example, the Detroit Council for Youth Service began the Job Upgrading Program in 1949. Coordinated with public and private agencies in the area, Job Upgrading organized six-week training programs to provide unemployed teenagers (sixteen and seventeen years old) with some job skills, attempt to place them with private employers, and continue contact with program clients for several months after placement (Miller, Saleem, and Bryce 1964: 93–94). Thus, existing counseling and vocational structures attracted dropout programs when educators designed them in the 1960s.

Both counseling and vocational programs were intended to assist teenagers in adjusting to the demands of school and work. Writers recommended additional counseling to identify potential dropouts and to convince them to stay in school or guide them through prevocational training. Advocates argued, for example, that counseling would improve students' ability to adapt to school (Murk 1960). A second recommended practice was expansion of work-experience programs (also called work study or cooperative education), sending students or dropouts to part-time jobs and teaching them the rest of the week in classes, including remedial instruction in reading and explicit guidelines for on-the-job behavior (New York City Board of Education 1962; New York Bureau of Guidance 1965). Supporters of expanded work-experience programs usually justified them for two reasons. First, part-time jobs could allow teenagers to stay in school when they were under pressure from families to produce income (Weinrich 1952: 128). Second, supporters claimed that work-experience programs would train students to enter the workforce with appropriate skills and possibly entry-level jobs. According to Charles Savitzky, the head of the New York School to Employment Program (STEP) quoted at the beginning of this chapter, STEP provided "opportunities to face real situations in the world of work with assistance" from counselors and other adults (Savitzky 1962: 54). Socialized into the formal and informal demands of the labor market, the dropout would be able to get and keep a job. The two common themes in dropout prevention proposals, counseling and work-experiences programs, were intimately connected. Good counseling and part-time work programs went hand in hand, in many writers' views. One psychologist said that the purpose of dropout prevention programs was to change potential dropouts' "perception of work and non-student days." The goal was a "guided and gradual entry into the role of wage earner" (French 1969).

The common prescriptions for the dropout problem omitted two important issues, however. First was the limit of formal education and job training. They could provide students and dropouts with concrete skills and the confidence to use them, but they did not guarantee a job. Skilled workers could be unemployed even after employment guidance and training. Proposed solutions to the dropout problem, though, implied that the labor market could absorb any number of skilled workers. The second common assumption of proposed solutions was that school bureaucracies would and could easily assimilate dropout programs into public school systems. Articles on the dropout program occasionally took the form of a checklist for action on the part of public schools. Others simply stated that certain programs should exist. Few articulated any idea of where dropout programs would fit within school organizations. Missing was a sense of who, precisely, would fulfill these mandates—or who might oppose them. After the scathing attacks on schools in the era of McCarthyism and the manpower debate, educators should have been more wary of short-sighted panaceas (Cremin 1961: Chap. 9; Tyack and Hansot 1982: Section 3). Yet they were not.

DROPOUT PROGRAMS

The model programs listed by bibliographies and articles at the time reflected a broad range of funding, operations, and results. Therefore, any schematic description must be hedged with the understanding that the most common characteristics applied to only a plurality of programs. In addition, records provide few clues about whom the programs served. Nevertheless, some routine elements existed. Work-experience programs, school counselor leadership, and publicity campaigns were common. Also common was a fragmentation of funding and control that made cohesion among different programs and coordination among different agencies difficult.

The most common component of a dropout prevention program was work experience in some form, usually aimed at male dropouts or potential dropouts. The Detroit Job Upgrading program mentioned above was an early example, and often-cited model, for this type of project. In Miami Springs, Florida, occupational training focused on junior high schools, which would attempt to identify potential dropouts and place them in job orientation and work-experience programs (Miller, Saleem, and Bryce 1964: 94). Other work-experience programs appeared in Kansas City, Missouri; Milwaukee, Wisconsin; San Francisco and Richmond, California; Tacoma, Washington; Chicago, Illinois; Jersey City, New Jersey; Lane County, Oregon; and Washington, D. C. (Schreiber 1962a: 55–59; Schreiber 1964b).

Second, counselors often directed or were critical staff members in programs. In Roanoke, Virginia, the Adult Education Program administered aptitude and interest tests to potential dropouts. In Lincoln, Nebraska, a special school counselor handled potential dropouts and their job prospects. Passaic, New Jersey, established a job referral system in 1948, run by the city psychologist's office (Miller, Saleem, and Bryce 1964: 96–97). One St. Louis, Missouri, high school established an experimental work-experience program for potential dropouts in 1960 (Varner 1967: 44; Wilkerson 1965). Almost all of the work-experience programs noted above involved counselors extensively in the selection, placement, and evaluation of individual students. In addition, a number of counselors and other educators ran small experimental programs designed to test the effects of counseling. Donald Davis, a professor in Western Michigan University's School of Education, organized a small control-group experiment (twenty-one students in each group) in which the primary treatment consisted of teacher training in "mental health, juvenile delinquency, holding power of schools, and under- and over-achievers," special counseling sessions for students, and a field trip to a professional basketball game (Davis 1962).

Third, some public relations campaigns tried to convince students to remain in school or dropouts to return to school. In the summer of 1963, Health, Education, and Welfare Department Secretary Anthony Celebrezze met with forty-five city superintendents, school board presidents and officials from urban programs "to see what could be done about getting additional numbers of young people to return to school in September." According to the memorandum from presidential assistant Ivan Nestingen on July 29, the meeting agreed to start "a special drive" to convince dropouts to return to school. In an August 2 memorandum to Celebrezze, President Kennedy approved $250,000 from the president's emergency fund for dozens of cities to hire school counselors. In sixty-three cities, a White House press release bragged on September 15, counselors walking door to door contacted over 23,000 dropouts, of whom 10,105 said they would return to school in the fall. Contrasted with the common supposition that 700,000 students dropped out of school annually, though, 10,000 returns were relatively small. While the Office of Education called the campaign a success, its limitations were clear: Very few dropouts actually returned to school as a result of the program (U. S. Department of Health, Education, and Welfare Subject Files, box 34; U. S. Office of Education 1964). The 1963 expenditure by the White House was only one of many similar publicity crusades. The NEA Project on School Dropouts, the armed forces, the U. S. Department of Labor, and other organizations produced films to convince students to stay in school (Philadelphia School District 1963: 1965). Various branches of the federal government had sponsored "Stay in School" campaigns since the early 1950s, continuing the trend of public crusades for attendance which had started with the Children's Bureau's campaign of 1918 (Zeitlin and Zeitlin 1952). These publicity campaigns attempted to use popular media to convince dropouts to return to school or potential dropouts to remain in school. They were rarely accompanied by other measures to keep students in school or enable dropouts to return to school.

Fourth, funding and other support frequently came from a variety of sources, including local school districts, state or federal budgets, community organizations, and local business leaders. Some school districts ran their own vocational programs in the early 1960s, or nominally coordinated vocational and job guidance programs with the state's employment referral service. Yet programs frequently relied on external financing. In some places, public schools cooperated with private organizations like the Chamber of Commerce or local Urban League to manage job referrals. In 1961, New York state created a job skills training project, the School to Employment Program. Some foundations sponsored programs designed to attack the dropout problem. For three years in the 1960s, the Ford Foundation underwrote a work-study program, which the New York City Board of Education and the city's personnel department jointly directed. Permanent commitments inside school systems, however, did not exist.

The federal government also sponsored dropout programs apart from publicity campaigns. Lyndon Johnson's legislation included projects that many described as dropout prevention (e.g., Varner 1967). The Economic Opportunity Act of 1964, commonly referred to as the omnibus War on Poverty bill, included several major job-training programs. One, the Neighborhood Youth Corps, was specifically designed to help ameliorate the dropout problem. It funded a variety of job training programs for adolescents sixteen to twenty-one years old, both in and out of school. The Labor Department allowed both public and private agencies to submit proposals for programs that would place adolescents in part-time jobs and also require them either to stay in school or to attend special training classes (Public Law 88-452, sections 111–16). Other federal programs included job-training programs funded by the Vocational Education Act and the Manpower Development and Training Act of 1963, guidance projects funded by Title V of the National Defense Education Act of 1958, the Adult Education Act of 1966, and a variety of programs based on Title I of the Elementary and Secondary Education Act of 1965. None of these were initially justified as dropout prevention programs, but educators and others occasionally described them as such.

Partly because of the fragmentation of funding, cohesion in dropout programs never fully developed, either in program goals or coordination among agencies. Thus, students, dropouts, and their parents faced a bewildering array of programs. In individual cities, dropout prevention never appeared as a package of programs. An individual project may have been rationalized as a jobs program, community action, dropout prevention, vocational education, or delinquency prevention. The boundaries between different goals were vague, and politics were as much a part of the framework of programs as the idyllic goal of dropout prevention. The best way to appreciate the organizational chaos involved is to examine programs in individual cities. New York City, Atlanta, and Philadelphia provide a range of case studies. New York City was the center of debate over the dropout problem. New York also provides evidence about the role of different actors within the school bureaucracy. Atlanta never was the site of innovative programs designed specifically to eliminate the dropout problem. Nonetheless, city and state educators were aware of the national debate over dropping out and occasionally called attention to the problem or claimed that one of their programs helped ameliorate the problem. Philadelphia, like Atlanta, had several programs aimed at the dropout problem. The fate of one particular work-experience program shows the way federal policies pitted the interests of Philadelphia's municipal government against those of community organizations.

"POSSIBILITIES OF . . . FUNDING"

David Rogers' (1968: 267–68) description of New York City's school system as a "sick bureaucracy" explains the irrationality of its dropout programs in the 1960s. Small, starved of funding commitments, and isolated in the bureaucracy, dropout programs were more symbolic than substantive. The school system administration and the Board of Education had a great incentive to *appear* to reform the school system. That veneer of innovation eased and diverted pressure to change the schools further. Thus, the Board of Education and superintendents in New York City supported some minor reform efforts while forestalling or watering down larger changes. The Board of Education and the superintendents approved of small dropout programs. They did not, however, change the policies that annually discharged thousands of students without high school diplomas.

New York educators at various times touted many programs aimed at the dropout problem. These included compensatory education, early academic counseling, job counseling, night schools, vocational courses, and work experience. All of these came layered on top of previous bureaucratic structures in the city schools that handled pupil counseling, dropouts, vocational education, and work experience. For example, by the early 1960s, the city school system had a wide counseling program, although high school counseling was done part time by teachers. The city also had special rules for dropouts sixteen years old. When New York state raised the compulsory attendance age from sixteen to seventeen in the 1930s, the city responded by creating a network of regulations specifically for sixteen-year-olds. Those who were out of school and without employment in 1960 had to attend a so-called continuation school until seventeen. The city's vocational schools were separate from the continuation school. In addition, the city had developed competing authorities to run vocational schools. State law required a lay Advisory Board for Vocational and

Extension Education, with representatives of business and labor, but the city's bureaucracy also had its own Department of Vocational Education. In addition to the vocational schools was a system of work-experience programs called cooperative education which had its own board of lay advisors (Kohler 1962: 17–18, 37–51). One could reasonably describe the city's public school organization in the 1960s as chaotic.

Most new projects in the 1960s were examples of the more commonly recommended dropout prevention programs. In 1961, the school district announced six programs aimed at dropout prevention; even a brief description of the programs listed on press releases of February 15–16, September 22, and December 14, 1961, shows the hodgepodge of programs (New York City Schools Office of Public Relations Records, box 16, folder 5; Byerly 1964). First, the city schools allowed 400 dropouts, sixteen years old, to attend evening school as a replacement for continuation school attendance. Second, one high school began an experimental work-experience program "intended for 16-year-old potential dropouts," serving forty-seven students. Third, the main continuation school and a Queens high school began an "intensive pre-employment course" for 400 dropouts to give them skills required to complete a job application. Fourth, the school district expanded to 108 students an existing work-experience program aimed at boys sixteen or seventeen years old. Fifth, New York City enrolled sixty students in the statewide School to Employment Program. Sixth, the school system's cooperative education division and the city's Personnel Department agreed to run jointly a work-experience program in which teenagers would fill vacancies in the civil service for part-time pay and go to school the rest of the week. For the latter program, the Ford Foundation agreed to fund the salaries of supervisors, teachers, and guidance personnel.

Easily apparent is the limited scope of these programs. The first six listed above served, altogether, fewer than 1,300 pupils. On the other hand, according to the system's newsletter on curriculum in the fall of 1961, New York City's public schools discharged over 27,000 students in 1959–60, and the city in 1960 had over 80,000 dropouts aged sixteen to nineteen (Municipal Cooperative Education Program Papers, section 5). While the programs listed above were only pilot projects in 1961, the city's school system never attempted to reach the majority of teenage dropouts. Even at the height of the War on Poverty, the school system's optimistic estimate of potential work-study programs included plans for 17,300 people, or easily less than a quarter of the potential client pool. According to minutes of an October 7, 1965, meeting of school officials to discuss expansion of work-study programs, New York City's STEP served 600, the local Vocational Education Act programs 1,038, and the city Manpower Development and Training projects 2,400 (Donovan Subject Files, box 26, folder 9). New York City's professional educators, with the most dropout programs in the country, never imagined that special programs would serve more than a small segment of the total dropout and potential dropout population.

Dropout programs had limited scope in part because the school system committed itself only as extra funding was available. The discussion of work-study programs by school bureaucrats in the October 1965 meeting focused on the funding potential of specific programs. The minutes' capsule summary of the School to Employment Program noted that 50-percent state funding of STEP "began [because it was] a Demonstration project, 5 years ago and for this reason may be soon phased out by the State Department [of Education]." The executive deputy superintendent demanded a plan within three weeks on how to fund STEP under the federal Vocational Education Act. Existing Vocational Education Act and Manpower Development and Training Act programs depended, according to the bureaucrats running them, on continuation of federal funds. One official promised to "explore the possibilities of a Ford Foundation funding for an extended work-study program with industry" along the lines of the municipal civil service cooperative education program. Note here that the question was not finding money within the system's operating budget but locating outside funding.

This focus on external funding was typical of New York's school bureaucracy. The reaction within the school district to the 1965 Elementary and Secondary Education Act (ESEA), with its Title I funds targeted at schools in poor neighborhoods, demonstrates the pervasive nature of pecuniary motives. Despite the act's explicit intention to fund additional rather than existing programs, as well as its call for input from other community institutions, the New York City school system rushed to apply for federal aid to subsidize the operating budget. A resolution on June 14, 1965, approving several projects very shortly after passage of the act, shows the speed with which the bureaucracy could move when it sensed funding (Shapiro Papers, folder 20). Flouting the spirit of the law, the superintendent's office and the Board of Education for several years sped through the annual proposal process in an effort to get federal funds, no holds barred (Rogers 1968: 339–42, 452–62). An internal memorandum from the 1960s, labeled simply "Use of ESEA Title I Funds," criticized the Title I proposal process in the city as blatantly illegal (Shapiro Papers, folder 21). In addition, the board centralized all control over external funding proposals in one office, according to a December 29, 1964, memorandum from Norman Brombacker (Shapiro Papers, folder 20). These abuses were typical of local and state reaction to the Elementary and Secondary Education Act (Washington Research Project 1965), and they crippled the long-term future of innovative projects, including dropout programs.

In addition to being limited to external funding, dropout programs had no logical place within the confused, overlapping jurisdictions of different school system components. Intense competition for legitimacy and funding discouraged any coherent approach to the dropout problem. The best example of that pattern is the Municipal Cooperative Education Program of the New York City Personnel Department and Board of Education. In 1961, the Ford Foundation agreed to fund a five-year work-experience program, which the New York City

Board of Education and the city's Personnel Department would run jointly. The Personnel Department claimed that job shortages had left vacancies in positions that teenagers could fill. According to the proposal, approved by the Ford Foundation, the city school system would initially select 250 tenth-grade students, each of whom would work one-half the hours of one position. The rest of the students' time in the program would be spent in remedial education and occupational orientation. The Ford Foundation's staff recommended the plan to the foundation Board of Trustees in June 1961 as follows:

The primary purpose of this program is to keep in the high school young people, including many from lower socioeconomic groups, who have good academic prospects but are in danger of dropping out. This is a demonstration program to show what a municipal government, with a dual interest as a representative of the public interest concerned with social problems and also as an employer, can do to help ameliorate the school dropout problem. (Municipal Cooperative Education Program Papers, section 1)

The Ford Foundation agreed to the project because it thought the program would be a model for dropout prevention.

The Ford Foundation's aims were frustrated, however, by the school system's obstinate bureaucracy. Over the course of the Ford Foundation grant, the New York Board of Education, the city Personnel Department, and the city's Manpower Utilization Commission feuded repeatedly over turf. The head of the city's Manpower Utilization Commission, O. William Ross, complained to the Ford Foundation in December 1961 about the attitude of Grace Brennan, who ran the Cooperative Education Program for the Board of Education. Ross had asked about "the need of training and orientation for City supervisors and mention[ed] the possibility that perhaps something similar might be required for Board of Education coordinators." In response, Brennan "explode[d] in all directions." Ross explained his concern:

I don't really care about Gracie's explosion. . . . [B]ut what *does* concern me is what appears to be a preremptory dismissal by Grace Brennan of the idea that maybe the school coordinators do need some special orientation in this program.

One of Brennan's supervisors then tried to stall the training program for city supervisors. A Ford Foundation program associate wrote in the margins of Ross' letter, "Tell them we'll stop making payments on funds unless they climb down from [their] high horse and start doing what's necessary" (Ross to Henry Saltzman, Municipal Cooperative Education Program Papers, section 4). This bureaucratic bickering occurred constantly over the course of the program, according to the evaluation report by Martin Hamburger in 1965 (Municipal Cooperative Education Program Papers, section 3). When Brennan wrote to David Hunter of the Ford Foundation on February 4, 1963, about possible extension of work experience to state civil service jobs, she sent copies to a number of officials but not to Theodore Lang, the head of the municipal Personnel Department (Municipal Cooperative Education Program Papers, section 4). At the end of the grant period, Lang suggested several projects. Brennan waged a short and bitter campaign to defeat his proposals. First, she responded to his plan for another Ford Foundation grant in a letter to city schools Superintendent Donovan on October 27, 1965:

This new plan is to have Federal Funds pay 90% of the students' wages and the firm 10%. This will eliminate all present Coop. firms who are adamant against this practice. . . . May I know if Ted Lang is to carry on here on this Municipal [Cooperative?] . . . I wanted your reaction to T. Lang's "taking over" this phase of our high school program. (Donovan Subject Files, box 26, folder 9)

Brennan's primary concern was to prevent Lang's "taking over" her program.

In December 1965, Brennan learned that Lang had written, without her knowledge, to the Ford Foundation regarding funds left over from the Municipal Cooperative Education grant. He had asked for and received permission to investigate a dropout recovery program operating out of the cooperative education office. She wrote a furious memo to the superintendent on January 3, 1966:

This has been done for two years by the Board of Education with a special program at Charles Evans Hughes High School . . . Careful evaluation (as suggested by Dr. Lang) was carried out by Dr. Hopkins, Dr. Namowitz and Miss Brennan. . . . It was a situation whereby boys could work every other week and stay home every other week or hang around the alternate week. . . . There is no need for the $18,186 dollars requested by Dr. Lang to "explore the feasibility of expansion of this type of return to school." (Donovan Subject Files, box 26, folder 9)

Superintendent Donovan sided with her and wrote to the Ford Foundation requesting that the funds be used for a male practical nursing program instead (Donovan to Chandler, January 14, 1966, in Donovan Subject Files, box 26, folder 9). The result of this bureaucratic feuding was the destruction of the program's chief aim: to serve as a demonstration project. In its immediate aims, to keep students in school, the program's evaluator thought the program did well. However, one of the chief criticisms of the Ford Foundation grant program by evaluator Martin Hamburger was the mismatch between goals and action on the part of Brennan's department:

Most coordination was administrative and not educational. Interviews with the students, teacher conferences and observations, and job visitations showed only a few situations where curriculum was flexible or where creative teachers had used the fact that the coops were working to "enrich" or improvise meaningful and motivating school experiences. (Municipal Cooperative Education Program Papers, section 3; emphasis in the original)

An internal Ford Foundation memorandum from John Coleman to McGeorge Bundy on August 28, 1967, after the end of the program, expressed the program associate's frustration with the school bureaucracy:

The grant was indeed a good one, but our attempts to get the Board to do it again with *private* industry involvement met with words of delight and mountains of inaction. We finally turned them off because they were so terribly slow in acting. (Municipal Cooperative Education Program Papers, section 4; emphasis in the original)

Intended originally as a model program, the Municipal Cooperative Education Program became a policy dead end because of bureaucratic rivalry. It serves as a powerful reminder of the limits of reform within a public school system.

Older bureaucratic structures often behaved defensively in the 1960s precisely because other structures threatened to encroach on their former rationales for existence. The behavior of Grace Brennan and the Cooperative Education Department is a case in point. New York's cooperative education program had begun during the Progressive Era, and the public-private commission to coordinate actions among the school system, businesses, and labor unions was dominated by heads of New York businesses. That domination by corporate leaders in itself was neither particularly unusual nor noteworthy among vocational programs in the United States, but it shaped the response to new institutional conditions. At the periphery of the school system by 1960, the cooperative education program faced competition for resources with the introduction of new programs such as Higher Horizons (one of the first compensatory education projects) and the War on Poverty. One response was to push for new programs under the jurisdiction of the office; Grace Brennan initially agreed to cooperate with the municipal Personnel Commission in running the Ford Foundation program. (Previously, cooperative education had meant work-study positions in private, not public, businesses.)

The alternative to cooperation within the bureaucracy was competition. Grace Brennan repeatedly tried to thwart any proposed deviation from what she and the Cooperative Education Commission saw as the legitimate aims of work-study programs. At one point, she requested that local Neighborhood Youth Corps programs remove the words "cooperative education" from its publications. As she explained in a letter to the superintendent on February 28, 1966, "If the extension of the Neighborhood Youth Corps into Municipal Government continues it will be another instance of competition among ourselves" (Donovan Subject Files, box 26, folder 9). Brennan's hostility toward Ted Lang mirrored the parochial attitude of the Cooperative Education Program advisory board. One meeting agenda from December 9, 1965, demonstrates that the board felt that the War on Poverty programs compromised its aims. Noting the "tremendous amounts of money available to various programs, i.e., [the New York City] Anti-Poverty Board," the agenda lamented that "anti-poverty programs [are] cutting Cooperative registers.... All militate against students' interest in 'real' work in the community" (Donovan Subject Files, box 26, folder 9). In this regard, New York was the extreme of internal bureaucratic belligerence. The same forces that limited change, though—the sponsorship primarily of small, model projects and internal squabbling—operated in other cities that claimed they ran programs responding to the dropout problem.

"THE QUITTER" AND OTHER SYMBOLS

Atlanta was very different from New York City. Its city schools were under court orders to reverse *de jure* segregation for most of the 1960s. It was a much smaller city, with a smaller public school system. As the next chapter will discuss, the racial politics of Georgia shaped school bureaucracy in a unique way. Nonetheless, it shared some common features with New York. No long-term commitment backed up the publicity surrounding dropout programs in Atlanta. The programs often existed for other reasons, served a small clientele (or one entirely different from the supposed dropout population), and disappeared within a few years.

In September 1963, the NEA Project on School Dropouts newsletter highlighted the programs putatively instituted by Atlanta's public schools to ease the dropout problem. The schools had hosted several conferences on dropping out, attended by "community leaders, business people, and representatives of labor and industry." Public service announcements on radio tried to discourage dropping out. The Atlanta public schools and a local television station produced and broadcast *The Quitter, a Portrait of a High School Dropout*, which half a million people viewed. Atlanta's Board of Education had plans to expand identification and counseling of potential dropouts, remedial reading programs, construction of comprehensive high schools and a regional vocational-technical school, and afternoon and evening classes "coordinated with the other provisions" of the dropout-prevention plan (NEA Project on School Dropouts Papers, section 3).

In addition to the programs announced in the NEA newsletter, Atlanta had other programs for dropouts. The Atlanta public schools participated in the summer 1963 program organized by the federal Office of Education to convince dropouts to return to school (Atlanta Board of Education agenda [hereafter "agenda"], August 12, 1963). Throughout the mid- and late 1960s, the Atlanta Board of Education operated training programs in the Atlanta metropolitan area funded by the Manpower Development and Training Administration. These programs, run by the Vocational-Technical Education Department, included projects at both predominantly white and black schools and had programs for preparation of nurse aides, diet kitchen helpers, custodians, mechanics, clerical workers, drafts workers, cabinet making, technical repair work, and cooking (June 8 and September 14, 1964, agenda). The school system later rented space in a local bank building to train 150 clerical workers (July 13, 1964, agenda). In the summer of 1965, the superintendent and his staff opened an in-school Neighborhood Youth Corps project. According to the original proposal, the program would provide "an opportunity to reduce the number of school drop-outs by providing meaningful work experiences for young men and women ages 16 through 21 years" (November 9, 1964, agenda). The Neighborhood Youth Corps enrollees' jobs included positions as clerical aides, gardeners, library aides, and warehouse assistants (October 11, 1965, agenda). Like other Neighborhood Youth Corps programs for students, this one required enrollees to work part time while attending school and represented cooperation between the school system and another authority (in this case, the Fulton County Board of Education). The program began with 250 students; in 1966, 2,000 were enrolled (Helping our youth 1966).

By 1967, therefore, the Atlanta Board of Education operated a broad range of programs that touched upon the social construction of the dropout program. According to the 1965–66 statistical report and reports to the board on August 8, 1966, and June 12, 1967, programs included the Manpower Development and Training projects, the program funded by the Ford Foundation, and projects funded by the Vocational Education Act of 1963 and by the Elementary and Secondary Higher Education Act and the Civil Rights Act of 1964. This list of programs is misleading, however. Atlanta's public schools committed themselves minimally to dropout prevention. As in New York, dropout programs in Atlanta were not large. For example, according to the annual report on vocational-technical and adult education in 1965, the Manpower Development and Training Program enrolled 1,010 students in 1964–65 (also see March 13, 1967, agenda). Yet high school enrollment was typically more than 30,000 each year during the 1960s. Furthermore, many of the programs were aimed at adults who enrolled part time in courses. According to the 1967–68 statistical report, the school system served 36,592 clients in its vocational programs, of which 2,793 (or 8 percent) were secondary school students. The others were largely evening students who came to programs after work or on weekends.

The Atlanta Public Schools also constantly delayed the construction of vocationally oriented schools and vocational workshops. In the spring of 1962, the Atlanta Board of Education approved an expansion and complete overhaul of the vocational education program, which the superintendent's office proposed to expand to all high schools and make "an integral part of the total educational program" (May 14, 1962, agenda and minutes). The board had to delay that plan in August 1963, however, because anticipated funds from a bond sale were unavailable (August 13, 1962, agenda). By 1964, Superintendent John Letson had scaled down the expansion. He wrote state Superintendent Claude Purcell on January 15, 1964, of a plan for one vocational-technical school, with later plans to build vocationally oriented high schools (Georgia Local School System Correspondence Files, box 2).

In February, Letson abandoned plans for one of the two planned vocational (as opposed to vocational-technical) schools (Clifford A. Nahser to "State Department of Education," July 29, 1964, in Georgia Local School Systems Correspondence Files, box 2). In May, his proposal was to allow seniors to attend regional vocational-technical schools (May 11, 1964, agenda). Several times in the mid-1960s, state officials wrote to the local superintendent to prod Atlanta to build an area vocational-technical school it had contracted to build with the state in 1961 (Purcell to Letson, August 18, 1964; Jack Nix to Letson, March 25, 1965, in George Local School Systems Correspondence Files, box 2). The annual report of the Georgia Department of Education in 1968 stated that Atlanta's vocational school finally had opened six years after the initial proposal. The leadership of the Atlanta public schools, if it was truly committed to job-training programs as a solution to the dropout problem, never showed it by completing the necessary facilities.

Many of the programs touted as dropout prevention originated for only distantly related reasons. For example, the area vocational-technical schools were planned not to ease the dropout problem but because the state Department of Education had embarked on a long-range plan to build regional vocational-technical schools across the state. In a memo to local superintendents on May 26, 1965, state vocational Director Jack Nix explicitly explained that they were not designed for dropouts and opposed what he thought of as a watering down of the vocational-technical program: "Area vocational high school programs shall not be used as a place to send students simply because 'they can't do anything else'" (Georgia State Superintendent General Administrative Records, box 12). When the Atlanta board claimed that the vocational-technical schools helped alleviate dropping out, it was directly contradicting the purposes as envisioned by state officials. The programmatic response to the dropout problem was a facade in Atlanta, as it was in New York.

"LEARN HOW TO GET ALONG"

In Philadelphia, competition between schools and other agencies thwarted a job-training program run by a neighborhood community council. Like other cities, Philadelphia had many programs that the school system and community groups mentioned when asked about the dropout problem. The problems of one community program, the Germantown Youth Corps, show the resistance of the federal government to anti-poverty programs initiated by nongovernmental groups. For dropout programs, structured competition between school systems and community organizations helped doom any possibility of coordinated action.

The city had several Neighborhood Youth Corps programs beginning in late 1965. One of the private agencies operating a Neighborhood Youth Corps program was in Germantown, a section of the northwest part of Philadelphia that had several multiracial neighborhoods and community organizations in the 1960s. Organized by the Germantown Community Council, a coalition that had existed since 1933, the Germantown Youth Corps program began operations in late 1965, continuously having seventy or eighty young men and women as enrollees. After a brief, intensive orientation, the program sent them out on part-time jobs in the area to work for nonprofit organizations, doing clerical work, clearing weeds from yards, and conducting neighborhood surveys.

Several parents vigorously defended the program later when its existence was threatened, as discussed below. They formed an auxiliary organization and argued that the program "has kept these youth in school" (Germantown Community Council Papers, box 35, folder 45). In particular, according to an outline for presentation by a Mrs. Pray in 1966, parents saw the separation of the program from the school district as essential:

Many youngsters who have been discouraged in school, or learning hostility [in] school situations, find relief and gain new insights and broader horizons by jobs OUTSIDE the school walls. If the School Board is to run the program, all these gains and assets will be lost.

Among the program's other virtues, the parents thought it created leadership in the community, developed self-esteem in their children, was a key ingredient in neighborhood stability, and provided "invaluable training for interim or permanent jobs" (Germantown Community Council Papers, box 35, folder 52).

The Germantown Youth Corps program faced several problems in everyday operations. One was the need to recruit employers to whom it could send its enrollees during and after the program. Program Director Mattie Humphrey and the Germantown Community Council sent out several mass mailings requesting positions for program enrollees. The Germantown Youth Corps also faced difficulties with the adolescents who were prospective enrollees, other neighborhood residents, and staff employees. On the demand side was a much higher call for positions than it could fill, as Humphrey reported to the federal government on January 31, 1966. In addition, as she noted in her July 1966 report, supervisors faced conflict with young men who "have heckled, harrasse[d], intimidated and [in] three cases assaulted an enrollee traveling to or from a work-site or the project offices" (Germantown Community Council Papers, box 32, folder 5). A report of an industrial injury on May 19, 1966, noted that a supervisor had dislocated his left thumb in one attack by harrassers: "The team leader pushed his thumb back into its socket and continued the direction of enrollees' work on the lot" (Germantown Community Council Papers, box 32, folder 11). Obviously, some of the Germantown Youth Corps staff were able to handle small crises well. Not all the staff was so competent, however, as Humphrey reported to the Greater Germantown Economic

Opportunity Committee (Germantown Community Council Papers, box 34, folder 21).

In the end, the most intransigent opponents of the Germantown Youth Corps were the federal officials who had approved it in the first place. The Labor Department cut off funding within a year (U. S. dooms youth corps 1966; Germantown youth project 1966). Because the Germantown program theoretically competed with school system programs for students, it had become politically unacceptable. Federal representative June Moore suggested on June 16, 1966, to Germantown Community Council Executive Director Frank Delany that the program continue with out-of-school teens, but she refused to continue the program with enrolled students (Germantown Community Council Papers, box 34, folder 15). Beginning in September 1966, only the Philadelphia Board of Public Education and the Philadelphia Archdiocese could run Youth Corps programs for enrolled students. Delany managed to wrangle a meeting with Labor Department officials and a promise for a new program in the summer of 1967, but finally had to settle for sending Germantown youth to a summer program run by the archdiocese (Germantown to regain youth corps 1966; U. S. aid asked 1966; U. S. officials agree 1966; Youth corps to help 1967).

The elimination of the Germantown program was part of a broader federal pattern favoring school system programs. At different points, the regional director blamed either the Vietnam War (Youth corps funds gone 1966; Youth corps here saved 1966) or the demands of rural Pennsylvania counties (Job training for youth cut 1966) for cuts in Philadelphia. Yet the regional office had consistently favored programs run by the local school systems (both public and Catholic). In the first year of Neighborhood Youth Corps program operations nationwide, the Labor Department approved citywide programs months before the Germantown project, an action that one official for the city's Redevelopment Authority thought "shows they favor what can be done easiest, instead of what will give the best results" (Germantown Youth Corps project balked 1965). After it eliminated the Germantown program, the regional office suggested that the Germantown Community Council work closely with the Philadelphia Antipoverty Action Committee (the city's official War on Poverty coordinating committee) to get another program. The regional director for the U. S. Labor Department knew, however, that the director of the Germantown program, Mattie Humphrey, had been an outspoken critic of the anti-poverty committee and was unlikely to be received kindly. He told one reporter: "We know that Germantown came to us in good faith. However, they must learn how to get along with the establishment in their local community" (U. S. aid asked 1966).

This political favoritism was part of a broad undermining of the principle of "maximum feasible participation" theoretically embodied in the Economic Opportunity Act of 1964. In a February 26, 1965, meeting, officials from the Office of Economic Opportunity had made a similar demand for local cooperation and unity before listening to grant proposals for Community Action Programs (Day to Longstreth, in Greater Philadelphia Chamber of Commerce Papers, box

15). And the public school district had struggled with Spring Garden College over who would be the primary local contractor for Manpower, Development and Training Administration programs (Binzen 1964c). Thus, the actions of federal officials in Philadelphia pitted the interests of neighborhood groups like the Germantown Community Council against the interests of local government authorities. After several years of the War on Poverty, the director of the Youth Corps program for the Delaware Valley Settlement Association thought the choice of cuts was, in a reporter's paraphrase, a device for "freezing out the private agencies in order to hand over a larger share of it to the city to be used for political advantage" (Youth corps faces 1968). Community initiative had died in part because of the political decisions of federal officials.

THE FATE OF COMPREHENSIVE SECONDARY EDUCATION

The problems dropout programs faced in the 1960s are, above all else, a testament to how bureaucratic intransigence can frustrate programmatic reform. No matter what criticism one can make of the projects themselves, most had no chance of long-term survival. Concern over the dropout problem left no institutional legacy because programs aimed at a broadly defined symptom do not have a permanent constituency. Dropouts may have seen themselves as individuals or as members of a community or other group, but they did not organize themselves as a potent political force *as dropouts* in the 1960s. When pilot projects expired or agencies cut funding, dropout programs disappeared. No law or coherent constituency placed sufficient pressure on politicians and educators to maintain dropout programs. Despite the calls for truly universal secondary education, public school systems maintained operating methods inimical to the aims of dropout programs. The pilot projects existed primarily as lip service to the ideal of comprehensive education.

The continuing rise in high school graduation was not, therefore, a result of deliberative efforts to increase graduation. Even the largest programs in the 1960s touched only a small fraction of the potential dropout population. Instead, the same factors that had pushed high school attendance up since the late nineteenth century—the common desire for education and the credential value of high school attendance and diplomas—kept operating. The long-term dilemma was that a diploma has the most credential value when it is limited. In the 1960s, though, that problem was not yet upon schools. There were plenty of people still left who had not graduated from high school. In addition, the framing of the problem and programs omitted key questions. Those silenced issues represented the gap between the myth of comprehensive high school education and the reality.

6

Omissions

The social construction of the dropout problem in the 1960s was irrational in at least three ways. First, the perceived crisis was not in response to a real demographic trend; graduation became more, not less, prevalent in the middle twentieth century. Rather, the perceived crisis reflected changing expectations and a connection between the institutional success of high schools and concerns about adolescence. Second, the perceived crisis did not lead to effective or even widespread policy changes. Most dropout programs were too small and isolated to affect most dropouts and potential dropouts. Third, the public debate over dropping out omitted issues and perspectives that a rational discussion should have included. Prior chapters discussed the first two weaknesses in the social construction of dropping out; this chapter discusses the third.

Omissions in programs in part reflected prejudices of the day. Certainly, dropout programs had biases. For example, many were only for male dropouts. Work-experience projects were especially likely to focus on males (Flynn, Saunders, and Hoppock 1954: 486; Novak 1968: 163; Schreiber 1964b: 251; Varner 1967: 44). Federally funded programs often required detailed proposals that engraved inflexibility into projects. For example, the form for Neighborhood Youth Corps proposals required statements of which jobs were for men and which for women. Those divisions, however, were not necessarily related to enrollee demand. Shortly after its inception, women flooded the Germantown Youth Corps seeking positions in the program. In her April 1966 report to the Labor Department, program Director Mattie Humphrey explained, "They are generally ineligible . . . since we have satisfied our quota of girls" (Germantown Community Council Papers, box 32, folder 5). The sexual division of work-experience assignments was a practice mandated neither by the legislation nor by the initial regulations by the federal government

(Neighborhood Youth Corps projects 1964). It existed entirely by the prejudice of program officers.

The discussion about dropping out went beyond the reflection of contemporary prejudices, however. Debate omitted or silenced obvious issues that could have been part of the social construction of dropping out. These issues included racial differences in educational attainment and the question of whether students have a right to an education. Southern (and some Northern) educators ignored evidence of racial disparities in educational outcomes. Most administrators in the 1960s also reaffirmed their belief that schools had the right to exclude students from an education. School officials shaped debate by ignoring critics insofar as they could. Embattled and defensive, many educators muted activists by responding selectively to criticism. The following sections first discuss the key issues omitted in much discussion and then focus on the local dynamics of silencing in Philadelphia.

"BLOCKING OFF ANY CONSIDERATION OF NEGRO DROPOUTS"

The dropout problem became a visible social concern in the decade after the Supreme Court's 1954 *Brown v. Board of Education* ruling outlawing explicit segregation in public schools. The fight to desegregate public education raised several issues to the forefront of public debate. The right to a decent education, the demand for equal school opportunities and participation in school politics, the authority of the federal government over states—all of these became critical issues in the conflict over segregation. Most of these issues could have been central to the discussion of and programmatic response to the dropout problem. In some ways, desegregation efforts and the dropout debate were intricately connected. Daniel Schreiber, director of the NEA Project on School Dropouts, had come straight from the administration of Higher Horizons and the Demonstration Guidance Project, a program that New York City's first commission on school desegregation had initiated. He attended a major 1961 conference on school desegregation sponsored by the U. S. Commission on Civil Rights (Dulles 1968). Thus, desegregation involved at least one of the major figures who raised the dropout problem to national visibility.

However, the relationship between the dropout problem and desegregation was rarely discussed in the open. Especially in the South, discussions of race entered the dropout debate only obliquely, if at all. The battles over school desegregation affected the dropout debate, though, in two significant ways. Bureaucratic defenses of segregation built a wall around the issue of race. Race became a taboo topic for many educators even on issues apart from desegregation. In a related manner, the same bureaucratic structures responsible for dropout programs were often those that helped schools defend the racial status quo. White school psychologists in the South were dependent on the local board and superintendent. When called upon to serve segregation, they usually answered. They had little freedom to advance dissenting views or explore new topics. Thus, public school officials' definition of the dropout problem avoided racial issues because confronting them would have been uncomfortable for those who felt obliged to defend segregation. The siege mentality of school districts, when faced with demands for desegregation, contributed to the rigidity of and limitations on dropout programs.

One example of the relationship, and the silence, between desegregation and the dropout problem was in Atlanta and the state of Georgia. When a group of black parents sued to desegregate Atlanta's school system, the schools responded to the court challenge with bureaucratic maneuvering. When faced with a series of court orders to desegregate the public schools in the early 1960s, the Board of Education decided to accept the letter of the law, but it instituted policies designed to slow integration. Delay tactics, including grade-by-grade integration, so-called "choice plans," and pupil assignment laws succeeded in significantly slowing public school desegregation throughout the South in the 1950s and 1960s (McCauley 1957: 130–46; U. S. Commission on Civil Rights 1962: 4– 16). Atlanta was no exception; its schools used all three methods mentioned above.

One measure was the slow desegregation of schools. The Atlanta Board of Education proposed integrating one grade at a time, beginning with high school seniors. Thus, in the fall of 1961 some black high school seniors were allowed to attend previously all-white schools. In the fall of 1962, the eleventh grade was to integrate, and so on. In the original grade-a-year plan, the public school system would not be desegregated from the first to the twelfth grade until 1972 (Integration made Kirkwood 1965).

The second tactic was the development of a "voluntary" integration plan, whereby parents could choose where to send students. In court testimony, Atlanta Superintendent John Letson admitted that the ability of white parents to transfer their children out of schools where black parents were transferring their children had resegregated several elementary schools (Dr. Letson admits in court 1965; Integration made Kirkwood 1965). According to the U. S. Commission on Civil Rights, the Atlanta superintendent's office had sent letters to the white parents of students in one elementary school, notifying them of the impending integration of the school and allowing them to transfer to other, all-white schools (U. S. Commission on Civil Rights 1967: 1:66). The voluntary nature of the transfer policy allowed white parents to stay one step ahead of the glacial desegregation of Atlanta's public schools. The bureaucratic tactics of the Atlanta public schools delayed integration long enough to allow white students to leave the Atlanta public schools, either by transferring to other all-white public schools or by moving.

The third major delay tactic was a local form of pupil assignment laws to slow integration without explicitly violating court orders. In 1960, the Atlanta Board of Education approved a set of pupil placement regulations, proposed by the superintendent's office, that established bureaucratic criteria for the transfer of students between schools. It explicitly declared that student assignment would be "without regard to race or color," but allowed the assignment of students based on putatively individual criteria, including the following:

the suitability of established curricula for particular pupils; the adequacy of the pupil's academic preparation; . . . the scholastic aptitude and relative intelligence or mental energy or ability of the pupil; the psychological qualification of the pupil for the type of teaching and associations involved; . . . the psychological effect upon the pupil of attendance at a particular school; the home environment of the pupil; the maintenance or severance of established social and psychological relationships with other pupils and with teachers; . . . the ability to accept or conform to new and different educational environments; the morals, conduct, health and personal standards of the pupil. (Atlanta Board of Education minutes, January 18, 1960)

The new regulations thus put the assignment of students on a supposedly race-neutral basis. A year later, the Atlanta Board of Education banned "reference to any terms designating race" in correspondence or reports, except where required by state law (August 14, 1961, minutes). The administration regulations for transfers from black to white schools, presented to the Board of Education on April 24, 1961, stipulated that school district counselors set up a series of tests for any applicant wanting to transfer between schools.

The effect of this bureaucratic race-neutrality was the continued segregation of Atlanta's high schools for several years. Supposedly on the basis of the standardized and psychological tests, the school district severely limited the numbers of black students who would begin desegregation in the city. Of more than 120 African-American students who applied to transfer to previously all-white high schools in 1961, only ten transfers were approved. Civil rights leaders in Atlanta interpreted the pupil placement laws, quite accurately, as an attempt to delay integration (Negroes tested 1961; Rejected Negroes planning appeal 1961).

The defense of segregation in Atlanta and the rest of the South directly limited the ability of school employees to discuss all facets of the dropout problem, especially to recognize racial differences in educational outcomes. The role of school counselors was critical in the bureaucratic tactics of the Atlanta public schools. Counselors gave the intimidating series of tests which the pupil placement regulations required of those African American students who wanted to attend integrated schools. The counselors wrote the reports on such students, reports that the school district used in its claim that it was refusing transfers solely on individual character traits and not on race. School counselors thus were essential instruments in the Atlanta Board of Education's stonewalling in the 1960s.

Counselors were also responsible in several ways for dropout prevention and dropout programs. Atlanta's superintendent relied on counselors to compile dropout statistics in the early 1960s. Atlanta's counselors were occasionally seen as experts on the issue statewide: In a 1964 proposal for a federally funded study of dropouts, Georgia Institute of Technology Professor John Fulmer cited Atlanta counseling statistics on the average IQ score of dropouts from city schools (Georgia State Superintendent Subject Files, box 9). That study proposal demonstrates the hypocrisy of the Atlanta Board of Education. The mental testing scores recorded in the study prospectus were broken down by race and sex, which explicitly violated the policy of official racial blindness in Atlanta. Despite the official silence in the Atlanta public schools, school counselors continued to separate white and black students in their internal assessments, and they shared these statistics with Fulmer. When in private communication, school employees still categorized students by race.

In public, however, school officials were silent on the possible connections between racial inequality and the dropout problem. Throughout Georgia, the structure of segregation, and the defensiveness about it, prevented discussion of racial differences in school resources and achievement. The state's association of white school counselors demonstrated a consistent concern over the dropout problem but never mentioned race. They also never met with the black association of counselors until 1970. All the association's conferences were held in segregated facilities and restricted to white school officials. For example, the June 1962 Georgia Association of School Counselors newsletter reported that the annual conference was to be held in the Athens Center for Continuing Education. The association was affiliated with the Georgia Education Association, the white teachers' association, and remained silent throughout the 1950s and 1960s on the topic of school desegregation. Of the conference programs for those years, not a single panel had desegregation or racial differences in educational outcome as the topic (Georgia Association of School Counselors Scrapbook).

The muffling of discussion on racial inequality was not limited to school counselors. Even those who acknowledged racial inequalities were reluctant to discuss the issue in the context of school dropouts. In 1962, Georgia's Department of Education co-sponsored a conference on dropping out whose participants included the state superintendent and several representatives from the Atlanta public schools. Frank Smith, a consultant for the Georgia Association for Mental Health, wrote Executive Director Frank McFall after the conference, on July 20, 1962. According to Smith, educators could not "much longer refuse to consider the implications of inferior Negro education." Nonetheless, he thought it more important to keep racial inequality out of the discussion: "We succeeded real well in blocking off any consideration of Negro dropouts, in the conference" (Georgia Director of Negro Education Subject Files, box 11).

Similar silences pervaded a June 1962 luncheon on vocational-technical schools. Held in an Atlanta motel (almost certainly segregated before the 1964 Civil Rights Act), the attendees included representatives from the Atlanta mayor's office and over twenty Atlanta businesses, as well as several dozen groups from outside Atlanta. The list of participants reported by state vocational Director Jack Nix on June 15, 1962, included no civil rights organization, and he probably had invited none (Georgia State Superintendent Subject Files, box 5). The state superintendent's speech included a substantial section on the dropout problem. He echoed one of the standard explanations of why dropping out was a problem:

Because the product of our schools will so directly affect the future of our nation and its economy, we are vitally concerned with providing the best education for ALL students. . . . We are, therefore, vitally concerned with the problem of the high school drop-out.

Nowhere, however, did Purcell discuss racial disparities in educational outcomes in Georgia (Georgia State Superintendent Subject Files, box 5).

Other school officials also ignored racial disparities in graduation. The head of Georgia's Pupil Personnel (or counseling) Services, Franklin Shumake, wrote in a letter on December 15, 1966, that "we have no official records that would verify whether the percentage of drop-outs among Caucasians is greater or less than the percentage of drop-outs among Negroes" (Georgia Deputy State Superintendent Subject Files, box 2). He was wrong; the state did have comparative figures. Figures from the state Department of Education's Office of Information on January 2, 1961, demonstrated a consistent gap in school achievement in high school graduation in the postwar years. Furthermore, those internal figures showed that, for grade cohort measures (for example, what proportion of first graders graduated twelve years later), the gap in high school graduation increased in the 1950s (Georgia Director of Negro Education Subject Files, box 11). Those statistics were flawed, but they existed. State school officials were unaware of their existence or ignored them.

A few white officials within the state education hierarchy were concerned about racial disparities in school attendance and outcome. The coordinator of Georgia's visiting teacher service (counselors who made home visits) consistently pressed for more attention to the dropout problem. Florrie Still created the first form in 1958 to count dropouts in Georgia's school districts. When the state contemplated eliminating the compulsory attendance law, she pointed out to state Superintendent Purcell on September 19, 1961, the discriminatory impact: "Which race do you think would show the greatest drop-out in percentage of attendance, as well as enrollment, with a repeal [of compulsory attendance]?" (Georgia State Superintendent Subject Files, box 11). Nonetheless, the dominant discussions of the dropout problem in Atlanta and Georgia excluded significant reference to racial differences in dropping out and the potential connection among desegregation, bureaucratic resistance to integration, and educational outcomes.

Southern school systems were not the only districts under pressure to desegregate, nor were they the only ones to soft-pedal racial disparities in education. The Philadelphia school district's monthly vocational guidance newsletter never mentioned race in any of its several dozen articles on the dropout problem in the early or mid-1960s. At a conference of the American Public Welfare Association in 1962, Philadelphia's Director of Pupil Personnel Robert Taber read a twenty-two-page paper on "School Dropouts—a Community Problem." He never once mentioned race. He did mention what he termed the problem of "culturally deprived children." He discussed a project funded by the Ford Foundation's Great Cities School Improvement Program, specifically designed to solve the problems associated with racial integration of schools, but never mentioned race, instead talking about "pupils of limited background" (Logan Papers, box 11).

The official use of euphemisms did not go unchallenged. The West Philadelphia Schools Committee disagreed with the official use of "cultural deprivation" as a term used to label racial minorities. Committee members explained why they distrusted conventional labels in a meeting with a district subcommittee reviewing the schools' nondiscrimination policy on May 16, 1963:

We believe that a majority of the Negro pupils in the segregated schools of West Philadelphia are handicapped not so much by cultural and family problems as by the serious deficiencies in the schools which they must attend. . . . Much of the talk about the "deprived" rests on clichés and half-truths, and has the effect of shifting all the blame for our poor achievement levels onto the pupils and their families. We are convinced that the conditions which exist in our elementary schools are equally responsible. (Citizens Committee on Public Education in Philadelphia papers, box 6)

Civil rights activists tried to fight stereotypical description by bringing racial inequality into open discussion. The West Philadelphia Schools Committee statement quoted above demonstrates its disagreement with the denigration of poor communities.

In both Northern and Southern cities, then, school officials often avoided discussing race when they wrote or spoke about the dropout problem. In many cities across the nation, bureaucrats tried to fend off desegregation with a variety of tactics. Those tactics made the discussion of racial inequality difficult in other contexts. A few school officials worried about inequality but were unable to bring it into open discussion, and little evidence exists of much official discussion of race in the context of the dropout issue. The dropout problem was one issue that could easily have led to analyses of racial differences in school outcomes. It did not, in part because public school districts had girded themselves for a siege.

"DENIAL . . . OF THE RIGHT TO ATTEND SCHOOL"

The public debate over the dropout problem did not change widespread school policies that pushed students out of school or denied public schooling to whole categories of children. In the 1960s, most educators insisted that they had the authority to determine who belonged in and out of school. This included the power to suspend students, remove pregnant students from classes, and place children in special education (or exclude them from schooling altogether) based on administrative prerogative alone. Educators' concerns about dropouts did not change those policies. The practices remained until court orders and federal legislation gave students and parents some modicum of procedural rights in schooling in the 1970s. These policies—discipline practices, responses to student pregnancy, and special education placement—could conceivably have been connected to the dropout discussion. All were visible concerns in the 1960s. Yet they were not explicitly tied to the dropout debate. The focus of the dominant dropout debate was not the effect of school policies on student achievement.

Discipline Policies

The power of school authorities to discipline students has been, historically, the most arbitrary cause of student attrition; public schools can force students out of school. School boards and superintendents consistently claimed that they had the legal and moral right to exclude some students from school. In March 1964, for example, the Atlanta Board of Education approved discipline policies that authorized principals to suspend students and the superintendent to expel students. According to the policy, "Denial to pupils of the right to attend school is an inherent power of the Board of Education which has been delegated, subject to approval, to the Superintendent of Schools or his representatives" (March 9, 1964, agenda).

In the 1960s, suspension policies became inextricably intertwined with desegregation issues. When previously all-white schools finally opened to African-American students in Atlanta, conditions remained poor. Black parents repeatedly complained not only of continuing segregation but of overcrowded classrooms and poor facilities (Culpepper 1966). Suspension policies were the target of the most vociferous complaints. The parents of black students in one Atlanta high school complained in 1966 of discriminatory suspension practices in the school. They called on an umbrella group of civil rights activists in the area to investigate mass suspensions. According to what the parents told the Atlanta *Inquirer*, "Students were being suspended from three to five days for the slightest infractions and on some occasions for no infractions." The school, which in the previous three years had gone from an all-white high school to one that almost no whites attended, had a mostly white faculty at the time. According to the complainants, the white principal frequently threatened "Negro students with bodily harm, such as 'I'll break your . . .'" (ellipsis in original article). The parents accused the staff of generally "cruel methods of addressing students, . . . harshness and lack of interest in the students" (Mass suspension of Negro students 1966).

The conditions in Atlanta schools after the end of legalized segregation were similar to those elsewhere in the South. Civil rights organizations throughout the late 1960s and early 1970s reported widespread harassment of African-American students within Southern school systems ordered by courts to desegregate. Once the federal government began collecting suspension statistics by race in most Southern school districts, civil rights activists could demonstrate wide racial disparities in suspension practices and discipline policies within school districts undergoing desegregation. According to civil rights activists, students at the frontier of desegregation faced the brunt of white resistance (Southern Regional Council 1973).

The complaints about discriminatory suspension practices did not mean, however, that local civil rights activists were unconcerned with discipline in schools. At least in one case, a community group in Philadelphia actively called for removing students from one high school. After repeated incidents of racial violence in South Philadelphia High School during 1967, a group of community organizations in Germantown recommended the transfer of troublesome students to other schools. In their view, "Many of these students, although enrolled in the school, are over 17 years of age, attend class infrequently and have manifested serious anti-social behavioral patterns." Unlike the city's police department, however, the coalition of community organizations thought that the size of the disruptive group in any individual high school was relatively small—twenty-five or thirty out of a school population of several thousand in a city high school (West Mount Airy Neighbors Association Papers, box 5). In general, community groups were alert to the discriminatory potential in student discipline policies.

Despite the complaints of unequal discipline practices, student placement and discipline policies did not change significantly in most public school systems until the late 1960s and early 1970s (Freidman 1982). As late as 1969, many public school systems still retained punitive sanctions against students for a variety of reasons (Goldstein 1969: 373–75). For example, New York City's public school suspension policy did not begin to change until the end of the 1960s, when court decisions forced the central bureaucracy to be more alert to the behavior of individual school principals. In 1969, the superintendent revised suspension guidelines (Robinson Papers, box 16, folder 55). Most prior policies, such as a March 5, 1964, circular on suspensions, simply reiterated the policy that gave school officials wide latitude in suspensions (New York City Superintendent of Schools Circulars, box 36). Most school district policies did not change until federal courts began to rule consistently that students had some rights within schools. The Supreme Court's 1969 *Tinker v. Des Moines Independent School District* (39 U. S. 503) opinion ruled unequivocally that students had many legal rights on school grounds that school officials could not arbitrarily override. This extended a 1964 decision, *In re Gault* (387 U. S. 1), which had changed juvenile justice procedures, on the grounds that Fourteenth Amendment protections applied to children as well as adults. In 1975, the Supreme Court ruled explicitly on a suspension case, *Goss v. Lopez* (419 U. S. 565), that students had some right to due process in school disciplinary proceedings. Throughout the late 1960s and early 1970s, civil rights organizations fought for state and federal court rulings that extended the procedural rights of students.

The result of these federal changes was a shift in the written policies of hundreds of school districts. By the mid-1970s, many school districts and state departments of education had written guidelines on substantive and procedural student rights (National School Public Relations Association 1972). While public schools did not necessarily follow such written procedures, the existence of a promise to respect student rights represents a dramatic change from the theory of *in loco parentis* (school acting as parent) commonly voiced through the late 1960s. Specifically, the acknowledgment of some moral (if not legal) right to an education shares an assumption with the dropout debate: A formal education is essential to economic and social participation in late twentieth century society. Yet the dropout literature of the 1960s entirely excluded suspension and discipline policies.

Student Pregnancy

One specific area of exclusion from school was of pregnant students and mothers. Until the late 1960s, most public school districts, including New York City and Philadelphia, summarily removed pregnant students from regular classes (Goldstein 1969: 373–75). Some activists tried to change this in the 1960s. For example, the Public Education Association in New York City issued a press statement April 16, 1968, urging the Board of Education to stop discharging pregnant students. Similarly, the Citizens' Committee for Children in New York explicitly linked pregnancy with the suspensions controversy in letters by committee members to school officials between 1967 and 1969 (Donovan Subject Files, box 7). While some school officials may have tried to work inside the bureaucracy to change policies, most high-placed bureaucrats refused to lift the ban on pregnant women attending regular classes (Goldstein 1969: 374 n.4).

Since the early twentieth century, the standard explanation for such policies was to protect other students "against moral pollution" (Goldstein 1969: 408). Throughout the 1960s, state court decisions were inconsistent on the question of whether to excluded married students from school, let alone on whether un-married pregnant students could be expelled (Goldstein 1969: 396 n.78). Finally, when Title IX of the 1972 amendments to the Elementary and Secondary Education Act banned sexual discrimination in schools accepting federal aid, the

Department of Health, Education, and Welfare ruled that excluding pregnant women from school constituted discrimination (Levine and Cary 1977: 101). As with other suspension and expulsion policies, however, the exclusion of pregnant women from classes remained unmentioned in discussions of the dropout problem.

Special Education

School systems also excluded or segregated students based on the school authorities' judgment of mental capacity. Through the end of the 1960s, thousands of children nationwide were excluded from schools because officials judged them uneducable. In addition, schools placed many children in segregated special education classes based on group-administered intelligence tests. Children whose first language was not English could be placed in special education even if the sole reason for their poor performance on tests might be their poor command of English. Since the early twentieth century, in addition, a disproportionate number of children in special education have been from ethnic and racial minorities or recent immigrant groups (Turnbull 1990: 13–18). The point here is that school officials reserved the right through the 1960s to make judgments about whether students belonged, and where they should be if they did belong.

Some critics of special education (and there were many) focused explicitly on the way that special education allowed school officials to lower academic expectations for students. In Philadelphia, civil rights activists complained in 1965 about the over-representation of Puerto Rican children in special education classes. One group, El Independiente, thought that the high proportion of Puerto Ricans classified as "retarded educables" was the result of psychological tests being "given in English." Special education, the group argued in a October 21, 1965, press kit, served only to guarantee failure: "The purpose of these classes is not to teach, but to keep the child 'jailed' until he reaches the 16th year of age and then put him on the street." These Puerto Rican activists explicitly connected student guidance practices with the dropout issue (West Philadelphia Schools Committee Papers, box 1). Few school officials, however, were willing to listen to such criticism. The administration of the West Philadelphia High School was defensive about its academic placement policies and strongly disagreed with the idea that parents knew their children's capacity. According to principal Jack Neulight in his 1961 biennial report, "The authority for course placement should rest with the school, not with the parent. The parents' refusal to accept the limited ability of their children is a major problem" (West Philadelphia Schools Committee Papers, box 1). The placement of pupils in various tracks, including special education, was intricately connected with expectations of future success, including high school graduation.

School officials and critics replayed this debate about academic placement, special education, and expectations across the country in the 1960s. One federal judge forbade Washington, D.C., schools from placing students in a set of classes called "Basic Track" because of its discriminatory impact on African Americans. School officials responded by creating a set of classes, with even more students, presumably based on behavior rather than academics (Tropea 1987). Special education in D.C. schools, as in many other places, continued to serve as a safety valve, relieving schools of responsibility to teach even while they were presumably trying to eliminate dropping out.

Eventually, special education changed. As a result of court orders and federal legislation in the 1970s, students acquired the right to an education regardless of the nature and degree of disability and procedural guarantees to eliminate arbitrary decisions by school officials (Turnbull 1990). (The extent to which those changes improved special education is a different question.) Yet this change did not come as a result of recognition of dropping out as a social problem. Change came much later, with concern over special education as a distinct issue. The way schools treated special education in the 1960s enabled the dropout problem to remain defined largely as the fault of students and their backgrounds, not of schools and their denial of student rights.

Possible Influences

In some way, perhaps, the dropout debate contributed to a growing recognition of a right to education, an idea that pointed out the conflict between arbitrary school decisions and the basic mission of public schools. One legal analyst wrote in 1970:

It is not surprising that judges, who have witnessed intensive school campaigns to convince drop-outs to return to school because of the crucial significance of education in our society, react unsympathetically ... to attempts by school administrators to deprive students of access to schools without first affording them adequate procedural safeguards. (Goldstein 1970: 616)

In general, however, one can draw no clear heritage descending from the 1960s dropout debate to the later development of student rights. The controversy over student rights was driven by court decisions and legislation, which usually expanded the rights of public school students and curtailed the powers of school authorities to arbitrarily place, suspend, and expel students without due process. The extension of procedural and substantive rights to children brought the right to an education to public attention and forced public schools to consider explicitly the rights of students. But that happened in the 1970s.

The rise in concern over the dropout in the early 1960s did not directly stimulate the expansion of student rights. None of the widely proclaimed dropout programs in the early 1960s changed longstanding policies that denied students the right to due process in suspension and expulsion cases, that denied pregnant women the right to an education, and that gave school officials wide power over assignment of students to special education or exclusion from school entirely.

Court decisions and legislation were responsible for changes in school policies affecting access to education. The definition of the dropout problem thus included a large blind spot: The dropout debate failed to address the question of whether students had a fundamental right to schooling. The issues were present in the 1960s. The outcry over the dropout problem could have led, for example, to the reinstatement of pregnant students and teenage mothers in regular classes. Yet the right of access to formal education remained outside the common definition of the dropout problem.

"THE REAL ROOTS . . . WOULD BE LEFT UNTOUCHED"

Both of the above issues, racial disparities in educational outcomes and the right to an education, were areas where local critics disputed the competence of school officials. This mirrored the fact that explanations of the dropout problem were not monolithic at the local level. Different individuals and groups had varied perspectives on the issue. Some, especially school officials, echoed the national stereotype. Outside the public schools, some agreed with the standard stereotype of the dropout, while others thought that the dropout problem was evidence of other problems rather than an issue by itself. (Thus, the issues analyzed separately for convenience in the section above were overlapping concerns for local school activists.) The construction of the dropout problem diverged dramatically at the local level. The following describes the dynamics in Philadelphia. The way in which official explanations and solutions omitted the perspective of school critics suggests the isolation of many urban public schools from the communities they served in the 1960s.

In Philadelphia, the language of school officials mirrored that of the national literature. The Philadelphia public school district's pedagogical library received all of Daniel Schreiber's bulletins and books. He also spoke at a staff meeting organized by the Division of Pupil Personnel and Counseling ($2,500 extra pay proposed 1961). Notices in the monthly newsletter echoed Labor Department warnings of dropout-related unemployment. The school district often cited new books or reports about dropouts produced in Washington and elsewhere (e.g., Education adds up 1966). One 1966 article, "Employment Outlook for the School Dropout," explained the importance of the dropout problem:

A recent release from the U. S. Department of Labor points out that automation and explosive technology demand much better educated youth to fill the demand for newly created jobs. Simultaneously, there is a significant decline in the number of job openings for uneducated and undereducated workers.

This explanation is almost identical to the language of the articles, reports, and books in the mainstream national literature.

Other organizations in Philadelphia echoed the standard social construction of the dropout problem. The director of the juvenile unit in the city's police department believed that "dropouts here contribute to delinquent acts to an inordinate degree" (Binzen 1964d). The Greater Philadelphia Chamber of Commerce printed a brochure describing the benefits of graduation and labeling dropouts as economic "pop-outs" (Binzen 1964d). The Commerce and Industry Council of the Chamber of Commerce described dropping out as evidence of the need to change the attitudes of youth and, as was common in the 1960s, connected dropping out to economic woes (Greater Philadelphia Chamber of Commerce Papers, box 6). These brief statements rarely explained anything more, but the language of delinquency and unemployment echoed the common construction of the dropout problem.

While several groups agreed with the common description of a dropout problem, others were more ambiguous about the issue. Teachers' organizations, for example, were ambivalent about the ideal of comprehensive education. When a 1965 school survey suggested that strict promotion policies were largely responsible for dropping out in Philadelphia, the Philadelphia Teachers Federation disagreed. In district meetings in response to the survey on June 1, 1965, a number of teachers rejected the conclusion out of hand, claiming that personal characteristics accounted for dropping out. Others suggested that more guidance and work-experience programs, not changes in promotion policies, were the appropriate response to concerns about dropouts (Philadelphia Federation of Teachers Papers, box 25). Ultimately, school officials agreed with teachers regarding the authority of school systems to place students. In Philadelphia as elsewhere, guidance and work-experience programs were the principal public school responses to the public construction of the dropout problem.

The primary dissenters from the school system's definition of the dropout problems were local civil rights activists. Some community groups disagreed vehemently with the school district's stated idea of what the "dropout problem" was and argued that unemployment in general was the critical issue. These activists pointed out that graduates as well as dropouts were unable to obtain good jobs. One coalition of desegregation activists offered a different view of juvenile delinquency in a press conference on October 21, 1965. Its perspective and proposed solution were strikingly at odds with the statements of James Conant and other nationally known writers:

We are concerned about the young people that are too often called "hoodlums" and "drop-outs." We don't want any more "hoodlums" and "drop-outs," and therefore we say, let's clear up the source. By the source we mean the slums and the lack of jobs for parents and young adults. Give us the means of getting homes that are not meant for pigs, homes that can be kept. Give us the recreation facilities that are needed in our neighborhoods. Help us to find jobs by creating them. Real jobs with a future; a future for us, the community, and the city. With these we could then let our minds rest more on education. (West Philadelphia Schools Committee Papers, box 1)

For the broad coalition of local activists pushing for integration, the school system's vocational training program was a failure. Students were not primarily at fault for school failure, in their view. The West Philadelphia Schools Committee even disagreed with the term "dropout" in its statement to the Board of Public Education on September 29, 1965. It described the group leaving high school not as dropouts but as "pushouts" (West Philadelphia Schools Committee Papers, box 2).

The West Philadelphia Schools Committee (WPSC) disagreed with the school district over dropout prevention programs in part because of a long-term dispute over the school district's programmatic priorities. The WPSC, an organization whose members had ties to other civic groups, congregations, and Home and School Associations, doubted whether job programs were worthwhile. It told a subcommittee reviewing nondiscrimination policy of the schools on May 16, 1963, "In the present labor market, such courses are a pitifully weak substitute for real vocational training. For this reason, and for the reason that they will surely be filled almost entirely by Negro pupils, we have called such a program 'bootblack education'" (Citizens Committee on Public Education in Philadelphia Papers, box 6). To the WPSC, Philadelphia's vocational education program was part of continued inferior education for African Americans. The WPSC had fought the district for several years over the public schools' plans to continue building neighborhood elementary, junior high, and senior high schools. In a February 16, 1965, report on a proposed junior high school, the committee argued that continued construction of buildings in the center of segregated neighborhoods would make it impossible to desegregate the school system. In addition, the committee told the Board of Public Education on November 15, 1961, most elementary schools in poor neighborhoods were overcrowded (Citizens Committee on Public Education in Philadelphia Papers, box 6).

For the WPSC, equal resource allocation was more important than the perceived dropout crisis. Thus, when one draft operating budget for the school system proposed occupational courses for potential dropouts in a planned junior high school, the West Philadelphia Schools Committee lambasted the school system's educational priorities. In a November 17, 1962, statement to the school board concerning the next year's budget, the committee calculated the additional money slated that year "for occupational courses and school-work programs, as a solution to the dropout problem." It noted, "We can only conclude that the Administration, in the face of the present fiscal crisis, proposes to devote a considerable sum to expanding this program for training secondary pupils in valet service, car-washing, short-order cooking, and so on." The committee argued that "the real roots of the dropout problem would be left untouched by such measures" as occupational training. The WPSC noted what they saw as the long-term costs of such a strategy:

If you attempt to solve the dropout and delinquency problems by this new policy of occupational training courses, without attacking the roots in the elementary schools, you can expect an endless drain upon your resources as the supply of pupils to the program mounts year by year.

Moreover, the committee claimed, when the school system refused to relieve elementary school overcrowding or ameliorate staff turnover in largely black schools, devoting resources to vocational programs was "based on massive discrimination" and a misuse of funds (Philadelphia Federation of Teachers Papers, box 29).

The committee had woven an implied theory of poverty and education into its argument to the board that vocational training was a poor response to the dropout problem. While it believed that dropouts were handicapped in the labor market, it was impossible to tell, from the committee's viewpoint, whether students were "years behind in critical reading skills" because they truly needed vocational education or because they had been denied a basic education. The committee agreed that "cultural and home conditions contribute to the difficulties of pupils," but argued that such problems did not absolve the schools of the burden for students' education: "It is too easy an out to talk in clichés of the culturally handicapped, the disadvantaged, the underprivileged. Behind such euphemisms is a half-truth, the judgment that the responsibility lies, after all, with the parents or with society, in some vague sense" (WPSC statement, November 17, 1962, 8-9, in Philadelphia Federation of Teachers Papers, box 29). The West Philadelphia Schools Committee believed that the public schools had a responsibility to parents and the community. That sense of institutional obligation was absent in the schools' construction of the dropout problem.

The statement quoted above was not an isolated disagreement. The WPSC consistently argued that schools should take primary responsibility for school outcomes. In 1963, the WPSC argued that, contrary to what the school's planning commission had claimed and the assistant director of Pupil Personnel and Counseling said publicly (Binzen 1964d), in-migrants from the South could not account for all the problems of the school district. In its statement to the subcommittee on nondiscriminatory policy, it reasoned that too few students grew up in or had parents from the South to account for higher African-American dropout statistics: "We know that we must be losing many thousands of talented youngsters every year. To place the blame for this state of affairs on in-migrants from the South is neither courageous nor constructive, however consoling it may be to 'old Philadelphia Negroes and whites'" (Citizens Committee for Public Education in Philadelphia, box 6). The WPSC thought that responsibility for community affairs in fact lay largely with the schools, whose actions would shape the future of many neighborhoods. To the Board of Public Education in 1962, it said "gray areas" that were not yet slums were between "pockets of severe blight": "If these areas do degenerate into slums, it will be because the school system has led the way" (Philadelphia Federation of Teachers

Papers, box 29). In the complex picture of poverty that the committee painted for the Board of Public Education, the public schools formed a prominent community institution. The West Philadelphia Schools Committee truly thought that the city school system could make or break children's lives.

The ambivalence of the November 1962 statement to the board is particularly noteworthy. On one hand, it went to a budget hearing to which it had been invited. It thought good schools were essential to the community. It publicly supported the district's attempts to get additional funding (see, for example, copy, Helen Oakes to Richardson Dilworth, May 23, 1968, in WPSC Papers, box 1). And yet it held the schools in extremely low regard. That ambivalence can be traced to the local focus of the West Philadelphia Schools Committee. While community groups certainly understood national politics and their consequences for Philadelphia's public schools, the object of hostility was the local school board. Not only the rhetoric of WPSC members, but also their perceptions of poverty reflected that local focus. Concern over specific issues existed, but explanations of causes became blurred. The WPSC did not repeat the claim of a linear relationship between dropping out and poverty that the district newsletter made. It also did not absolve students and parents of all responsibilities. Instead, the West Philadelphia Schools Committee made its judgments of parents, students teachers, principals, and the Board of Public Education in different gradations. In its view, however, the board had been a culpable actor in its decision in 1962 to spend money on vocational programs rather than on improving elementary schools.

The West Philadelphia Schools Committee was unusually articulate and focused in its critique of the school district's construction of the dropout problem. However, its isolation from the public schools' bureaucracy was symptomatic of community relationships with the public schools. The WPSC statements are evidence that important civil rights organizations in Philadelphia disagreed with the school district's public posture on the dropout problem. Many civil rights activists were more concerned with the broader problems of classroom overcrowding, resource allocation, and desegregation than solely with the discrete issue of the dropout. Conversely, the discussion by school and other government officials never acknowledged dissenting views.

Representative of that gulf between official and dissenting interpretations of dropping out was a series of six articles on the dropout problem in the Philadelphia *Evening Bulletin* in early 1964. The series, by education reporter Peter Binzen, began with fairly typical drama: "The word is 'dropout.' In America today, it's a word of warning and reproach" (Binzen 1964d). In the articles, Binzen explored several aspects of the dropout debate. In the first article, he repeated the most common claims of Schreiber and other authors, including their concerns about the economic consequences of the problem, the connections people made with juvenile delinquency, and the 1963 summer campaign sponsored by the White House. The later articles discussed public-private school relationships, vocational schools, preschool training, and reading curricula.

In some important ways, Binzen pointed out the discrepancies in official portraits of the dropout problem. He noted that the Philadelphia public schools maintained a longstanding practice of dismissing some students, so-called "asked to withdraw" cases, while the district claimed it wanted to eliminate the dropout problem. However, he primarily used administrative sources in his series. He cited Daniel Schreiber, officials in the federal Office of Education, state Department of Education employees, public and private school personnel, and a few faculty members of graduate schools of education. In one article, he interviewed a handful of dropouts, and he asked businesses whether they required diplomas for jobs. In no case did he quote, directly or indirectly, local critics of the Philadelphia schools. Even when discussing the "asked to withdraw" policy, he quoted Philadelphia public schools' pupil personnel and counseling director, an associate superintendent, and several counselors. Activist groups, however, were invisible in his series on the dropout problem. That omission meant that substantial dissent from the social construction of the dropout went unmentioned in newspapers.

Despite the common use of dropouts as a trope for urban problems, no consensus existed within cities about what the dropout problem was and what its solutions should be. Many local school critics saw dropping out as evidence of other problems, but not something about which the schools should obsess. School officials, despite the disagreement, continued to echo the stereotypical explanations of the problem. Few school officials appeared to respond to dissenting assessments by civil rights activists of the labor market, of dropouts, or of the schools' responsibilities to teach students.

LOCAL DYNAMICS AND A NATIONAL DISCUSSION

One must be cautious in interpreting the fragmentary record of dynamics between civil rights activists and public schools at the local level, let alone the amorphous mass I have casually labeled as "public debate" or "discussion." Nonetheless, the omission from dropout literature of racial disparities in educational outcomes and the right to an education suggests the existence of dissonance within the dropout debate in the 1960s. Faced with an apparent problem—students leaving school before graduation—school officials and other writers ignored the possibility that public policies helped push students out of school. On the local level, at the very least, it was not convenient to acknowledge dissenting views.

The gap between public school systems and local critics also helps explain the transience of dropout programs and policies. As described earlier, public school programs died in part because they were bereft of long-term grass-roots support. This is not to say that similar programs did not have support; the record of the Germantown Youth Corps suggests that community groups did support work experience in some forms. Rather, the dropout programs that operated within public school systems existed at the initiative of school officials, supported largely when external funding was available, and made little permanent connection with the community. In part because school officials isolated themselves from dissenting views of schooling (including the dropout problem), they had no opportunity to build a deep base of support for innovative programs. Then, when external funding ended, so did the programs. With the end of projects designed explicitly to help ameliorate the dropout problem, no institutional memory remained. As the next chapter describes, school officials responding to another wave of concern over dropping out in the 1980s reinvented many of the explanations and programs of the 1960s. Institutional amnesia, in part caused by the insulation of school officials in the 1960s, prevented them from using any historical perspective on this supposedly "new" problem.

7

Dropout Tides

Since the end of the 1960s, interest in the dropout problem has waned and waxed several times. The number of newspaper and periodical articles on the subject fluctuates by year, without the sudden rise in interest that happened in the early 1960s. Nonetheless, several developments since 1970 are notable. First was the rapid growth in alternative credentials in the 1970s and early 1980s. Second was the aborted attempt to link attrition to issues of school equity in the early 1970s. Third was the more intense debate over dropping out in the 1980s that led, ultimately, to the inclusion of the second national goal as part of the America 2000 reform document. Throughout, though, we have continued to use the word "dropout" in describing those who fail to graduate from high school, with a tendency to use the 1960s stereotypes as the core of discussion.

The contemporary debate over dropping out (since the mid-1980s) has included more explicit discussion of equity in schools than did the original literature. Current authors also use a different vocabulary than the 1960s discussion included (especially in the use of "at-risk" to describe a wide variety of populations). Yet "dropping out" and many connotations of that term have remained as a common way of describing the failure of schools and their students. High school dropouts do face economic hardships; a real stigma exists. Nonetheless, the use of the same word implies some structural continuity. The survival of the term, between the sudden drop in interest in the mid-1960s and its reappearance two decades later, suggests that something more is involved in our collective vocabulary than a catchy label. The word "dropout" remains in common parlance because it reflects an age norm with relatively deep (if newly developed) roots.

U. S. residents still use the word "dropout" in part because of a historic obsession we have had with the behavior of post pubescent Americans. However, we also still use "dropout" because the norm of high school graduation, solidified in the 1960s, has remained. A higher proportion of teenagers today graduates from high school than did in the 1960s, and (partly because of that) we still expect the vast majority to acquire diplomas. The sudden rise in concern over dropouts, and the retention of the term after the 1960s, come from the interweaving of demographic changes with recurrent anxieties about adolescence in America.

"Dropping out" is a term whose roots lie both in institutional developments and concerns of the moment. For many decades, educators had been concerned about attendance patterns and the way teenagers left school for work. In the 1960s, that general concern gelled into a definition of a discrete problem because high school graduation had become an expectation of all youth. The widespread recognition of dropping out as a unified social concern was almost certain, yet prevalent views and prejudices still helped determine its definition. The common description of the dropout problem could have been framed in many ways, as the 1950s articles demonstrate. Once well defined, dropout stereotypes have remained common because they are easy ways of describing the minority of adolescents who have failed to graduate from high school since the 1960s.

However, the value of a high school diploma in itself has come under fire. Those warning the public of the dropout problem three decades ago often argued that dropping out was becoming more of a problem because of economic changes the country was experiencing. Increased automation, many claimed, would make skilled jobs more plentiful in the future and unskilled jobs very rare (Schreiber 1964b). Thus, everyone needed a high school diploma. Since the mid-1970s, several critics have observed an apparent surplus of college and high school graduates seeking jobs and questioned the use of a diploma, by itself, as an economically useful item (Berg 1970; Freeman 1976; Sedlak et al. 1986: Chap. 2). In addition, complaints from business and higher education about the "quality" of high school graduates now testify that few employers or colleges trust a diploma as an affidavit of skills learned.

THE RISE OF THE GED

The 1970s witnessed an unprecedented expansion of alternatives to high school diplomas, primarily with the growth of General Educational Development (or GED) diplomas. Alternative credentialing is perhaps the only program explicitly for dropouts that has had a sizable influence on the demographics of graduation. The growth of the GED illustrates the failure of the social construction of dropping out to address the nature of credentialing. Because credentials are valued relative to their rarity, any expansion of a credential tends to dilute its value. Many employers—including the military, which created the GED—treat GED diplomas today as less valid than a high school diploma, assuming that they are easier to acquire. This was inevitable with the expansion of the program, yet the GED is still touted as part of the solution to the dropout problem. Thus, a misunderstanding of the nature of credentials has led to the irony that the most "effective" dropout solution has, in fact, been largely worthless.

The GED remained largely in the background during the 1960s dropout debate and emerged only later. The U. S. Armed Forces Institute and American Council on Education created a high school equivalency test during the second World War for soldiers as part of a larger effort to organize social services within the military. After the war, the American Council on Education started a Veterans' Testing Service. Over the next several decades, states adopted policies that gave equivalency certificates to individuals who achieved a certain level of proficiency on standardized tests administered through the American Council of Education. In the 1950s, the American Council on Education began offering the test to nongraduates, and the GED became available to civilians nationwide (Stewart 1992). In November 1963, for example, Georgia expanded its GED program to allow nonveterans to take the test and earn the credential (Georgia Deputy State Superintendent Subject Files, box 9). However, alternative credentialing was neither important demographically nor did any advocate it as a viable solution to the dropout problem in the 1960s. When federal support for adult basic education became part of the Economic Opportunity Act of 1964 (later authorized separately in the Adult Education Act of 1966), it was a minor footnote. Federally supported programs were restricted to adults and were supposed to stress basic literacy skills rather than credentials (DeSanctis 1979: 7–11).

Yet, as adult education programs grew, pressure came from the states to change the focus of the federal program. Besieged by dropouts wanting credentials, state directors of adult education wanted to spend more effort on credential-related activities rather than basic skills. In 1970, they received what they had wanted, as amendments allowed dropouts sixteen years old to enroll in federally supported programs and allowed the programs to lead to high school equivalency degrees (DeSanctis 1979: 15–16). Eventually, despite nominal limits on equivalency-related expenditures, GED programs dominated adult education, as the pressure from state directors prevented the federal government from maintaining any focus on literacy as opposed to credentialing (DeSanctis 1979: 29). By 1980, approximately 40 percent of GED recipients came from federally supported adult education programs (Cameron and Heckman 1993: 39–40). In addition, federal support for higher education created an incentive for dropouts to acquire GEDs, as students in nonselective colleges (including proprietary training centers) became eligible to receive federal support.

The result of both policies was an expansion in the number of GED recipients. In the 1970s, the number of people receiving GED diplomas snowballed, reaching 294,000 in 1974, and 489,000 received GED degrees in 1981. In the 1980s, the number of people passing the GED dropped somewhat, as did the number of regular high school graduates (National Center for Education Statistics 1994: Table 101). The number of GEDs when compared to regular high school diplomas, however, has continued to rise. For 1991, 1992, and 1993, GEDs accounted for more than 15 percent of all credentials (GEDs and high school graduations) reported to the federal government (National Center for Education Statistics 1994: Tables 99, 101). In addition, GED diplomas are disproportionately distributed by race. A higher proportion of African-American and Hispanic males reaching adulthood in the late 1970s and early 1980s had alternative credentials compared with non-Hispanic white males in the same period (Cameron and Heckman 1993: Table 1). As discussed in the first chapter, GEDs and other alternative credentials may be a more important part of educational strategies for African Americans who do not receive regular diplomas than for other dropouts.

Unfortunately, the expansion of GED programs has not led to the amelioration of labor market problems that high school dropouts face. Economic research suggests that, for young men in the 1980s, a GED recipient was no better off than high school dropouts without alternative credentials (Cameron and Heckman 1993). Perhaps a GED was valuable in the immediate postwar years. Then, however, GED recipients were mostly veterans with military experience, which may have translated into credible value in the labor market. In addition, the number of GED recipients was small. The expansion of GED programs in the 1970s, however, diluted any potential value that had existed before. Even the U. S. military, which helped initiate equivalency degree programs, stopped accepting GEDs as a true equivalent of high school diplomas in 1991 (As more earn 1992).

Alternative credentials may have become the most important dropout "solution" in the past three decades, but they do not solve the labor market problems that dropouts face. Nonetheless, some tout them as an appropriate response to dropping out (Toby and Armor 1992). One school participating in New York City's Dropout Prevention Initiative in the 1980s created a GED program as its "alternative education" for potential dropouts (Grannis et al. 1990: 94). As part of dropout prevention, this school created a program to hand teenagers a dubious replacement credential. In doing so, it directed what had been merely potential dropouts to actual dropout status (albeit dropouts with a GED). I cannot find a better example of how a school can create dropouts in the name of dropout prevention.

EQUALITY AND SCHOOL ATTRITION

By 1970, dropping out had lost its status as a critical problem in education. Other issues had crowded it out. The initiation of desegregation suits in the North, the spread of busing as a proposed remedy, and President Nixon's backing away from strict enforcement of the Civil Rights Act of 1964 dominated education policy debates. In addition, the late 1960s witnessed (among other developments) the creation of Head Start, compensatory education, growing power of teacher unions, the limited decentralization of New York City's public schools, and federal aid to college students. Some of this could be coopted as issues related to dropping out, but the reverse was more likely. When Congress authorized grants for specific dropout prevention programs in Title VIII of the 1968 amendments to the Elementary and Secondary Education Act, some programs focused on elementary compensatory education (Langley and Ewing 1973).

It was, however, in the early 1970s that civil rights activists explicitly connected dropping out to issues of educational equity in national publications. Both the Southern Regional Council and the newly formed Children's Defense Fund sought to place the exclusion of children from school in the framework of civil rights. In 1973, the Southern Regional Council published a study of suspension policies, *The Student Pushout*, which argued that discriminatory discipline procedures were unfairly denying African-American high school students the right to an education. In many school districts undergoing forced desegregation across the South, the report noted, suspension rates for blacks were far higher than those for white students. The result, according to the Southern Regional Council (1973: 34), was a clear violation of rights:

Those public school officials who are responsible for racially discriminatory policies and practices which result in suspensions and expulsions or which induce minority students to withdraw from school, are violating the law and are subject to challenge in the courts.

The report called for congressional and executive investigation of the "pushout" phenomenon. It also recommended judicial and administrative relief of discriminatory suspension and expulsion practices (62–72).

In the year after the *Student Pushout* report, the Children's Defense Fund published *Children out of School in America*, which claimed that millions of school-age children were not attending school. Barriers to adequate schooling included textbook and transportation fees, misclassification of students in special education classes, and discriminatory and extensive use of suspension as a discipline measure. The Children's Defense Fund argued, like the Southern Regional Council, that the denial of access to education was wrong:

To continue to deny our children schooling or to give them as little as we can is so unfair to the children denied, and so costly to the rest of us in future dependency, as to be intolerable. That we single out some groups of children who are different for special deprivation of education is downright cruel. It profoundly violates American pretensions to provide equal opportunity to all within its fold. (Children's Defense Fund 1974: 7)

The Children's Defense Fund study followed a task force report on discriminatory suspension and expulsion practices in the Boston public schools (Task Force on Children out of School 1971). All three reports tried to appropriate the dropout problem as a civil rights issue. All argued that education was a right of Americans and that school districts often denied access to education, violating that right.

The attempts to return the dropout problem to front-page headlines failed, however. When newspapers covered the Children's Defense Fund or Southern Regional Council, they often relegated them to the back pages of news sections (e.g., New unit to fight 1973; Two rights groups 1973). More fundamentally, civil rights activists failed to change the impetus of federal policy on the question of students' rights to an equitable education. By 1973, both the Supreme Court and the federal Office of Civil Rights had retreated significantly from the battle over educational equity. In the 1973 decision, *San Antonio Independent School District v. Rodriguez* (411 U. S. 1), the Supreme Court decided that public education was not a constitutionally mandated right. Several years earlier, the Nixon administration had taken several steps to soften the federal government's stance on desegregation. By 1970, the administration announced that it would not attempt to bar de facto segregation (resulting from housing segregation rather than statutes) without a Supreme Court decision, even in Southern cities (Nixon 1971: 315–16).

As reported by the *New York Times* on March 25, 1970, the Nixon administration had signaled to civil rights activists and their opponents that it was not fully committed to federal enforcement of desegregation regulations. Without a supporting voice from either the executive or judicial branches of the federal government, civil rights activists were unable to stir sustained interest in access to education as a federal civil rights issue (Orfield 1988: 348–50). Often frustrated by inaction on equity issues, the Children's Defense Fund has moved on to other issues, including day care and health policies, as a focus of advocacy. Educational equity, especially that of school financing, has continued to be an issue that state courts have considered repeatedly in the last twenty years (Ballot 1991). But the national debate on school equity essentially ceased in the early 1970s, and the potential for connecting equity to the dropout problem dwindled along with it.

NEW ISSUES

A resurgence of interest in equity and dropping out came in the 1980s as a response to the movement to apply stricter standards to student promotion and graduation. It is not entirely true that dropping out disappeared as a topic of interest between the 1960s and the middle 1980s. However, dropping out was not the headline issue it had become in the early 1960s. That changed, however, as public school critics called for stricter standards for schools (e.g., National Commission on Excellence in Education 1983). Some academics and educators worried, however, that imposing mandatory standardized testing and other graduation requirements on high school students would lead to higher proportions of students dropping out of school (Hamilton 1987; Kreitzer, Madaus, and Haney 1989; McDill, Natriello, and Pallas 1987).

Many of the writings on dropping out in the 1980s represent perspectives largely unspoken in the 1960s discussion. Most prominent is the discovery that dropping out by women is sometimes related to pregnancy. None of the mainstream discussion of the dropout problem in the 1960s discussed adolescent pregnancy, and many schools still excluded pregnant teenagers and mothers from classes until Title IX regulations in the 1970s. Researchers have legitimate questions and debates as to whether being pregnant is a barrier to graduation beyond the material problems of maternity (Anderson 1993; Rindfuss, St. John, and Bumpass 1984; Upchurch and McCarthy 1993). However, model dropout programs sometimes incorporate child care as part of a broad-based dropout strategy to enable continued attendance by adolescent mothers (Orr 1987: 70–79). Critically, the relationship between gender and dropping out has become an open topic for debate (Fine and Zane 1989). That, by itself, is unprecedented.

In addition, many since the early 1980s (more than in the 1960s) pointed to dropping out as evidence of inequities in schooling and denial of educational rights. Michelle Fine (1991: 26) wrote that dropping out served as an icon for broader educational inequities:

Dramatically different patterns of dropping out by social class, race, ethnicity, gender, and disability characterize U. S. public schools. The patterns stand as evidence that the promise of equal opportunity is subverted institutionally by the guarantee of unequal educational outcomes.

Issues raised by those concerned about equity included the role of suspensions and grade retention in dropping out, financial inequities, and the avoidance of responsibilities by school systems (e.g., U. S. House of Representatives 1986: 155–63). Jon Blyth, program officer of the Charles Stewart Mott Foundation, testified before the House of Representatives that dropout prevention would require reducing financial inequities in schooling and targeting resources at poor and disabled children (U. S. House of Representatives 1991: 52, 54). Renee Marie Montoya, an official with the Chicago urban reform organization Designs for Change, used her testimony in front of a House of Representatives (1986: 169) subcommittee to point out that dropping out was part of a larger problem with Chicago schools:

We have a two-tiered high school system in Chicago. Some schools are designed for the best students drawing the highest achieving students away from inner city neighborhood schools. Others seem to be dumping grounds for the worst prepared students. The opportunity we have is not just keeping at risk students in school, but providing them with educationally worthwhile experiences. The public school is obligated to create an environment in which youth can experience success and develop aspirations.

To Montoya, dropping out was not primarily a concern about future dependency but a symptom of systematic inequities that undermined the notion of educational opportunities.

Another concern of some in the 1980s was the possibility that higher promotion and graduation standards would intensify dropping out. The movement in many states to create minimum competency tests and higher standards for promotion in the late 1970s and early 1980s concerned Edward McDill, Gary Natriello, and Aaron Pallas with the potential for creating further inequities. They argued that reform reports, which generally excluded dropping out as an issue, may "exacerbate the unnoted dropout problem." The potential result was dire: "The reports' neglect of the dropout problem together with their recommendations that are likely to aggravate this problem may be a blueprint for failure in the nation's schools" (McDill, Natriello, and Pallas 1987: 169).

Ethnographic studies have also pointed more recently to the importance of school structures and cultures in promoting dropping out. While the 1960s debate discussed student attributes and recommended personal guidance, perhaps in combination with vocational programs, the debate in the 1980s sometimes focused on how the organization of schools in general promoted attrition. The discussion ranged widely from the silencing of dropping out as an issue in schools to the "assumption of incompetence" in poor children to the deleterious effects of tracking minority youth into sports (Fine 1991; Gilmore and Smith 1988: 90; Solomon 1989). What is important is that the discussion of dropping out in the 1980s did not entirely mirror the limited consensus of the 1960s.

Despite these new themes in the past fifteen years, some similarities exist between recent and older discussions of dropping out. One is an obsession with statistical analysis, in part because numbers have visible power in public debate. As Carol Weiss (1988: 168) has written,

The media report the proportion of the population that has been out of work for fifteen weeks or more, characteristics of high schools which have the highest dropout rates, reasons given by voters for choosing candidates. These kinds of data become accessible and help to inform policy debates.

Writers have noted, once again, the problems with official school statistics and repeated the perennial call for standardized measures of dropping out (Hammack 1987). As a result of this, the National Center for Education Statistics has defined three measures of dropping out (McMillen, Kaufman, and Whitner 1994). This discussion unwittingly mirrored earlier attempts to define dropout statistics in a rigorous fashion (National Education Association Research Division 1963). One could even point to Edward Thorndike's study as the first to argue for consistent reporting of attrition. The establishment of three statistical measures is certainly better than the morass of noncomparable statistics in the 1960s. Nonetheless, the only statistics typically available for individual schools and school systems are still grade-based. Reporting student statistics by age and focusing on graduation rather than the administrative calculation of dropouts would be more useful for comparative purposes than grade-based measures.

In addition to the reappearance of debates over statistics, the renewed debate over dropping out has retained concerns over the economic consequences of dropping out and fears of dependency. Jon Blyth and Renee Marie Montoya, quoted above, were some of the few witnesses in several sets of congressional hearings who spoke of equity concerns (U. S. House of Representatives 1986, 1991; U. S. Senate 1985, 1987, 1988). Most did not. Certainly, the members of Congress present focused on dependency as the primary reason to be concerned about dropping out. Typical was the statement of Rhode Island Senator John Chaffee:

Dropouts disappear from high school corridors, but they do not disappear from society. Rather, their names show up on the welfare rolls; they become drug abuse statistics, or they wind up in our overcrowded prison system. . . . The dropout exodus is increasing the number of those who live on the margin of society, while our social welfare costs and, too frequently, our penal institutions pay the costs. (U. S. Senate 1985)

The language of Chaffee and others descends directly from the 1960s dropout debate and concerns about dependency. In addition, the belief that technology was changing the workforce was again driving concerns about dropouts. The National Center on Education and the Economy published a report in 1990, *America's Choice*, which argued that changing technological requirements of work would increase the need for skilled workers. The thesis of the report was that the United States has a fundamental choice for its economy: Train workers to be the backbone of a new postindustrial economy or doom a large proportion of the population to permanently low wages. The dependency of dropouts, according to the report, presaged disaster for the society: "Our welfare and unemployment systems, our prisons, and, ultimately, the national economy are continually drained by the cost of sustaining an uneducated, unproductive individual in our society" (Commission on the Skills of the American Workforce 1990: 47). Even liberal Democrats use the rhetoric of the 1960s. In part of a speech justifying federal education aid, Representative George Miller (1987: H3901–2) explained his concerns about the connection between dropping out and dependency:

Without a high school education, few will be able to compete in the new, high-technology centered labor market. Dropout prevention programs are essential to securing family self-sufficiency and to preventing the cycle from starting over again with a new generation of children.

Yet again, the view of dropping out as impending dependency has remained the staple concern of mainstream political debate. Alternative views remain largely marginalized, visible mostly in academic journals and books.

RENEWED FAILURES

Once again, schools and the federal government clamored to create dropout prevention programs (Orr 1987; Wehlage et al. 1989; West 1991). For example, an Atlanta school official proposed extensive outreach to individuals in combination with extensive social supports (Jonas 1987). In 1988, as part of the omnibus Elementary and Secondary School Improvement Amendments, Congress included several provisions specifically aimed at high school dropouts (Public Law 100-297, section 6006). This authorized federal spending for remedial reading courses, work-experience programs, programs for the identification of potential dropouts, and publicity campaigns. Publicity campaigns have again emerged as one of the most visible responses to the dropout issue. Professional basketball stars, among others, now appear regularly in televised public service announcements urging high school students to "Stay in School." Model programs in the 1980s and 1990s, as several decades before, have concentrated on vocational training for potential and actual dropouts. Still, there are a few differences. Primary among them is the recognition of pregnancy and parenting as a barrier to high school attendance. Thus, some programs offer child care as a component of social services attached to dropout programs. Anecdotal evidence, however, suggests that these programs are limited, and that many schools still place obstacles in the paths of pregnant and postpartum students, including practices that violate Title IX prohibitions against discrimination (Dunkle 1990).

As in the past, many initiatives have had little measurable influence on demographic patterns of leaving school. Two notable examples from the 1980s were the Boston Compact and the New York City Dropout Prevention Initiative. In 1982, Boston's largest corporations, universities, and the public school system signed an agreement to provide incentives for better schooling of adolescents. The public schools promised to improve student achievement and increase the proportion of students who graduated. In return, universities promised substantial financial aid for Boston residents, and the corporations involved in the agreement promised a steady job for every high school graduate in the city. The results after five years were mixed. The Private Industry Council provided hundreds of jobs to high school graduates, and universities and corporations gave millions in financial aid to college enrollees from the city. Yet the school system had not lived up to its part of the bargain. Achievement test results and official dropout statistics showed little, if any, improvement over the first five years of the Compact, and some deterioration (Farrar and Cipollone 1988). The Compact has continued, but it no longer is the promising solution to the dropout problem it seemed to be at first.

In the middle 1980s, New York City's public schools announced a Dropout Prevention Initiative in thirteen high schools and twenty-nine middle schools. It was supposed to target individual students for guidance, career education, remedial instruction, and close tracking of attendance. The results, as in Boston, were meager. Evaluators of the program wrote several years later that they saw little measurable improvement in attendance or the proportion of courses passed as a result of the Dropout Prevention Initiative (Grannis et al. 1990). What is equally ominous is that the evaluators had no plan to track the influence of the project on dropping out itself, though they foresaw no improvement.

The failures of these two highly visible efforts present disturbing evidence, once again, of the limits of targeted dropout programs. The New York City failure was perhaps predictable from the mix of activities that replicated the isolated, ineffective policies of the 1960s. Evaluators of the Dropout Prevention Initiative noted that many of the outreach activities never occurred for a high proportion of the targeted population. Once again, schools did not show sufficient commitment to implementing a program completely. The story in Boston is more complicated. One would presume that, with the guarantee of a job, high school graduation would have become a solid credential that students would have wanted more than before the job guarantee. Yet, according to Eleanor Farrar and Anthony Cipollone, the chaotic politics of Boston's public schools prevented long-term commitment to instructional change, and the business community's efforts became entangled in bureaucratic politics. School intransigence turned a radical venture into a symbolic gesture with little reciprocation: "More than anything else, school staff view the Compact as a jobs program and a way of involving business in the schools" (Farrar and Cipollone 1988: 26). Yet again, school bureaucracies thwarted reform.

It is difficult to imagine either program improving high school graduation by itself, even if well implemented. The New York City Dropout Prevention Initiative was a combination of approaches discussed for more than thirty years. The attempt to encourage individuals to remain in school through various means is well intentioned, but it changes neither the broad policies that encourage dropping out nor the economic circumstances that still shape the odds of graduating. Among the in-school reasons that students drop out are retentions and failures, which make students older on average than their peers (Roderick 1993; Shepard and Smith 1989). I know of no evidence that the Dropout Prevention Initiative changed broader school policies. The problems of the Boston Compact are more puzzling; 1980s Boston was in the midst of an economic boon, and the offer of a job to every high school graduate appeared credible. In part, public school bureaucracies thwarted an energetic reform movement started from outside. Thus, the internal dynamics of school systems are important in shaping the educational experiences of teenagers. Yet in Boston, as in New York, the persuasive power of a full-time job may be limited, for several reasons. First, some economic factors affect teenagers before graduation, represented by the effects of home ownership and household income on the odds of graduating since 1940. Thus, the attraction of a job at the end of schooling may not suffice to keep students in school. In addition, one cannot expect higher graduation from labor market changes any more. Teenagers are now largely excluded from full-time work. In fact, teenagers are increasingly likely to work in part-time jobs since World War II (Greenberger and Steinberg 1986). This is perhaps an explanation why the proportion of students graduating from high school has stagnated.

The growth of part-time work represents the decay in all the older assumptions about the relationship of schooling to work. Schooling no longer keeps teenagers from working. The availability of part-time jobs introduces teenagers early into work, yet they are neither a final break from schooling nor a credible introduction into full-time work. If anything, access to work for adolescents may break down the attraction of the high school credential; students' peers can evidently find work without having a degree. This deterioration of the barrier between the labor market and schooling has ominous implications for debates about school policy. It implies that generic vocational training in school may have little effect on how teenagers experience and understand the labor market. In addition, it suggests that our assumptions about the legitimacy of teenage dependency may be outdated. As high school enrollment and graduation grew, we increasingly relied on school as a justification for why teenagers do not work: They are preparing for adult life. Yet the existence of part-time work, coexisting with schooling, suggests that we can no longer justify teenage dependency with the explanation that their "job" is education. That change in teenage experience may well be undermining our trust in schools as the place to prevent dependency.

8

The Demeaning Dropout Debate

In the late 1980s, two conservatives argued in *The Public Interest* magazine over whether we should be concerned about dropping out. Chester Finn, former U. S. Education Department appointee in the Reagan administration, noted that a higher proportion of adolescents acquired diplomas than ever before. Nonetheless, he thought it important to keep adolescents in school, lest we see "a burgeoning population of unskilled, semiliterate men and women" (Finn 1988: 132). Thus, states should coerce teenagers into remaining in school: "So long as school graduation is optional, so long as attendance through age eighteen is required in few places, and so long as enforcement of existing attendance laws is lackadaisical, we surely convey the message that high school completion is not one of our societal absolutes" (Finn 1987: 12). Here, in a nutshell, was the conservative rationale for a response to dropping out: Society needed to socialize and train all adolescents.

Rutgers University sociologist Jackson Toby, on the other hand, wrote that "in order for schools to be safer and more concerned with education, some kids *ought* to drop out" (Toby 1988a: 9; emphasis in the original). To Toby, as to junior high school Principal Michael Rovello more than two decades before, most dropouts were behavior problems who should stay out of schools. Encouraging dropouts to remain would ruin the chances of improving schools by raising their standards: "Compelling unwilling adolescents to remain in school for their own good lowers the instructional level for other students and increases the level of school violence" (Toby 1988b: 134). In Toby's response one finds the conservative rationale for not worrying about dropouts. For him, schools have to exclude some children in order to guarantee a quality education. Toby recognized the dilemma of trying to educate everyone while maintaining a credential; the explicit goals of socializing and sorting conflict at some level. (Finn was also concerned about the potential for dropout prevention to dilute the

1980s standards movement. Nonetheless, he still considered coercion the appropriate response.)

The debate in the pages of *The Public Interest* accurately mirrored the tensions brought by increasing high school attendance since the early twentieth century. Since Joseph Van Denburg's 1911 opinion about the need to select efficiently, educators have been torn between the urge to select graduates and the urge to socialize everyone. Selective high schools are more prestigious, both for students and educators. Yet, at the same time, administrators have also been under some pressure to increase promotion and graduation. Sometimes the pressure is external to schooling, as when political pressures to open up access to high schools eliminated the monopoly of Philadelphia's Central High School. Sometimes the pressure is from inside the profession, as in the reports of Thorndike and Ayres accusing schools of inefficiency. Schools have tried to resolve this tension in a variety of ways. In many school systems, the co-existence of selective and nonselective high schools has served to maintain a limited credential in a time of increasing high school attendance (Labaree 1988).

Ultimately, though, this debate between two conservative goals of schooling is repetitive. With some minor variation, Finn and Toby were replaying a conversation implied for several decades. One should not be surprised at this. The debate of educators in the 1960s was also on the whole conservative because successful school administrators have generally been socially conservative, especially in how they justified their actions or proposals. (In practice, schools have tended to side with Toby, taking few broad steps on their own since 1960 to encourage students to continue schooling.)

The apparent choice between coercion and selection is not only old; it is also demeaning to students and a limited vision of education. As City University of New York education Professor Michelle Fine (1991) has noted, Finn and Toby wrote about dropouts as though the only consideration was some form of social utility. I will not dispute that a good education can improve the careers and lives of students afterward and by so doing help a country. The problem comes in using education primarily as a means for controlling behavior and privileges, either by universal socializing, on the one hand, or confirming the status of a limited set of citizens, on the other. The way we have rationalized our expectation of graduation, with the stereotype of the high school dropout, has focused on the most superficial aspects of education—providing or maintaining the worth of credentials and preventing dependency and criminality. The social construction of the dropout problem has thus continued our national obsession with education either as a panacea for social problems or as the last bulwark against urban chaos.

The way we view graduation and dropping out does not have to imprison education inside a crude instrumentalist framework. We have done so since the 1960s in part because school systems are successful at insulating themselves from dissenting perspectives. Nonetheless, the history of the dropout problem suggests that different views of dropping out were available. The West

Philadelphia Schools Committee saw dropping out as an issue of equity, not socialization. One may say the same about the Southern Regional Council's concerns about "pushouts." More recently, advocates of reform in Chicago's public schools began their crusade with a series of exposés about horrific dropout statistics. These isolated incidents suggest that educational inequity has been, since the early 1960s, an alternative way of explaining both the causes and consequences of the dropout problem.

In short, demographic patterns and the importance of credentials should not determine how we define social problems. Age-related expectations are particularly limiting. Linking social problems as closely to age as most rhetoric about dropouts does ignores economic changes that affect people across ages. Ultimately, these cross-age changes are more important than the limited time in which most people acquire high school diplomas. In that way, concern over dropouts has distorted our understanding of economic change. In addition, we must understand the limits of credentialism. I recognize that civil rights activists have not excluded the importance of credentials for adulthood from their discussions of dropping out. On the contrary, the importance of credentials has been a key motivator in discussing dropping out. Yet (in contrast to supporters of alternative credentialing programs), civil rights activists have generally gone beyond the credential to discuss equity and the purposes of education and child welfare more broadly. Among the concrete lessons of the history of dropping out as a social construction is the danger of seeing the credential out of its social context.

The history of dropout policies does have some implications for school policy. First is the urgent need to reduce our dependence on high school credentials for adult education. The dynamics of credentials has fostered an artificial demand for alternative credentials that has supplanted, instead of advancing, adult education. In addition, the limits of 1960s and later programs suggest the need for broad programs to assist students rather than limited, "pilot" projects that will never become permanent features of schools. Finally, these programs need to rely on permanent constituencies and rationales beyond the prevention of dropping out. The shallowness of the social construction of dropping out has served school programs poorly over more than three decades.

The creation of the dropout as a social problem represents, ultimately, one sign of our society's discomfort with dependency. For more than 100 years, North Americans have built institutions and age norms to obscure and rationalize the existence of dependents, the large number of people not in the labor force. The expansion of high schools represents one of the best successes of that strategy, with its dominance of adolescence and the growing expectation that everyone should graduate. That success led to criticism of high schools because the new expectation implied that those who did not graduate were problems. The way the dropout stereotype developed, with suggestions of imminent criminality and dependency on the part of dropouts, reinforced the belief that schooling was necessary to prevent dependency—even though full-time schooling represents guaranteed dependency for a large portion of a person's life. Schools' failure to prevent dropping out also suggests that age norms and age-related institutions have failed to resolve our collective concerns about dependency.

The obsession with dropouts as an impending sign of social chaos, finally, must end. It is a superficial way of describing education's problems, and it has smothered alternative frameworks of school failure. The rhetoric of the dropout stereotype demeans its target and has led to little fruitful action. In the 1960s, school dropout programs were more symbolic than substantive. Later, the expansion of GED programs failed to address the central dilemma of credentialing. It is time to step away from the stereotype of the dropout problem and approach it as one (but only one) aspect of education's problems.

CAPTURING THE DEBATE

The prior chapter suggests that, despite a vivid literature describing dropping out as a crisis in educational equity, the same stereotype of dropping out that dominated the 1960s captured the debate by the end of the 1980s. In part, that may be the result of tactical decisions about rhetoric: It is easier to scare politicians with the immediate dangers of the next generation than to describe their potential in compelling terms. Yet the rhetoric also suggests the timidity of public officials, especially school administrators. Social criticism, and alternative ways of viewing social problems, are buried under the avalanche of other concerns. Daniel Schreiber's personal history is emblematic of the response to the dropout problem and the ways in which a bureaucratic setting can divert reform. His partial resume from the 1960s suggests his growing prominence as an educational innovator (Shapiro Papers, box 6). He was the principal of the junior high school where the Demonstration Guidance Project made an impressive impact as compensatory education and inspired Higher Horizons. Plucked from the leadership of Higher Horizons, for three years he crusaded across the country in an effort to convince the public that a dropout crisis existed. He wrote and talked at length about the economic consequences of the dropout problem and what he saw as model policy responses.

Toward the end of his tenure at the NEA Project on School Dropouts, he began to explore alternative ways to respond to employment problems. Instead of focusing on schools, Schreiber turned to the labor market as a target of change. On August 11, 1964, Schreiber wrote a letter to Ford Foundation officer Paul Ylvisaker proposing a project to challenge corporate employment practices. After serving as an advisory to the Urban League, for example, he had decided that standardized achievement scores could work to discourage employment of African Americans:

Quite frequently the employer, based on his experience, sets up various "cut-off" points for different specific jobs, and too many Negro applicants score below these points.... As far as the employer is concerned the achievement tests used do screen in the kind of workers the company wants. Obviously, *they* are satisfied with the results and will continue to use the tests. Yet, Negro youth, who if they had had the same educational background and experiences would pass, be hired, and eventually promoted to higher jobs, are screened *out*. (emphasis in the original)

Schreiber proposed that a large corporation sponsor a project to hire people who met minimum competency requirements for a group of jobs. In this project, "the company would substitute an on-the-job training" program for standardized application tests. Schreiber hoped that the project would be a model for change in employment practices: "If the experimental groups turns out to be proficient, at least to the same extent as groups that are hired normally, then I think that the original company will continue this new practice, and other companies will give it a try" (NEA Project on School Dropout Papers, section 4). He had moved from a focus on schools as the primary agent of change to seeing a need to change labor market practices.

For the most prolific proselytizer of the dropout problem, this proposal was a fundamental change in approach. Before this letter, Schreiber had consistently praised programs that emphasized the school's role in changing the employment prospects of dropouts. Most work-experience programs implied that pre-employment training would raise the prospects of dropouts and graduates alike. In his letter quoted above, however, Schreiber proposed that businesses take up some of the burden by *first* hiring people and *then* training them. A flurry of notes inside the Ford Foundation followed Schreiber's letter. Two program associates wrote back to Schreiber, encouraging him to develop his proposal. Ylvisaker wrote him on August 17, 1964, "Keep writing letters like that, they recharge our batteries" (NEA Project on School Dropouts, section 4).

Schreiber did not follow up on the encouragement, however. The papers of the Project on School Dropouts contain no later letters about the proposal. He returned to New York as the assistant superintendent in Harlem, immediately taking a prominent place in the school bureaucracy. Whatever lessons he may have learned as head of the Project on School Dropouts, he failed to apply them to the growing controversy over desegregation in New York City. As a district superintendent in Harlem, he approved (without consulting any community organization or holding open meetings) a gerrymandered attendance zone that ensured school segregation for a junior high school. The controversy over the zoning at IS 201 became one of the chief points of conflict between the city's school system and civil rights activists in the mid-1960s, as community groups and parents' associations repeatedly pointed out the hypocrisy with which the school system treated their own desegregation goals (Rogers 1968: 364–65). In two years, Schreiber had gone from challenging existing employment practices to approving the creation of segregated schools. Maybe his social criticism at the NEA was just bluster; perhaps it was sincere. After he returned to the bureaucratic fold, it became meaningless.

Schreiber's professional fate represents one person's limits in the dropout debate. One must be cautious about interpreting his return to New York. Nonetheless, he was among the most articulate of crusaders against dropping out, and his story suggests how bureaucratic routines, especially the defense of segregation, could override personal opinions. Back in a school bureaucracy, Schreiber contributed to the type of inequities he had denounced while at the NEA.

ALTERNATIVE PERSPECTIVES

Fortunately for the future of education, one does not have to focus on schools either as socializers or as selectors. (Those goals are also not mutually exclusive; schools always socialize in some way, even if implicitly. Sorting by schools can facilitate the socialization of adolescents into marginality as adults (Bowles and Gintis 1974; Willis 1977). Nonetheless, the two explicitly conservative goals of high schools are, at least superficially, at odds.) The existence of a civil rights perspective on dropping out, side by side with more conservative views since the early 1960s, suggests that we do not need to see dropping out as a crisis of impending dependency and criminality. Instead, civil rights activists have seen dropout statistics as a confirmation of fundamental inequalities in education and a rallying point for deeper reform.

In Chicago, the dropout problem became the basis for one of the most deep-reaching educational reforms in any urban city this century. A series of reports on dropping out in the middle 1980s suggested that half or more of Chicago children never graduated from high school. Despite the attempted manipulation of statistics by school system officials, the reports provided substantial evidence of the fundamental incompetence of the schools in providing a decent education for the city's children. The activists who wrote the reports did not stop, however, with documenting the magnitude of dropping out. They instead presented what they saw as the reasons for the crisis: the dysfunctional central bureaucracy, principals' lifetime tenure, and the incompetence of the system at all levels. The initial flurry of attention helped provoke the dismissal of the city superintendent, and several years of work produced a wide-ranging reform in 1988 (Hess 1991: 7–21; Kyle and Kantowicz 1991).

Dropout statistics alone did not bring school reform; that would not have been possible. It took a broad coalition of interests and several years of activism to get a reform bill through the Illinois legislature (Katz 1992). Yet, in Chicago, the dropout problem became part of a broader discussion about the dysfunction of the school system. As with the West Philadelphia Schools Committee, Chicago activists saw the dropout problem as one element of a holistic, evolving criticism of public schools. At the center was the ideal that schools should provide a decent education for all the city's children. Notable is what activists did not emphasize: work-experience programs, counseling, or publicity campaigns.

Instead, they saw education as a right of citizenship and dropping out as evidence that schools were failing to guarantee those rights.

The notion of education as a right and requirement of citizenship is a messy one. Certainly, parents are concerned about their children's future jobs, and they look to schools to provide both usable skills and credentials. Yet they rarely see education purely in such a fashion. In contrast to the stereotype of the dropout problem, there perhaps should be no easy match between schools and society except the notion that children have a birthright to education. As Ira Katznelson and Margaret Weir have argued, public primary schooling became noncontroversial in the North as the franchise spread for white males in the early nineteenth century (Katznelson and Weir 1985: Chap. 2). Similarly, African Americans have struggled from before the Civil War to acquire decent schooling for their children, an attribute of citizenship so clearly denied them for decades. In this country, the meanings of citizenship and educational politics have been intertwined for well over a century. The stereotype of dropping out since the 1960s has obscured that debate with a shallow, instrumental view of schooling. The social construction of dropping out has concealed the existence of other, deeper meanings of schooling.

DISTORTIONS OF AGE NORMS

One of the ways in which the social construction of dropping out has limited public understanding has been its emphasis on age norms, on the expectation that a person's adolescence determines her or his life course. The focus of concern over dropping out on adolescents—or on any age-specific group—distorts our perceptions of social change. It makes historical transitions appear specific to individual generations. The concerns with automation and the economic consequences of dropping out implied that workers in the future would find an altered job market. It suggested that the postwar generation of high school students would be the first for whom technological changes would dramatically affect their careers. To some degree, adolescents have been on the cutting edge of the economy. Young women were among the first factory workers in the United States. Young women played an important role in the creation of a white-collar class of workers at the end of the nineteenth and beginning of the twentieth centuries. After World War II, increasing segmentation, or division, of the labor market affected both young men and young women.

Yet it is misleading to see economic and social change as primarily generational. It is mostly intergenerational. Adolescents have been among the first of the groups limited by growing occupational segregation, but they are only a minority within that. One consequence of labor market segmentation has been the relegation of most teenagers to a peripheral job market. Yet the critical detail is that teenagers share peripheral job markets with many other people, of all ages. The increased part- and full-time work of married women was as important a development in the postwar labor market as were changes in job opportunities for teenagers. McDonald's may employ thousands of teenagers, but poorly paid service work is as much the realm of older workers as of adolescents. Instead of isolating the changing economic circumstances of teenagers, we must put them in a broader historical perspective. Economic and social changes cross several generations. The problem with many age norms is that they do not necessarily reflect the broad nature of historical transitions. Demographic patterns do exist; age is a relevant factor in considering social change. Yet the reification of patterns into normative expectations is unwise.

In some sense, the focus on adolescents comes from the complexity of historical developments. Large-scale social change in the United States usually has a demographic component. People alter their fertility behavior, migrate, enter or leave the workforce, or have to react to consequences of mortality, fertility, residential, or career changes. Along with demographic change, however, come different social judgments about the value and role of children, old age, place, and work. The perceived dropout problem of the 1960s (as well as the perceived teenage pregnancy crisis of the 1970s) was a reaction to changes in both demographic behavior and social judgment. Partly because more teenagers graduated from high school, but also because high school diplomas became widespread economic credentials, the stigma of those without diplomas became highly visible. Thus, the construction of the dropout problem involved changing educational achievement and an evolving economic value of education.

Perhaps the comprehension of complex changes is easier when one thinks only about a narrow age range. It seems simpler to examine the changing condition of adolescents than society-wide demographic changes. One consequence of this simplification, however, is the loss of perspective on the role of institutions. Since the early nineteenth century, most demographic change has revolved around, or had serious consequences for, social institutions. The dropout problem is no different. Conventional wisdom defined it by reference to an institution, the high school, as though a high school education had become a natural part of life by the middle of the twentieth century.

Over the last several decades, educators and economists have often talked about the need for a transition from school to work. The rise of concern over dropouts was, in part, the origin of such theorizing (Barton and Fraser 1980; Coleman et al. 1974; Herman, Sadofsky, and Rosenberg 1968; National Commission for Manpower Policy 1976; Survey Research Center 1971). That phrase, "transition from school to work," implies a neat fit between formal education and the labor market. The close coordination of transitions from childhood dependence to adult independence, however, is a recent phenomenon. Until the development of a wage-labor economy, transitions to adulthood in the United States often covered a broad span in a person's life. The acts of moving out of parents' households, having children, leaving school, or entering the workforce usually happened at different times. Urban children often began work while they lived with parents, going to school when they could not find or keep a job. By the mid-twentieth century, that transition to adulthood had narrowed, on average occurring within a shorter span for individuals than it had in the middle of the nineteenth century (Modell, Furstenberg, and Hershberg 1978).

Thus, the close timing of transitions to adulthood reflects historical changes. It has required the high school attendance of most teenagers. It has required the exclusion of adolescents from most (and well-paying) jobs. We often take the existence and much of the shape of public schooling for granted. When we describe the problems of adolescents, we rarely examine the basic choices we have about the shape of institutions. When we examine the history of the dropout problem, we can see that the definition of the dropout required the development of secondary schools. That, however, was not inevitable in the nineteenth century.

Specifically, the dropout problem became a coherent issue because high school diplomas have served as credentials for labor markets and colleges. People leave school for many reasons. Yet we often think of dropping out as a single problem, or at least a single symptom of related problems. We perceive a dropout problem because being a dropout carries an economic and social stigma. Some of that stigma may come from skills or information that could have been learned if the former student had remained in school. Most of it comes, however, because employers will hire a high school graduate before hiring a dropout and because colleges require a high school diploma before admission. Dropping out is a coherent issue because a diploma by itself has a value in this society. The dropout debate of the 1960s distorted the process of historical change in two major ways, therefore. First, it focused attention about economic changes on adolescents, leading discussion away from broader patterns and the development of peripheral job markets. Second, the dropout debate assumed that the credentialing function of a high school diploma was natural and reasonable. This last assumption led to the rationalization of GED programs as a replacement for graduation without understanding the context of credentials.

THE DILEMMA OF CREDENTIALS

The use of high school diplomas as a credential for college and labor markets is ubiquitous. Neither the ideal of education as a broadly defined right of citizenship nor the artificiality of the age norm of graduation eliminates that fact of modern life. Individuals who complete high school have better lives as adults than dropouts, in a variety of ways. Nonetheless, we must keep the value of a credential in context. While part of the value of a school credential lies in the concrete skills acquired through education, part also accrues from the relative rarity of the credential and the implied difficulty of acquisition. The expansion of General Educational Development (GED) programs in the 1970s and 1980s as a means of providing alternative credentials ignored the dynamics of credentials. By providing a degree that, by implication, was easier to acquire than high school graduation, GED programs have provided largely worthless credentials to its enrollees. The domination of adult education programs by the GED and other alternative credentials illustrates the shallowness of dropping out as a social construction. Unfortunately, one of the targets of the Goals 2000 legislation is based solely on credentials: "The Nation must dramatically reduce its school dropout rate, and 75 percent of the students who do drop out will successfully complete a high school degree *or its equivalent*" (Public Law 103-227, section 102; emphasis added). Equally ominous is the evidence that most adult education programs have a narrow range of curriculum geared to the GED (Grubb and Kalman 1994: 61). If the best an adult education program can provide dropouts is a GED, it is a failure.

Similarly, arbitrary targets for graduation—such as the national goal of 90 percent graduation—have no inherent rationale. They are automatic reflections of the expectations we hold for teenagers. I can find no evidence that having 90 percent of the population with high school diplomas is any more valuable than having 75 percent graduating, apart from what students learn. As in the 1960s, I can find no magical threshold we have passed that requires a certain level of education related to production needs. The primary goal should be on those skills and habits of mind, as Ted Sizer (1992) writes, that schools are supposed to teach. Focusing on the piece of paper is a trivial task.

Yet it is important to track graduation statistics as a measure of schooling equality, if not for the absolute level of graduation in a society. The historical evidence suggests that poverty has remained a sizable disadvantage in completing high school, beyond what may be associated with the prior generation's education, family size, nativity, and the person's sex. The crime is not that fewer than 90 percent of students graduate, but that household income and property ownership still provide an advantage in education. Because of residential segregation by both race and class, differences will show up among schools and school systems. For this reason, dropout and graduation statistics (if collected appropriately by age, an important caveat) can still be one measure of how well schools educate everyone.

In addition, one can reduce the importance of the high school diploma by eliminating it as a requirement for public colleges. In practice, this would not change admissions procedures for selective colleges and universities, which would continue to require a certain amount of coursework or skills to matriculate. However, nonselective institutions should not demand a high school credential for entrance. This requires potential students without diplomas to waste their time acquiring a GED or other alternative, instead of the more valuable task of attending classes. If we are concerned as a society about dropouts, it makes little sense to make it more difficult for them to re-enter schooling.

DROPOUTS AND POLICY

Reducing our reliance on diplomas as credentials is one lesson the history of dropout policies suggests. Historians have to be wary of making policy recommendations, but my reading of dropout programs is that their justifications come from distorted understandings of relationships between schooling and society. The growth of GED credentials is the most obvious mistake in the history of dropout policies. The GED does not serve as an appropriate alternative credential, and it distracts from substantive adult education. GED programs provide an excuse for schools and social critics to ignore the real disparities in educational opportunities between poor and wealthy. By suggesting that dropouts can easily replace four years of high school education with a test, proponents of the GED reduce the mission of secondary education, for poor children at least, to providing a piece of paper and little else. Thus, the nominal emphasis in the Goals 2000 legislation on replacement credentials is unwise.

The limitations on dropout programs in the 1960s and more recently also suggest that small programs are less useful and less politically viable than broader policy changes in schools. Severely limiting the use of suspensions and grade retention would help keep students in or return dropouts to school. In general, it is more effective to implement broad policy changes than small, innovative programs, simply because district-wide practices affect more students. In addition, however, small programs with a narrow rationale are less politically viable in the long run than programs with a broader rationale than dropout prevention. In the 1960s, narrowly targeted programs disappeared when funding dried up. Since World War II, special school programs have had financial stability when they have had a powerful constituency or when legislatures have mandated that local public schools support them.

Since dropping out is a complex phenomenon, dropout programs do not need a narrow rationale. A day care center at a high school may help young mothers to stay in school, but it is also a public service with a potential constituency independent of the justification that it prevents dropping out. The existence of day care in a high school can appeal not only to a student mother, but also to the grandparents of the child, neighborhood organizations, social workers, and school employees with their own children. One can make similar arguments about vocational education and other programs that have been justified as dropout prevention or remediation. Each specific project will probably survive better with a broad rationale than simply as a dropout program.

Consider the defense of federal dropout prevention programs in 1995 as an object lesson. As the Republican Congress threatened to cut programs or eliminate the Department of Education, Democrats railed against the proposals on the floors of both houses. Yet, when Massachusetts Senator Edward Kennedy defended federal dropout programs, it was in terms that James Bryant Conant would have understood:

[We need] dropout prevention programs, demonstration programs which are targeted at some 400,000 young people who drop out of school every year. [Dropouts] are the principal cause of violence in our society and the principal individuals that have the challenges with teenage pregnancy. We have a small program that is having some positive effects, and it is targeted to be eliminated. (Kennedy 1995: S6438)

Kennedy offered no defense of these programs except as prevention of criminality and dependency. Though he has been one of the staunchest liberals in the Senate, Kennedy had nothing but a conservative rationale for dropout prevention. In contrast, threatened cuts to programs for children with disabilities have encountered much heavier opposition, because these programs have a natural constituency in the parents. When the House of Representatives eliminated funding for several programs in the original appropriations bill for education for the 1996 fiscal year, parents and other advocates responded with fury. Senator Bill Frist of Tennessee, chair of the Senate Subcommittee on Disability Policy, quickly mailed letters to constituents in early August 1995 promising to help reverse the cuts. The fate of the Department of Education and many of its programs (including both dropout prevention aid and discretionary programs in special education) is in doubt as I write. Yet what is clear is that a shallow justification for dropout prevention has not served the cause well.

Finally, the history of dropout policies suggests the limits of vocational education as a remedy for young adult unemployment. As explained above, it masks the fact that unemployment and underemployment have become a feature of life at all ages with continuing labor market segmentation. In addition, vocational programs have rarely matched students to jobs well. Two aspects of education are relevant here. First is the insulation of schools from the community and from pressures to reform. The failure of the Boston Compact to increase graduation in the early 1980s suggests that, even when graduates are guaranteed jobs, schools are frequently unable to improve sufficiently to enable students to graduate and earn the promised positions.

In addition, vocational programs in schools weather a tension between training students for specific jobs, which may not exist after training, and giving general education with some ill-defined vocational orientation. The recent "tech-prep" movement, which suggests that technical education can combine vocationalism with academics, illustrates that tension (Mendel 1994). Ironically, some of the vocational programs with the best results are supported employment programs for individuals with moderate to severe disabilities (such as mental retardation) that first place individuals in jobs and then train students in the technical and social requirements of the job (Rusch and Hughes 1989). Beyond intellectual capacities, two critical differences in orientation separate supported employment from vocational education in general. Supported employment programs penetrate the job environment, unlike most vocational programs that may place but not continue training after formal schooling ends. This is critical to understanding the limitations of traditional vocational education, which continues to rely on the assumption that skills are sufficient to ensure employability. Supported employment programs, on the other hand, view labor markets as well as the individual as problematic. For supported employment, schooling is only a partial solution to the problematic future of teenagers with disabilities.

Furthermore, programs for training adolescents for supported employment developed under the auspices of federal laws that made the education of individuals with disabilities a right. While some justify transition programs as a way to reduce later costs of institutionalization, the argument about social cost is only part of the rationale. The larger framework is the federal law that guarantees individuals with disabilities a right to an education and habilitation; help in securing supported employment for adolescents is part of that guaranteed education, not all of it. This framework of rights, bolstered by the Americans with Disabilities Act of 1990, suggests the shallowness of viewing schools solely as instrumental. It was not inevitable that we framed dropping out as a problem of social cost; it could have been, and still can be, an issue of the right to an education.

Ultimately, the power of schools to warehouse children is eroding, and that development undermines vocational orientations to dropout prevention. Why should children attend school for vague vocational preparation, when some part-time jobs exist for students? Some vocational or technical programs do attract students, but their power may rely as much from selectivity as academic programs do. A vocational program that requires entrance exams is presumably more difficult than one that does not, and it is impossible to disentangle the influence of selectivity on the value of graduation from that of the concrete skills learned. Yet we continue to debate the merits of vocational education as dropout prevention, as the barrier between school attendance and employment on the periphery of labor markets decays and the warehousing function of schools becomes more irrelevant.

DROPOUTS AND DEPENDENCY

The creation of the dropout problem represents the institutional success of age norms in the United States. High schools became so successful at accommodating adolescents out of the labor force that it became expected for teenagers to spend four years in school. Now, most parents expect to support their children through at least eighteen years of dependency. There are three ironies in this apparent victory of high schools. One is the dilemma explored in this book: Growing attendance at high schools and graduation made it possible to criticize high schools for failing to educate everyone. In addition, however, is the illusion that extended schooling eliminates dependency. While the dropout stereotype speaks to fears of welfare use and jails, in truth childhood schooling is the surest form of dependency in this society.

Finally, demographic and economic changes were beginning to undermine age norms and the success of age-specific institutions while institutions at both ends of the age spectrum were showing signs of dominance. Consider that the expectation of high school graduation became common at the same time, roughly, as the postwar expansion of Social Security (Myles 1988). Poverty rates among those 65 and older dropped from 35 percent in 1959 to 13 percent in 1992 (U. S. Bureau of the Census 1993b: 4). Yet, at the same time, the apparent success of high schools and retirement in keeping people comfortably out of the labor market was eroding. Since World War II, teenagers have re-entered the work force, reversing a century-long trend of withdrawal from labor during the primary ages of school attendance (Greenberger and Steinberg 1986). Also, the aging of the population began to erode expectations and institutions of retirement.

The erosion of retirement came in part from decreases in mortality. As a higher proportion of the population reached the age of retirement, fewer younger adults existed to support each Social Security recipient. Simultaneously, the existence of pensions and Social Security rules regarding allowable income for those under seventy encouraged additional withdrawal from the labor market through the early 1980s (Leonesio 1993). Thus, while Social Security has become successful in reducing poverty in old age, its solvency came under a cloud of suspicion. In addition, Social Security and pensions—even when solvent—do not always pay very much. Thus, the success of Social Security and pension systems in promoting retirement may have encouraged the very dependence on retirement income that so frightens people today.

Yet, once again, demographics do not explain everything. Social Security rules regarding income have been important in shaping retirement patterns (also see Estes 1983). At the other end of the life span, changes in consumption and labor patterns have led the erosion of age norms. After World War II, companies began to focus advertising and product promotion on specific age groups in a conscious market segmentation (Pope 1983: Chap. 7). Thus, while advertisers have looked to adolescents for some time as a market (Hollander and Germain 1992), postwar advertising has increasingly aimed marketing and promotion at specific age groups, and products have been developed for the elderly and the young. Some of that is healthy, but it can also lead to juvenile crime committed for the sake of expensive sneakers or jewelry (Nightingale 1993: Chap. 5). The development of age-specific consumption patterns and marketing has provided incentives for disposable income by teenagers—and thus an incentive for early entry into working (Greenberger and Steinberg 1986: 28–34).

That incentive for disposable income has reinforced further segmentation of labor markets since World War II. Teenagers in cities are now more likely to work and attend school simultaneously than at any time since the nineteenth century. The proportion of sixteen- and seventeen-year-olds who both work and attend school has climbed from under 4 percent in the 1940 public use samples and 12 percent in 1950 to 25 percent in 1990; those figures may well underestimate in-school working (Greenberger and Steinberg 1986: 16–17).

Adolescents work primarily in low-wage, part-time jobs. Older workers, also, are likely to be in part-time positions at the periphery of the labor market. The long-term trend toward withdrawal from the labor market for older men appeared to reverse in the middle 1980s, as older women have also been more likely to work (Taeuber 1992: Chap. 4). The development of more dead-end jobs, in combination with technological advances that allow the reorganization of work, has enabled corporations to lower labor costs. This, in turn, has made it impossible for many families to survive on a single income, leading to more women entering the labor market, often needing part-time work. The entry of women into the labor force has fed labor market segmentation even further.

The erosion of age-related institutions erected around the labor market is now forcing a redefinition of dependency. We can no longer rationalize dependency as preparation for the labor market (schooling) or withdrawal from it (retirement). It may be no accident that the latest wave of concern with dropouts came as debates about the solvency of Social Security began in the 1980s. Older Americans are concerned about retirement security, and adults are concerned about what the next generation will do. Once again, concerns about intolerable dependency have dominated discussion about age-related policy. Yet the questions about retirement institutions in combination with the inability of schools to eliminate dropping out make institutional, age-related solutions doubtful. High schools, at least, need something more than vocationalism as their purpose, and schooling cannot solve poverty. The current construction of dropping out, which we have largely inherited from the 1960s, serves neither schools nor poor children well.

Bibliography

MANUSCRIPT SOURCES

Atlanta Board of Education agendas and minutes. Atlanta Public School Archives, Atlanta.

Atlanta Public School annual reports. Atlanta Public School Archives, Atlanta.

Binzen, Peter, articles. 1964. Pamphlet box 379.23, Philadelphia School District Pedagogical Library, Philadelphia.

Citizens Committee on Public Education in Philadelphia papers. Accession 427, Temple University Urban Archives, Philadelphia.

Donovan, Bernard, subject files, III/A/2. New York City Board of Education archives. Record group 1, Milbank Memorial Library, Columbia University Teachers College, New York.

Georgia Association of School Counselors scrapbook. Atlanta Public School Archives, Atlanta.

Georgia Department of Education annual reports. Record group 12, subgroup 2, series 29, Georgia State Department of Archives and History, Atlanta.

Georgia Deputy Schools Superintendent subject files. Record group 12, subgroup 34, series 79, Georgia State Department of Archives and History, Atlanta.

Georgia Director of Negro Education subject files. Record group 12, subgroup 6, series 71, Georgia State Department of Archives and History, Atlanta.

Georgia local school system correspondence files. Record group 12, subgroup 2, series 26, Georgia State Department of Archives and History.

Georgia School Superintendent general administrative records. Record group 12, subgroup 2, series 27, Georgia State Department of Archives and History, Atlanta.

Germantown Community Council papers. Accession 49, Temple University Urban Archives, Philadelphia.

Greater Philadelphia Chamber of Commerce papers. Record group 1997, Historical Society of Pennsylvania, Philadelphia.

Logan, Floyd, papers. Accession 469, Temple University Urban Archives, Philadelphia.

Municipal Cooperative Education Program papers. PA61-266, Ford Foundation Archives, New York.

National Education Association Project on School Dropouts papers. PA61-208, Ford Foundation Archives, New York.

New York City School Office of Public Relations records, IV/A/3. New York City Board of Education archives. Record group 1, Milbank Memorial Library, Columbia University Teachers College, New York.

New York City Schools Superintendent circulars, IV/A/1/c. Record group 1, Milbank Memorial Library, Columbia University Teachers College, New York.

Philadelphia Federation of Teachers papers. Accession 509, Temple University Urban Archives, Philadelphia.

Philadelphia School District *Occupational Notes*. Philadelphia School District Pedagogical Library, Philadelphia.

Robinson, Isaiah, papers. Series 378, Milbank Memorial Library, Columbia University Teachers College, New York.

Shapiro, Rose, papers. Series 385, Milbank Memorial Library, Columbia University Teachers College, New York.

U. S. Department of Health, Education, and Welfare subject files. 1963 Summer Dropout Campaign. Record group 51, series 60.3a, National Archives, Washington.

West Mount Airy Neighbors Association papers. Accession 274, Temple University Urban Archives, Philadelphia.

West Philadelphia Schools Committee papers. Accession 306, Temple University Urban Archives, Philadelphia.

DATA SOURCES

The analysis of graduation and attendance patterns since 1940 relied on public use samples of the decennial United States census made available by the Inter-University Consortium for Political and Social Research (ICPSR). These included the 1940 1 percent sample (ICPSR set 8236), the 1950 1 percent sample (ICPSR 8251), the 1960 1/1000 sample (ICPSR 54), the 1970 1/1000 sample (from ICPSR 18), the 1980 1/1000 A sample (ICPSR 8210), the 1990 1/10,000 sample (ICPSR 6150), and the 1990 1 percent sample (ICPSR 9951).

The size of the public use samples analyzed here varied, largely from practical considerations of availability and computing resources. Thus, multivariate analysis of the 1940 census relied on half of the twenty subsamples that compose the 1 percent sample, whereas multivariate analysis for 1960, 1970, and 1980 relied on one-in-one-thousand samples, and 1990 on the full 1 percent sample. Analysis of the proportion of sixteen- and seventeen-year-olds at both work and school used different samples for 1940 (one of the twenty subsamples) and 1990 (the one-in-ten-thousand sample). Recalculations based on different samples may result in different estimates, but the differences would not change the substantive conclusions.

PUBLISHED SOURCES

Anderson, Douglas K. 1993. Adolescent mothers drop out. *American Sociological Review* 58: 735–38.

Anderson, James D. 1982. The historical development of black vocational education. In *Work, youth, and schooling*, edited by Harvey Kantor and David B. Tyack. Stanford: Stanford University Press.

———. 1988. *The education of blacks in the South, 1860–1935.* Chapel Hill, N.C.: University of North Carolina Press.

Andrus, Ethel Percy. 1956. Operation salvage. *California Journal of Secondary Education* 31: 57-81.

Angus, David. 1965. The dropout problem. Unpublished Ph.D. diss., Ohio State University, Columbus, Oh.

Angus, David, Jeffrey E. Mirel, and Maris A. Vinovskis. 1988. Historical development of age stratification in schooling. *Teachers College Record* 90: 211–36.

As more earn equivalency diploma, its value is debated. 1992. *New York Times* (21 October).

Ayres, Leonard P. 1909. *Laggards in our schools.* New York: Survey Associates Inc.

Balliet, Thomas M. 1903. Discussion. *Proceedings of the National Education Association*: 800–801.

Ballot, Richard D. 1991. State constitutional law. *Seton Hall Law Review* 21: 445–81.

Bard, Bernard. 1966. Why dropout campaigns fail. *Saturday Review* 17 (September): 78–79.

Barnard, Henry. 1865. History of common schools in Connecticut. *American Journal of Education* 15: 276–331.

Barton, Paul, and Byrnn Shore Fraser. 1980. *Between two worlds.* Washington, D.C.: Government Printing Office.

Berg, Ivar. 1970. *Education and jobs.* New York: Praeger Publishers.

Bestor, Arthur E. 1953. *Educational wastelands.* Urbana, Ill.: University of Illinois Press.

Binzen, Peter. 1964a. *Dilemma of the dropout.* Philadelphia: Philadelphia Evening Bulletin. In Philadelphia School District Pedagogical Library, pamphlet box 379.23. Also in Urban Archives, Accession 246, Citizens Committee on Public Education in Philadelphia Papers, box 4.

————. 1964b. Those who quit school are witnesses to toll of frustration and boredom. In *Dilemma of the dropout*. Philadelphia: Philadelphia Evening Bulletin.

————. 1964c. Vocational schools are considered the stepchildren of education. In *Dilemma of the dropout*. Philadelphia: Philadelphia Evening Bulletin.

————. 1964d. 700,000 a year quitting school and heading for economic cellar. In *Dilemma of the dropout*. Philadelphia: Philadelphia Evening Bulletin.

Bledsoe, Joseph C. 1959. An investigation of six correlates of student withdrawal from high school. *Journal of Educational Research* 53 (September): 3–6.

Book, William F. 1904. Why pupils drop out of the high school. *Pedagogical Seminary* 11: 204–32.

Bound, John, and Richard Freeman. 1992. What went wrong? *Quarterly Journal of Economics* 107: 201–32.

Bowles, Samuel, and Herbert Gintis. 1976. *Schooling in capitalist America*. New York: Basic Books.

Boynton, F. D. 1902. High school attendance. *School Review* 10: 558–65.

Braverman, Harry. 1974. *Labor and monopoly capital*. New York: Monthly Review Press.

Brooks, Stratton D. 1902. Relation of temperament to withdrawal from school. *School Review* 10: 446–55.

Burke, Walter J. 1965. The dropout problem. *Clearing House* 40 (September): 44–46.

Byerly, Carl. 1967. A school curriculum for prevention and remediation of deviancy. In *Profile of the school dropout*, edited by Daniel Schreiber. New York: Random House.

Callahan, Raymond E. 1962. *Education and the cult of efficiency*. Chicago: University of Chicago Press.

Cameron, Stephen V., and James L. Heckman. 1993. The nonequivalence of high school equivalents. *Journal of Labor Economics* 1: 1–47.

Carr, J. W. 1903. Discussion. *Proceedings of the National Education Association*: 798–800.

Caswell, Hollis L. 1933. *Non-promotion in elementary schools*. Nashville, Tenn.: George Peabody College for Teachers, Division of Surveys and Field Services.

Cervantes, Lucius F. 1965. *The dropout*. Ann Arbor, Mich.: University of Michigan Press.

Chafe, William H. 1980. *Civilities and civil rights*. New York: Oxford University Press.

Chandler, Alfred D. 1977. *The visible hand*. Cambridge, Mass.: Belknap Press.

Children's Defense Fund. 1974. *Children out of school in America*. Washington, D.C.: Children's Defense Fund.

Chudacoff, Howard P. 1989. *How old are you?* Princeton, N.J.: Princeton University Press.

Churaman, Charlotte V. 1992. How families finance college education. *Journal of Student Financial Aid* 22 (Spring): 7–21.

Cohen, Sol, ed. 1974. *Education in the United States*. New York: Random House.

Coleman, James, et al. 1974. *Youth: Transition to adulthood*. Chicago: University of Chicago Press.

Commission on the Reorganization of Secondary Education. 1918. *Cardinal principles of secondary education*. U. S. Bureau of Education Bulletin No. 35. Washington, D.C.: Government Printing Office.

Commission on the Skills of the American Workforce. 1990. *America's choice*. Rochester, N.Y.: National Center on Education and the Economy.

Conant, James Bryant. 1959. *The American high school today*. New York: McGraw-Hill.

———. 1961. *Slums and suburbs*. New York: McGraw-Hill.

Coplein, Leonard E. 1962. Techniques for study of dropouts. *Clearing House* 36 (May): 526–530.

Counts, George Sylvester. 1922. *The selective character of American secondary education*. Chicago: University of Chicago.

Cravens, Hamilton. 1993. Child saving in modern America 1870s–1990s. In *Children at risk in America*, edited by Roberta Wollons. Albany, N.Y.: State University of New York Press.

Cremin, Lawrence A. 1961. *The transformation of the school*. New York: Random House.

———. 1970. *American education: The colonial experience*. New York: Harper and Row.

———. 1990. *Population education and its discontents*. New York: Harper and Row.

Culpepper, Claude. 1966. Call on school board to end discriminating ways. Atlanta *Inquirer* (30 July).

Dan Schreiber, 71, educator who worked with poor youths. 1981. *New York Times* (March 9).

Davies, Margery. 1982. *Woman's place is at the typewriter*. Philadelphia: Temple University Press.

Davis, Donald A. 1962. An experimental study of potential dropouts. *Personnel and Guidance Journal* 40: 799–802.

Dentler, Robert A., and Mary Ellen Warshauer. 1965. *Big city dropouts and illiterates*. New York: Praeger.

DeSanctis, Vincent. 1979. *The Adult Education Act 1964–1979*. Upper Montclair, N.J.: National Adult Education Clearinghouse. Educational Resources Information Center Reproduction Document No. ED 218 517.

Dillon, Harold J. 1946. *Work experience in secondary education*. New York: National Child Labor Committee.

———. 1949. *Early school leavers*. New York: National Child Labor Committee.

Dr. Letson admits in court transfers leave desegregation. 1965. Atlanta *Daily World* (16 February).

Dropout tragedies. 1960. *Life* (May 2): 106A–113.

Dulles, Foster Rhea. 1968. *The Civil Rights Commission*. East Lansing, Mich.: Michigan State University Press.

Dunkle, Margaret C. 1990. Schools today aren't making the grade. *Public Welfare* 48 (Summer): 9–15.

Education adds up to job security. 1966. *Occupational Notes* 22 (November).

Educational Policies Commission. 1944. *Education for all American youth.* Washington, D.C.: National Education Association and American Association of School Administrators.

Ekstrom, Ruth B., et al. 1987. Who drops out of high school and why? In *School dropouts*, edited by Gary Natriello. New York: Teachers College Press.

Elder, Glen H., Jr., John Modell, and Ross D. Parke. 1993. Introduction. In *Children in time and place*, edited by Glen H. Elder, Jr., John Modell, and Ross D. Parke. New York: Cambridge University Press.

Ellis, A. Caswell. 1903. The percentage of boys who leave the high school and the reasons therefor. *Proceedings of the National Education Association*: 792–98.

Employment outlook for the school dropout. 1966. *Occupational Notes* 22 (October).

Engs, Robert F. 1979. *Freedom's first generation.* Philadelphia: University of Pennsylvania Press.

Estes, Carroll L. 1983. Social Security. *Milbank Memorial Fund Quarterly* 61: 445–61.

Farrar, Eleanor, and Anthony Cipollone. 1988. *The business community and school reform.* Educational Resources Information Center Document Reproduction No. ED 348 405.

Fasick, Frank A. 1988. Patterns of formal education in high school as *rites de passage. Adolescence* 23: 457–68.

Featherman, David L., and Robert M. Hauser. 1976. Equality of schooling. *Sociology of Education* 49: 99–120.

Fine, Michelle. 1987. Why urban adolescents drop into and out of high school. In *School dropouts*, edited by Gary Natriello. New York: Teachers College Press.

———. 1991. *Framing dropouts.* Albany, N.Y.: State University of New York Press.

Fine, Michelle, and Nancy Zane. 1989. Bein' wrapped too tight. In *Dropouts from school*, edited by Lois Weis, Eleanor Farrar, and Hugh G. Petrie. Albany, N.Y.: State University of New York Press.

Finn, Chester. 1987. The high school dropout puzzle. *The Public Interest* 87 (Spring): 3–22.

———. 1988. Dropouts and grownups. *The Public Interest* 96 (Summer): 131–34.

Flynn, Henry J., Norma Saunders, and Robert Hoppock. 1954. Course for dropouts. *Clearing House* 28 (April): 486–87.

Freeman, Richard. 1976. *The overeducated American.* New York: Academic Press.

———. 1980. Why is there a youth labor market problem? In *Youth employment and public policy.* Background papers for the Arden House Assembly on Youth Employment, August 1979. Englewood Cliffs, N.J.: Prentice-Hall.

Freeman, Richard B., and Harry J. Holzer. 1986. The black youth employment crisis. In *The black youth employment crisis*, edited by Richard B. Freeman and Harry J. Holzer. Chicago: University of Chicago Press.

Freidman, Lawrence M. 1982. Limited Monarchy. Paper prepared for the Institution for Research on Educational Financing and Government's Seminar on Law in Education, Project Report No. 82-A25.

French, Joseph L. 1969. Characteristics of high school dropouts. *National Association of Secondary-School Principals Bulletin* 53 (February): 67–79.

Furstenberg, Frank F., Jr. 1991. As the pendulum swings—teenage childbearing and social concern. *Family Relations* 40: 127–38.

Germantown to regain youth corps program. 1966. Philadelphia *Evening Bulletin* (8 December).

Germantown Youth Corps project balked. 1965. Philadelphia *Evening Bulletin* Suburban North edition (16 December).

Germantown youth project laid to rest. 1966. Philadelphia *Evening Bulletin* (1 September).

Gilbert, James Burkhart. 1986. *A cycle of outrage.* New York: Oxford University Press.

Gilmore, Perry, and David Smith. 1988. Mario, Jesse and Joe. In *What do anthropologists have to say about dropouts?*, edited by Henry T. Trueba, George Spindler, and Louis Spindler. New York: Falmer Press.

Goff, Aaron. 1950. They dropped out of school. *Education* 70 (January): 330–32.

Goldberg, Arthur J. 1961. Keep them in school. *NEA Journal* 50 (April): 9.

Goldin, Claudia. 1981. Family strategies and the family economy in the late nineteenth century. In *Philadelphia*, edited by Theodore Hershberg. New York: Oxford University Press.

Goldstein, Stephen R. 1969. The scope and sources of school board authority to regulate student conduct and status. *University of Pennsylvania Law Review* 117: 373–430.

———. 1970. Reflections on developing trends in the law of student rights. *University of Pennsylvania Law Review* 118: 612–20.

Goodman, Paul. 1964. *Compulsory mis-education and the community of scholars.* New York: Vintage Books.

Gordon, David M., Richard Edwards, and Michael Reich. 1982. *Segmented work, divided workers.* New York: Cambridge University Press.

Graebner, William. 1980. *A history of retirement.* New Haven, Conn.: Yale University Press.

———. 1989. *Coming of age in Buffalo.* Philadelphia: Temple University Press.

Grannis, Joseph C., et al. 1990. *Evaluation of the New York City Dropout Prevention Initiative.* New York: Institute for Urban and Minority Education.

Greenberger, Ellen, and Laurence Steinberg. 1986. *When teenagers work.* New York: Basic Books.

Greene, Bert I. 1966. *Preventing student dropouts.* Englewood Cliffs, N.J.: Prentice-Hall.

Greenwood, J. M. 1900. Report on high school statistics. *Proceedings of the National Education Association*: 340–50.

Grossman, James R. 1989. *Land of hope.* Chicago: University of Chicago Press.

Grubb, W. Norton, and Judy Kalman. 1994. Relearning to earn. *American Journal of Education* 103: 54–93.

Haber, Carole. 1983. *Beyond sixty-five*. New York: Cambridge University Press.

Hamilton, Stephen F. 1987. Raising standards and reducing dropout rates. In *School dropouts*, edited by Gary Natriello. New York: Teachers College Press.

Hammack, Floyd Morgan. 1987. Large school systems' dropout reports. In *School dropouts*, edited by Gary Natriello. New York: Teachers College Press.

Hampel, Robert L. 1986. *The last little citadel*. Boston: Houghton Mifflin.

Hareven, Tamara K. 1982. *Family time and industrial time*. New York: Cambridge University Press.

Harlan, Louis R. 1972. *Booker T. Washington: The making of a black leader, 1856–1901*. New York: Oxford University Press.

Harrison, Bennett, and Lucy Gorham. 1992. Growing inequality in black wages in the 1980s and the emergence of an African-American middle class. *Journal of Policy Analysis and Management* 11 (Spring): 235–53.

Helping our youth. 1966. *Atlanta Journal* (17 January).

Herman, Melvin, Stanley Sadofsky, and Bernard Rosenberg, eds. 1968. *Work, youth, and unemployment*. New York: Thomas Y. Crowell.

Hess, G. Alfred. 1991. *School restructuring, Chicago style*. Newbury Park, Calif.: Corwin Press.

Hilgartner, Stephen, and Charles L. Bosk. 1988. The rise and fall of social problems. *American Journal of Sociology* 94 (July): 53–78.

Hollander, Stanley C., and Richard Germain. 1992. *Was there a Pepsi generation before Pepsi discovered it?* Lincolnwood, Ill.: NTC Business Books.

Hollingshead, August B. 1949. *Elmtown's youth*. New York: John Wiley & Sons.

Integration made Kirkwood nearly all-Negro, Letson says. 1965. Atlanta *Constitution* (15 February).

Jaynes, Gerald David, and Robin M. Williams, Jr., eds. 1989. *A common destiny*. Washington, D.C.: National Academy Press.

Jencks, Christopher, et al. 1972. *Inequality*. New York: Basic Books.

Job training for youth cut here to start projects in rural areas. 1966. Philadelphia *Evening Bulletin* (6 September).

Johnson, Elizabeth S. 1948. Teenagers at work. *The Child* 14 (October): 55–58.

Johnson, Elizabeth S., and Caroline E. Legg. 1948. Why young people leave school. *National Association of Secondary Schools Principals Bulletin* 32 (November): 14–24.

Jonas, Edward D., Jr. 1987. *The Atlanta dropout prevention plan*. Atlanta: Atlanta Dropout Prevention Collaborative.

Joncich, Geraldine M. 1968. *The sane positivist*. Middletown, Conn.: Wesleyan University Press.

Jones, Jacqueline. 1985. *Labor of love, labor of sorrow*. New York: Basic Books.

Kaestle, Carl F., and Maris A. Vinovskis. 1980. *Education and social change in nineteenth-century Massachusetts*. New York: Cambridge University Press.

Kantor, Harvey A. 1982. Vocationalism in American education. In *Work, youth and schooling*, edited by Harvey A. Kantor and David Tyack. Stanford: Stanford University Press.

———. 1988. *Learning to earn*. Madison, Wis.: University of Wisconsin Press.

Katz, Michael B. 1968. *The irony of early school reform*. Cambridge, Mass.: Harvard Universtiy Press.

———. 1992. Chicago school reform as history. *Teachers College Record* 94: 56–72.

Katz, Michael B., Michael J. Doucet, and Mark J. Stern. 1982. *The social organization of early industrial capitalism*. Cambridge, Mass.: Harvard University Press.

Katznelson, Ira, and Margaret Weir. 1985. *Schooling for all*. New York: Basic Books.

Kennedy, Edward M. 1995. Opposing the elimination of the Department of Education. *Congressional Record* (May 10).

Kennedy, John F. 1964. *The public papers of the presidents: John F. Kennedy 1963*. Washington, D.C.: Government Printing Office.

Kessler-Harris, Alice. 1982. *Out to work*. New York: Oxford University Press.

Kett, Joseph K. 1977. *Rites of passage*. New York: Basic Books.

———. 1995. School leaving. In *Learning from the past*, edited by Diane Ravitch and Maris A. Vinovskis. Baltimore: Johns Hopkins University Press.

Kirby, Jack Temple. 1987. *Rural worlds lost*. Baton Rouge, La.: Louisiana State University Press.

Kirschenman, Joleen, and Kathryn M. Neckerman. 1991. "We'd love to hire them, but. . ." In *The urban underclass*, edited by Christopher Jencks and Paul E. Peterson. Washington, D.C.: The Brookings Institute.

Kohler, Mary Conway. 1962. *Work and youth in New York City*. New York: Taconic Foundation.

Kohler, Mary Conway, and André Fontaine. 1962. We waste a million kids a year. *Saturday Evening Post* (March 10): 15–23.

Kreitzer, Amelia E., George F. Madaus, and Walt Haney. 1989. Competency testing and dropouts. In *Dropouts from school*, edited by Lois Weis, Eleanor Farrar, and Hugh G. Petrie. Albany: State University of New York Press.

Krug, Edward A. 1964. *The shaping of the American high school*. New York: Harper & Row.

———. 1972. *The shaping of the American high school. Vol. 2, 1920–1941*. Madison, Wis.: University of Wisconsin Press.

Kyle, Charles, and Edward Kantowicz. 1991. Bogus statistics. *Latino Studies Journal* 2 (May): 34–52.

Labaree, David F. 1988. *The making of an American high school*. New Haven, Conn.: Yale University Press.

Langley, Janis, and Lonnie Ewing. 1973. *Project KAPS*. Baltimore: Baltimore City Public Schools.

Lazerson, Marvin. 1971. *Origins of the urban school.* Cambridge, Mass.: Harvard University Press.

Lazerson, Marvin, and W. Norton Grubb. 1974. Introduction. In *American education and vocationalism,* edited by Marvin Lazerson and W. Norton Grubb. New York: Teachers College Press.

Leonesio, Michael V. 1993. Social Security and older workers. *Social Security Bulletin* 56 (Summer): 47–57.

Levine, Alan H., and Eve Cary. 1977. *The rights of students,* 2nd ed. New York: Avon Books.

Licht, Walter. 1992. *Getting work.* Cambridge, Mass.: Harvard University Press.

Lieberson, Stanley. 1980. *A piece of the pie.* Berkeley: University of California Press.

Lynd, Robert S., and Helen Merrell Lynd. 1928. *Middletown.* New York: Harcourt, Brace and Company.

Mare, Robert D. 1980. Social background and school continuation decisions. *Journal of the American Statistical Association* 75: 295–305.

———. 1981. Change and stability in educational stratification. *American Sociological Review* 46: 72–87.

Margo, Robert A. 1990. *Race and schooling in the South, 1880–1950.* Chicago: University of Chicago Press.

Margo, Robert A., and T. Aldrich Finegan. 1993. The decline in black teenage labor-force participation in the South, 1900–1970. *American Economic Review* 83: 234–47.

Mass suspension of Negro students. 1966. Atlanta *Inquirer* (2 April).

McCauley, Patrick E. 1957. 'Be it enacted.' In *With all deliberate speed,* edited by Don Shoemaker. New York: Harper Brothers.

McDill, Edward L., Gary Natriello, and Aaron M. Pallas. 1987. A population at risk. In *School dropouts,* edited by Gary Natriello. New York: Teachers College Press.

McMillen, Marilyn M., Phillip Kaufman, and Summer D. Whitner. 1994. *Dropout rates in the United States: 1993.* Washington, D.C.: Government Publications Office.

Mendel, Richard. 1994. *The American school-to-career movement.* Washington, D.C.: American Youth Policy Forum.

Miller, George. 1987. *Congressional Record* (21 May).

Miller, Leonard M. 1965. Dropouts: Selected references. United States Office of Education Bulletin No. 7. Washington, D.C.: Office of Education.

Miller, Seymour Michael, Betty L. Saleem, and Herrington Bryce. 1964. *School dropouts.* Syracuse, N.Y.: Syracuse University Youth Development Center.

Modell, John, Frank F. Furstenberg, Jr., and Theodore Hershberg. 1978. Social change and transitions to adulthood in historical perspective. In *The American Family in Social-Historical Perspective,* 2nd ed., edited by Michael Gordon. New York: St. Martin's Press.

Moore, Bernice Milburn. 1965. Mothers, homemakers, and wage earners. *NEA Journal* 54 (May): 22–23.

Moss, Philip, and Chris Tilly. 1991. Why black men are doing worse in the labor market. Background paper prepared for the Social Science Research Council Subcommittee on Joblessness and the Underclass.

Murk, Virgil. 1960. A follow-up study on students who drop out of high school. *National Association of Secondary-School Principals Bulletin* 44 (February): 73–75.

Myles, John. 1988. Postwar capitalism and the extension of Social Security into a retirement wage. In *The politics of social policy in the United States*, edited by Margaret Weir, Ann Shola Orloff, and Theda Skocpol. Princeton, N.J.: Princeton University Press.

National Center for Education Statistics. 1994. *Digest of educational statistics.* Washington, D.C.: Government Printing Office.

National Commission for Manpower Policy. 1976. *From school to work.* Washington, D.C.: Government Printing Office.

National Commission on Excellence in Education. 1983. *A nation at risk.* Washington, D.C.: Government Printing Office.

National Education Association. 1893/1894. *Report of the Committee of Ten on secondary school studies.* New York: American Book Company.

National Education Association Research Division. 1963. Research Memo 1965-10 (April). Washington, D.C.: National Education Association.

National Manpower Council. 1957. *Womanpower.* New York: Columbia University Press.

National School Public Relations Association. 1972. *Student rights and responsibilities.* Arlington, Va.: National School Public Relations Association.

National stay in school campaign. 1960. *Occupational Notes* 16 (October).

Natriello, Gary, Aaron M. Pallas, and Edward L. McDill. 1987. Taking stock. In *School dropouts*, edited by Gary Natriello. New York: Teachers College Press.

Negroes tested for transfer. 1961. Atlanta *Constitution* (19 May).

Neighborhood Youth Corps projects for unemployed youth. 1964. *Federal Register* 29 (25 December): 18419–22.

New unit to fight for children's rights. 1973. *New York Times* (23 May).

New York Bureau of Guidance. 1965. *Developing work-study programs for potential dropouts—a manual, STEP.* Albany: New York State Education Department.

New York City Board of Education. 1962. *Curriculum resource materials for meeting school retention and pre-employment needs.* New York: New York City Board of Education.

Newman, Harold. 1965. Dropout Case No. 22. *Clearing House* 39 (May): 544–46.

Nightingale, Carl Husemoller. 1993. *On the edge.* New York: Basic Books.

Nixon, Richard M. 1971. *The public papers of the presidents: Richard M. Nixon, 1970.* Washington, D.C.: Government Printing Office.

Norrell, Robert J. 1985. *Reaping the whirlwind.* New York: Knopf.

Novak, Benjamin J. 1968. Controlled group guidance. *Education* 89 (November): 162–65.

O'Neill, John H. 1963. High school drop-outs. *Education* 84 (November): 156–59.

Oppenheimer, Valerie Kincade. 1970. *The female labor force in the United States.* Berkeley: Institute of International Studies.

Orfield, Gary. 1988. Race and the liberal agenda. In *The politics of social policy in the United States,* edited by Margaret Weir, Ann Shola Orloff, and Theda Skocpol. Princeton, N.J.: Princeton University Press.

———. 1993. *The growth of segregation in American schools.* Alexandria, Va.: National School Boards Association, Council of Urban Boards of Education.

Orr, Margaret Terry. 1987. *Keeping students in school.* San Francisco: Jossey-Bass.

Osterman, Paul. 1980. *Getting started.* Cambridge, Mass.: MIT Press.

Papagiannis, George J., Robert N. Bickel, and Richard H. Fuller. 1983. The social creation of school dropouts. *Youth and Society* 14: 363–92.

Paterson, Fiona M. S. 1989. *Out of place.* New York: The Falmer Press.

Perlmann, Joel. 1988. *Ethnic differences.* New York: Cambridge University Press.

Philadelphia School District. 1963. Resources for dropout prevention activities for students and parents. *Occupational Notes* 19 (October).

———. 1965. Dropout prevention films. *Occupational Notes* 20 (January).

Pope, Daniel. 1983. *The making of modern advertising.* New York: Basic Books.

Rawlins, V. Lane, and Lloyd Ulman. 1974. The utilization of college-trained manpower in the United States. In *Higher education and the labor market,* edited by Margaret S. Gordon. New York: McGraw-Hill.

Reese, William J. 1995. *The origins of the American high school.* New Haven, Conn.: Yale University Press.

Rejected Negroes planning appeal. 1961. Atlanta *Journal* (5 June).

Ribicoff, Abraham. 1961. Plain words from Mr. Ribicoff on dropouts. *School Life* 44 (November–December): 14–15.

Riches, N. 1957. Education and work of young people in the labor force. *Monthly Labor Review* 80 (December): 1457–63.

Rindfuss, Ronald R., Craig St. John, and Larry L. Bumpass. 1984. Education and the timing of motherhood. *Journal of Marriage and the Family* 46: 981–84.

Roderick, Melissa R. 1993. *The path to dropping out.* Westport, Conn.: Auburn House.

Rogers, David. 1968. *110 Livingston Street.* New York: Random House.

Rothman, David J. 1980. *Conscience and convenience.* Boston: Little, Brown.

Rovello, Michael J. 1965. Dropouts. *Clearing House* 39 (March): 402–6.

Rumberger, Russell W. 1987. High school dropouts. *Review of Educational Research* 57: 101–21.

Rury, John L. 1991. *Education and women's work.* Albany: State University of New York Press.

Rusch, Frank R., and Carolyn Hughes. 1989. Overview of supported employment. *Journal of Applied Behavior Analysis* 22: 351–63.

Savitzky, Charles. 1962. Work experience programs for potential dropouts. *National Association of Secondary-School Principals Bulletin* 46 (November): 53–59.

———. 1964. Job guidance and the disadvantaged. *Clearing House* 39 (November): 156–57.

Scholarship and Guidance Association. 1962. *The drop-outs*. New York: Free Press of Glencoe.

Schreiber, Daniel. 1962a. School dropouts. *NEA Journal* 51 (May): 50–59.

————. 1962b. The school dropout—fugitive from failure. *National Association of Secondary-School Principals* 46 (May): 233–41.

————. 1964a. *The holding power of large-city school systems*. Washington, D.C.: National Education Association.

————. 1964b. An introduction to the school dropout. In *Guidance and the school dropout*, edited by Daniel Schreiber. Washington, D.C.: National Education Association.

————. 1967. Work-experience programs. In *Profile of the school dropout*, edited by Daniel Schreiber. New York: Random House.

Sedlak, Michael, et al. 1986. *Selling students short*. New York: Teachers College Press.

Sharp, Selby. 1957. Automobiles and pupil adjustment. *Clearing House* 32 (October): 83–85.

Shepard, Lorrie A., and Mary Lee Smith. 1988. Escalating academic demand in kindergarten. *Elementary School Journal* 89: 134–45.

————, eds. 1989. *Flunking grades*. New York: Falmer Press.

Simons, Alfred E., and Nelson S. Burke. 1966. The probable syndrome in terms of educational experiences which precipitates dropouts, delinquency, and eventual incarceration. *Journal of Negro Education* 35: 27–34.

Singleton, Robert, and Paul Bullock. 1963. Some problems in minority-group education in the Los Angeles Public Schools. *Journal of Negro Education* 32: 137–45.

Sizer, Ted. 1992. *Horace's school*. Boston: Houghton Mifflin.

Snepp, Daniel W. 1956. Can we salvage the dropouts? *Clearing House* 31 (September): 49–54.

Snyder, Thomas D., ed. 1993. *One hundred twenty years of American education*. Washington, D.C.: U. S. Department of Education.

Solomon, Barbara Miller. 1985. *In the company of educated women*. New Haven, Conn.: Yale University Press.

Solomon, R. Patrick. 1989. Dropping out of academics. In *Dropouts from school*, edited by Lois Weis, Eleanor Farrar, and Hugh G. Petrie. Albany, N.Y.: State University of New York Press.

Southern Regional Council. 1973. *The student pushout*. Atlanta: Southern Regional Council.

Spring, Joel H. 1989. *The sorting machine revisited*. New York: Longman.

Steele, W. L. 1899. To what extent should the high-school pupil be permitted to elect his work? *Proceedings of the National Education Association*: 331–36.

Stern, Mark J. 1987. *Society and family strategy*. Albany: State University of New York Press.

Stewart, David W. 1992. GED: 50 years at a glance. In *GED testing program*, edited by Colleen A. Allen and Edward V. Jones. Washington, D.C.: American Council on Education.

Strayer, George Drayton, and Edward L. Thorndike. 1913. *Educational administration.* New York: Macmillan Company.

Survey Research Center. 1971. *Youth in Transition.* Ann Arbor, Mich.: University of Michigan Institute for Social Research.

Taeuber, Cynthia M. 1992. *Sixty-five plus in America*, rev. ed. Current Population Reports P23–178RV. Washington, D.C.: Government Printing Office.

Task Force on Children out of School. 1971. *The way we go to school.* Boston: Beacon Press.

Tennessee Department of Education. 1950. *Annual statistical report of the Department of Education.* Nashville, Tenn.: Tennessee Department of Education.

————. 1960. *Annual statistical report of the Department of Education.* Nashville, Tenn.: Tennessee Department of Education.

The facts about school "dropouts." 1963. *US News and World Report* (August 26): 11.

The tragedy of drop-outs. 1961. *Ebony* (September): 48.

Thorndike, Edward L. 1907. *The elimination of pupils from school.* U. S. Bureau of Education Bulletin No. 4, Whole No. 379. Washington, D.C.: Government Printing Office.

Toby, Jackson. 1988a. Of dropouts and stay-ins. *The Public Interest* 95 (Spring): 3–13.

————. 1988b. Coercion or choice? *The Public Interest* 96 (Summer): 134–36.

Toby, Jackson, and David J. Armor. 1992. Carrots or sticks for high school dropouts? *The Public Interest* 106 (Winter): 76–90.

Topetzes, Nick John, and John M. Ivanoff. 1962. The dropout. *Catholic School Journal* 62 (February): 35–36.

Trattner, Walter I. 1970. *Crusade for the children.* Chicago: Quadrangle Books.

Tropea, Joseph L. 1987. Bureaucratic order and special children: Urban schools, 1950s–1960s. *History of Education Quarterly* 27: 339–61.

Tucker, Susan. 1988. *Telling memories among Southern women.* Baton Rouge, La.: Louisiana State University Press.

Turnbull, H. Rutherford, III. 1990. *Free appropriate public education*, 3d ed. Denver: Love Publishing Co.

Two rights groups charge resistance to school desegregation has led to expulsion of many blacks. 1973. *New York Times* (29 November).

$2,500 extra pay proposed for difficult teaching jobs. 1961. Philadelphia *Bulletin* (13 December).

Tyack, David B. 1974. *The one best system.* Cambridge, Mass.: Harvard University Press.

Tyack, David B., and Elisabeth Hansot. 1982. *Managers of virtue.* New York: Basic Books.

————. 1990. *Learning together.* New Haven, Conn.: Yale University Press.

Tyack, David B., Robert Lowe, and Elisabeth Hansot. 1984. *Public schools in hard times*. Cambridge, Mass.: Harvard University Press.

U. S. aid asked by job unit in Germantown. 1966. Philadelphia *Evening Bulletin* (9 September).

U. S. Bureau of the Census. 1953. *Special reports: Education* (PE No. 5B). Washington, D.C.: Government Printing Office.

———. 1975. *Historical statistics of the United States: Volume 1*. Washington, D.C.: Government Printing Office.

———. 1992. *1990 census of population: General population characteristics* (CP-1-1). Washington, D.C.: Government Printing Office.

———. 1993a. *1990 census of population: Social and economic characteristics* (CP-2-1). Washington, D.C.: Government Printing Office.

———. 1993b. *Poverty in the United States: 1992* (CPR P60-185). Washington, D.C.: Government Printing Office.

U. S. Commission on Civil Rights. 1962. *Civil rights U.S.A.* Washington, D.C.: Government Printing Office.

———. 1967. *Racial isolation in the public schools*. Washington, D.C.: Government Printing Office.

U. S. Department of Commerce. 1994. *Statistical abstract of the United States*. Washington, D.C.: Government Printing Office.

U. S. Department of Education. 1991. *America 2000*. Washington, D.C.: Government Printing Office.

U. S. dooms youth corps project hailed by Germantown residents. 1966. Philadelphia *Evening Bulletin* Suburban North edition (21 August).

U. S. House of Representatives. 1986. Committee on Education and Labor. *H. R. 3042, the Dropout Prevention and Reentry Act*. 99th Congress, second session.

———. 1991. Committee on Education and Labor. *Hearing on dropout prevention and workplace literacy*. 102d Congress, first session.

U. S. Office of Education. 1952. *Biennial survey of education in the United States, 1950–52*. Washington, D.C.: Government Printing Office.

———. 1964. *The 1963 Dropout Campaign*, Office of Education Bulletin No. 26, 1964.

U. S. officials agree to discuss Germantown youth job program. 1966. Philadelphia *Evening Bulletin* Suburban North edition (4 September).

U. S. Senate. 1985. Committee on Labor and Human Resources. *Dropout Prevention and Reentry Act of 1985*. 99th Congress, first session.

———. 1987. Committee on the Budget. *The School Dropout Retention and Recovery Act of 1987*. 100th Congress, first session.

———. 1988. Committee on Appropriations. *School dropouts and dropout prevention*. 100th Congress, second session.

Upchurch, Dawn M., and James McCarthy. 1993. Childbearing and schooling. *American Sociological Review* 58: 738–40.

Van Denburg, Joseph King. 1911. *Causes of the elimination of students in public secondary schools of New York City*. Teachers College Contributions to Education, No. 47. New York City: Teachers College, Columbia University.

Varner, Sherrell E. 1967. *School dropouts*. Research Summary 1967-S1. Washington, D.C.: National Education Association Research Division.

Vinovskis, Maris A. 1985. *The origins of public high schools*. Madison, Wis.: University of Wisconsin Press.

————. 1988. Have we underestimated the extent of antebellum high school attendance? *History of Education Quarterly* 28: 551–67.

Voss, Harwin L., Aubrey Wendling, and Delbert S. Elliott. 1966. Some types of high school dropouts. *Journal of Educational Research* 59: 363–68.

Walters, Pamela Barnhouse, and Carl M. Briggs. 1993. The family economy, child labor, and schooling. *American Sociological Review* 58: 163–81.

Washington Research Project. 1965. *Title I of ESEA*. Washington, D.C.: Southern Center for Studies in Public Policy and the NAACP Legal Defense and Education Fund Inc.

Wehlage, Gary G., et al. 1989. *Reducing the risk*. New York: Falmer Press.

Weinrich, Ernest F. 1952. How can a school increase its holding power of youth? *National Association of Secondary-School Principals* 36 (March): 125–30

Weiss, Carol H. 1988. Interview study. In *Reporting of social science in the national media*, edited by Carol H. Weiss and Eleanor Singer. New York: Russell Sage Foundation.

Wellesley College Center for Research on Women. 1992. *How schools shortchange girls*. Washington, D.C.: American Association of University Women Educational Foundation.

West, Lynda L., ed. 1991. *Effective strategies for dropout prevention of at-risk youth*. Gaithersburg, Md.: Aspen Publishers.

White House Conference on Child Health and Protection. 1932. *Child labor*. New York: Century Co.

Wilkerson, Doxey. 1965. Programs and practices in compensatory education for disadvantaged children. *Review of Educational Research* 35: 426–40.

Willis, Paul E. 1977. *Learning to labour*. Farnborough, Eng.: Saxon House.

Wills, Claude C., Jr. 1956. A program to decrease the number of early school leavers. *National Association of Secondary-School Principals Bulletin* 40 (September): 93–97.

Wright, Gavin. 1986. *Old South, New South*. New York: Basic Books.

Young, Joe M. 1955. Can counseling reduce dropouts? *Clearing House* 30 (September): 22–23.

Youth corps faces more job cuts. 1968. Philadelphia *Evening Bulletin* (20 May).

Youth corps funds gone, workers told. 1966. Philadelphia *Evening Bulletin* (16 August).

Youth corps here saved by $800,000 U. S. grant. 1966. Philadelphia *Evening Bulletin* (17 August).

Youth corps to help provide summer jobs. 1967. Philadelphia *Evening Bulletin* (6 July).

Zeitlin, Herbert, and Eugenia Zeitlin. 1952. Navy's material helps keep them in school. *Clearing House* 27 (October): 83–85.

Zelizer, Viviana A. 1985. *Pricing the priceless child.* New York: Basic Books.

Index

About the Author

SHERMAN DORN is Research Assistant Professor of Special Education at Peabody College of Vanderbilt University in Nashville. He holds history degrees from Haverford College and the University of Pennsylvania.

ISBN 0-275-95175-8

9 780275 951757

HARDCOVER BAR CODE